W0006374

Credits

Author
Micheal Lanham

Reviewer
Francesco Sapio

Commissioning Editor
Amarabha Banerjee

Acquisition Editor
Reshma Raman

Content Development Editor
Jason Pereira

Technical Editor
Prashant Mishra

Copy Editor
Charlotte Carneiro

Project Coordinator
Sheejal Shah

Proofreader
Safis Editing

Indexer
Tejal Daruwale Soni

Graphics
Jason Monteiro

Production Coordinator
Shantanu Zagade

About the Author

Micheal Lanham is a solutions architect with petroWEB and currently resides in Calgary, Alberta, in Canada. In his current role, he develops integrated GIS applications with advanced spatial search capabilities. He has worked as a professional and amateur game developer building desktop and mobile games for over 15 years. In 2007, Micheal was introduced to Unity 3D and has been an avid developer, consultant, and manager of multiple Unity game and graphic projects since.

Micheal has previously written *Augmented Reality Game Development*, also published by Packt Publishing in 2017.

I would really like to thank the team at Packt Publishing for all their support and assistance in making this book so easy and enjoyable to write. It has been a joy working with the team, which is composed of nothing but dedicated professionals. I would especially like to thank Reshma Raman and Jason Pereira. Reshma, the Senior Acquisition Editor, understood and agreed with the vision I had for this book. Jason, the Content Development Editor, has been a joy to work with and has worked hard assisting me when needed. Of course, no book would ever make it past the first draft if it were not for the dedication and hard work of the reviewers. So I would also like to make a special thanks to all the dedicated and hard work of the reviewers.
Writing a book would not be possible if I didn't have the support of my family and friends, Especially, with the help of my little tester and ideas contributor, Ava, who has been a great asset in developing several of the books exercises. Yet, none of this would be possible without the help and support of Rhonda. Rhonda has been gracious enough to draw some of the initial diagrams, lend her musical ear, and help with those first draft reviews.
I found this book a pleasure to write, and none of it would have been possible without any of the people I mentioned above.

About the Reviewer

Francesco Sapio obtained his Computer Science and Control Engineering degree from Sapienza University of Rome, Italy, with a couple of semesters in advance, graduating summa cum laude. He is currently studying a Master of Science in Engineering in Artificial Intelligence and Robotics at the same university.

He is a Unity 3D and Unreal expert, a skilled game designer, and an experienced user of the major graphics programs. He developed *Gea 2: A New Earth* (Sapienza University of Rome), an educational game for high school students to learn concepts of physics, and *Sticker Book* (series) (Dataware Games), a cross-platform series of games for kids. In addition, he worked as consultant for the (successfully funded by Kickstarter) game *Prosperity – Italy 1434* (Entertainment Game Apps, Inc), and for the open online collaborative ideation system titled *Innovoice* (Sapienza University of Rome). Moreover, he has been involved in different research projects, such as Belief-Driven-Pathfinding (Sapienza University of Rome), a new technique of pathfinding in videogames that was presented as a paper at the DiGRA-FDG Conference 2016; and Project Anima (Royal Melbourne Institute of Technology), which included developing a recommendation system for games.

He has authored several books for Packt. He is an active writer on the topic of game development. Recently, he authored the book *Getting Started with Unity 5.x 2D Game Development*, which takes your hand and guides you through the amazing journey of game development, the successful *Unity UI Cookbook*, which has been translated into other languages, and teaches readers how to develop exciting and practical user interfaces for games within Unity, and a short e-guide called *What do you need to know about Unity*. In addition, he co-authored the book *Unity 5.x 2D Game Development Blueprints*. Furthermore, he has also been a reviewer for the following books: *Game Development Patterns and Best Practices*, *Game Physics Cookbook*, *Mastering Unity 5.x*, *Unity 5.x by Example*, and *Unity Game Development Scripting*.

Francesco is also a musician and a composer, especially of soundtracks for short films and video games. For several years, he worked as an actor and dancer, where he was a guest of honor at the theatre Brancaccio in Rome. In addition, he is a very active person, having volunteered as a children's entertainer at the Associazione Culturale Torraccia in Rome.

Finally, Francesco loves math, philosophy, logic, and puzzle solving, but most of all, creating video games — thanks to his passion for game designing and programming.

You can find him at www.francescosapio.com.

Acknowledgments

I'm deeply thankful to my parents for their infinite patience, enthusiasm, and support throughout my life. Moreover, I'm thankful to the rest of my family, in particular to my grandparents, since they have always encouraged me to do better in my life with the Latin expressions "Ad maiora" and "Per aspera ad astra".

Finally, a huge thanks to all the special people around me whom I love, in particular to my girlfriend; I'm grateful for all of your help in everything. I do love you.

www.PacktPub.com

For support files and downloads related to your book, please visit www.PacktPub.com.

Did you know that Packt offers eBook versions of every book published, with PDF and ePub files available? You can upgrade to the eBook version at www.PacktPub.com and as a print book customer, you are entitled to a discount on the eBook copy. Get in touch with us at service@packtpub.com for more details.

At www.PacktPub.com, you can also read a collection of free technical articles, sign up for a range of free newsletters and receive exclusive discounts and offers on Packt books and eBooks.

https://www.packtpub.com/mapt

Get the most in-demand software skills with Mapt. Mapt gives you full access to all Packt books and video courses, as well as industry-leading tools to help you plan your personal development and advance your career.

Why subscribe?

- Fully searchable across every book published by Packt
- Copy and paste, print, and bookmark content
- On demand and accessible via a web browser

Customer Feedback

Thanks for purchasing this Packt book. At Packt, quality is at the heart of our editorial process. To help us improve, please leave us an honest review on this book's Amazon page at `https://www.amazon.com/dp/1787286452`.

If you'd like to join our team of regular reviewers, you can e-mail us at `customerreviews@packtpub.com`. We award our regular reviewers with free eBooks and videos in exchange for their valuable feedback.

Help us be relentless in improving our products!

To my father Leslie, who taught me how to love and appreciate music of all forms.

Table of Contents

Preface	1
Chapter 1: Introducing Game Audio with Unity	7
Introduction to game audio	8
Main game audio components	8
Diegetic versus non-diegetic sound	9
Audio layers or groups	10
Getting started with unity	11
Downloading unity	11
An introduction to unity	17
Downloading and importing project assets	20
A tour of the village	24
Importing audio into unity	26
Inspecting the imported audio files	31
Audio sources and listeners	35
Adding an audio source	38
3D sound and spatial blending	42
Summary	48
Chapter 2: Scripting Audio	49
Introduction to scripting in Unity	50
Building a musical keyboard	54
Importing and playing notes	58
Enhancing the virtual keyboard	62
Weapons and sound	65
Throwing the ax	70
Understanding the axController script	75
Playing sounds on collision	78
Randomizing audio	81
Background music	84
Summary	86
Chapter 3: Introduction to the Audio Mixer	87
Introducing the Unity Audio mixer	88
Creating mixer groups	93
Shaping audio with effects	95

Visualizing audio equalization   98
The master mixer and controlling signal flow   101
Routing audio signals in the mixer to effects   104
  Audio effects breakdown   110
    Equalization effects   110
      Lowpass and Lowpass simple   110
      Highpass and Highpass simple   111
      ParamEQ   111
    Delay effects   111
      Echo   111
      SFX reverb   112
      Flange   113
      Chorus   114
    Other effects   114
      Pitch Shifter   114
      Normalize   115
      Compressor   115
The duck volume effect   118
Summary   123

Chapter 4: Advanced Audio Mixing   125
Recording audio changes with snapshots   126
  Pausing the scene   128
Audio Mixer scripting with parameters   132
A dynamic audio wind effect   133
Creating environmental audio zones   142
Dynamic music mixing   153
Summary   158

Chapter 5: Using the Audio Mixer for Adaptive Audio   159
Introducing adaptive audio   160
Building adaptive audio cues   162
Creating mood with adaptive music   170
Vertical remixing with the Audio Mixer   172
Footsteps with adaptive sound   182
Summary   191

Chapter 6: Introduction to FMOD   193
Getting started with FMOD Studio   194
  Installing FMOD Studio   194
Back to the basics   199
Effects and mixing   207
Mixing in a reverb effect   210

Parameters, snapshots, and triggers	217
Summary	223

Chapter 7: FMOD for Dyanmic and Adaptive Audio — 225

Dynamic wind and environmental zones	226
Scripting with FMOD	233
Revisiting the footsteps example	241
Adaptive music with FMOD	245
Transition timelines and stingers	251
Summary	259

Chapter 8: Visualizing Audio in Games — 261

Analyzing audio with Fast Fourier Transform (FFT) windows	262
Audio spectrum	262
Deconstructing signals using FFT and windowing	265
Examining an audio visualizer	268
Uncovering the details	269
Visualization performance and windowing	275
Audio-driven lighting	278
Microphone-driven visualizations	283
Summary	288

Chapter 9: Character Lip Syncing and Vocals — 289

Real-time lip syncing	290
Speech and phonemes	297
Blend shape animation	303
Real-time character lip sync	309
Recording vocals	314
Summary	317

Chapter 10: Composing Music — 319

Getting started with Reaper	320
MIDI and virtual instruments	322
Virtual instruments	327
Basic music theory	332
Chords and chord progressions	332
Chord progression	336
Melody and scale	339
Enhancing the composition	343
Recording music and vocals	348
Recording and optimizing vocals	349

Summary   352

Chapter 11: Audio Performance and Troubleshooting   353

Audio performance considerations   354
Profiling performance with Unity   356
Audio optimization tips and tricks for Unity   362
    Memory optimization tips and tricks   363
    Effects optimization tips and tricks   368
FMOD performance and optimization   370
Audio troubleshooting   379
Summary   381

Index   383

Preface

From those exotic sound effects that improve game fun and playability to that dark musical score that sets the entire atmosphere of a scene or game audio is essential to any great game. Yet it is perhaps one of the most often overlooked assets in the development of a game by new or indie developers. Instead, they dedicate the bulk of their effort to graphics and other visuals, often deferring the audio portion until the later stages of production. They do this not because good audio is not a critical aspect to any good game, but as a single or indie developer they feel AAA game quality audio is out of reach. Of course, that is far from the truth, especially with the great audio system built into Unity and the many freely available commercials plugins and tools.

This book was written to introduce the reader to the extensive audio framework built within Unity and other freely available commercials tools and plugins. Often, audio development tools expect a certain level of knowledge in sound, mixing and music. By following through the books material and exercises a reader should be able to master all the essentials of audio development. From the basics of implementing an audio source; to spatial sound, mixing, effects and dynamic and adaptive audio system. As well there will be time spent learning professionals like FMOD Studio for game audio and Reaper for music composition. While the book assumes no prior knowledge of working with Unity or audio, there will be enough new and interesting content that even the more advanced developer will find useful.

What this book covers

This book starts from the fundamentals of starting game audio development with Unity and progresses to using advanced commercial tools for professional game audio and music composition. It is assumed the reader will follow the chapters in sequential order as many chapters build from previous exercises. Each of the chapters is listed below with a quick summary:

Chapter 1, *Introducing Game Audio in Unity*, Unity is introduced and the reader is guided through installation of the software and setup of the first project. Which includes importing audio assets, audio source essentials and setting up spatial sounds.

Chapter 2, *Scripting Audio*, the basics of scripting in Unity is introduced with the writing of a simple musical keyboard. Followed by; scripting weapons, sound effects, physics and implementing ambient sounds and music.

Chapter 3, *Introduction to the Unity Audio Mixer*, introduces the basics of the Audio Mixer, mixing audio sources and effects, with further coverage on mixer signal routing and using the Duck Volume effect.

Chapter 4, *Advanced Audio Mixing*, covers using advanced capabilities of the Audio Mixer. From mixer parameter scripting, snapshots, snapshot transitions, and developing audio transition zones.

Chapter 5, *Using the Audio Mixer for Adaptive Audio*, introduces adaptive audio and covers techniques for mixing adaptive music. The rest of the chapter is spent implementing adaptive audio in sound and music.

Chapter 6, *Introduction to FMOD*, starts with the installation and setup of FMOD Studio. Then, it goes over the similarities and differences between the Unity Audio Mixer and FMOD.

Chapter 7, *FMOD for Dynamic and Adaptive Audio*, builds upon previous advanced examples and converts or adapts them to use FMOD. The chapter covers several advanced techniques of working with FMOD Studio.

Chapter 8, *Visualizing Audio in Games*, starts with a background of how sound can be broken down by frequency with mathematical techniques know as FFT Windowing. Those techniques are then used to create stunning audio-visual dancing lights and graphics.

Chapter 9, *Character Lip Syncing and Vocals*, builds upon previous work and builds a real-time character lip syncing demo. By covering character bone and vertex animation, lip-sync animation with phonemes, and recording with Unity.

Chapter 10, *Composing Music*, introduces the basics of music composition with Reaper using some simple music theory. It covers the installation and setup of Reaper, MIDI basics, virtual instruments, audio rendering and recording.

Chapter 11, *Audio Performance and Troubleshooting*, covers the fundamentals of audio performance with Unity and FMOD. From performance profiling to the tips and tricks of optimizing and troubleshooting performance issues.

What you need for this book

In order to be successful with this book you will need to have an eagerness to learn the basics and master game audio development. No previous game or audio development knowledge is required. Although, it may be helpful to have some knowledge of scripting with a C language like C#, JavaScript or C++, but it is not essential. Covering some of the material may be easier if you know how to play an instrument or understand sound or music theory, but again this is not required. You should have a desktop or laptop computer running Windows XP+, Mac OS, or Linux to complete the book's essential exercises.

Who this book is for

This book is for anyone who wants to learn how to create better sound for their games or just have a better understanding of how audio works in games. While this book is directed at the individual or indie development team, it certainly could be put to good use by sound designers or audio enthusiasts.

Conventions

In this book, you will find a number of styles of text that distinguish between different kinds of information. Here are some examples of these styles, and an explanation of their meaning.

Code words in text, database table names, folder names, filenames, file extensions, pathnames, and user input are shown as follows: "As the scene is running, be sure to select the `VirtualKeyboard` object in the **Hierarchy** window."

A block of code is set as follows:

```
public int transpose = 0; //after this line
private List<int> notes = new List<int>();
private int index = 0;
public bool record;
public bool playback;
```

New terms and important words are shown in bold. Words that you see on the screen, in menus or dialog boxes for example, appear in the text like this: "Click on the checkbox next to the **Record** setting on the **Keyboard** component. Click on the mouse in the **Game** view and then type some keys to play the virtual instrument."

Warnings or important notes appear in a box like this.

 Tips and tricks appear like this.

Reader feedback

Feedback from our readers is always welcome. Let us know what you think about this book-what you liked or disliked. Reader feedback is important for us as it helps us develop titles that you will really get the most out of.

To send us general feedback, simply e-mail feedback@packtpub.com, and mention the book's title in the subject of your message.

If there is a topic that you have expertise in and you are interested in either writing or contributing to a book, see our author guide at www.packtpub.com/authors.

Customer support

Now that you are the proud owner of a Packt book, we have a number of things to help you to get the most from your purchase.

Downloading the example code

You can download the example code files for this book from your account at http://www.packtpub.com. If you purchased this book elsewhere, you can visit http://www.packtpub.com/support and register to have the files e-mailed directly to you.

You can download the code files by following these steps:

1. Log in or register to our website using your e-mail address and password.
2. Hover the mouse pointer on the **SUPPORT** tab at the top.
3. Click on **Code Downloads & Errata**.

4. Enter the name of the book in the **Search** box.
5. Select the book for which you're looking to download the code files.
6. Choose from the drop-down menu where you purchased this book from.
7. Click on **Code Download**.

Once the file is downloaded, please make sure that you unzip or extract the folder using the latest version of:

- WinRAR / 7-Zip for Windows
- Zipeg / iZip / UnRarX for Mac
- 7-Zip / PeaZip for Linux

The code bundle for the book is also hosted on GitHub at `https://github.com/PacktPubl ishing/Game-Audio-Development-with-Unity-5X`. We also have other code bundles from our rich catalog of books and videos available at `https://github.com/PacktPublishing/`. Check them out!

Downloading the color images of this book

We also provide you with a PDF file that has color images of the screenshots/diagrams used in this book. The color images will help you better understand the changes in the output. You can download this file from `https://www.packtpub.com/sites/default/files/down loads/GameAudioDevelopmentwithUnity5X_ColorImages.pdf`.

Errata

Although we have taken every care to ensure the accuracy of our content, mistakes do happen. If you find a mistake in one of our books-maybe a mistake in the text or the code-we would be grateful if you could report this to us. By doing so, you can save other readers from frustration and help us improve subsequent versions of this book. If you find any errata, please report them by visiting `http://www.packtpub.com/submit-errata`, selecting your book, clicking on the **Errata Submission Form** link, and entering the details of your errata. Once your errata are verified, your submission will be accepted and the errata will be uploaded to our website or added to any list of existing errata under the Errata section of that title.

To view the previously submitted errata, go to `https://www.packtpub.com/books/conten t/support`and enter the name of the book in the search field. The required information will appear under the **Errata** section.

Piracy

Piracy of copyrighted material on the Internet is an ongoing problem across all media. At Packt, we take the protection of our copyright and licenses very seriously. If you come across any illegal copies of our works in any form on the Internet, please provide us with the location address or website name immediately so that we can pursue a remedy.

Please contact us at copyright@packtpub.com with a link to the suspected pirated material.

We appreciate your help in protecting our authors and our ability to bring you valuable content.

Questions

If you have a problem with any aspect of this book, you can contact us at questions@packtpub.com, and we will do our best to address the problem.

1
Introducing Game Audio with Unity

Welcome to our journey into game audio and audio development with Unity. It is the leading cross-platform game engine that provides an abundance of features to make developing games easy. For this book, it doesn't matter if you are completely new to game audio, Unity, or game development. We will start with the assumption that you are a complete novice and build from there. With each new chapter, we will be introducing new concepts and additional material. Of course, if you are an experienced Unity developer with basic knowledge of audio development, you may want to skim over the first couple of chapters. Regardless of if you are a novice or master, the later chapters in this book will cover plenty of Unity features and tools to give you the knowledge of developing **AAA** game quality audio for your games.

In this chapter, we will cover the basics of Unity and add audio to a project and scene in Unity. As this is the first chapter, we will be covering a quick introduction to game audio and then spend some time installing and configuring Unity. From there, we will introduce the core Unity components and how they function. Here is a summary of what we will cover in this chapter:

- Introduction to game audio
- Getting started with unity
- Importing audio into unity
- Audio sources and listeners
- 3D sound and spatial blending audio

As with most of the chapters in this book, it is expected that you follow along and complete each of the exercises. Completing the exercises hands on will reinforce all the concepts and provide you with a good foundation for the more complex material introduced in later chapters. All the material required to complete the exercises will either be provided via the book's downloaded source code or will be freely available online. Therefore, in almost all cases, you will be required to have an internet connection. If you feel that you understand the content in a chapter and just want to review the completed examples, then follow the instructions provided in the book's download to build the final examples.

Introduction to game audio

Chances are, if you have played a few computer, video, or mobile games in your life, you are already quite familiar with what great game audio should sound like. Perhaps; you even cherish the audio from a couple of your favorite games. However, if someone asked you how they composed or mixed that audio, unless you were a professional audio technician, you would likely be at a loss on how the audio in a game mixes together. Fortunately, in this section, we will start to introduce some of the basic concepts of game audio, which we will of course build upon in later chapters in this book.

Main game audio components

Game audio, unlike audio a sound designer would compose for film or television, will typically be broken down into three distinct areas as listed here:

- **Music**: This includes content such as theme or background music, in-game music such as a radio or a band playing, and can even include certain audio effects. Creating or obtaining unique music for your game could be as complex as recording a music track in a sound studio to purchasing rights to a music track of the asset store. In Chapter 10, *Composing Music*, we will explore how to compose your own unique tunes.
- **Sound**: This generally includes sound effects, such as creaking doors, explosions, footsteps, clicking, beeping, and many others. Most sound designers or developers will often browse through many of the free or paid sound effects sites to find a sound they like. Another option is to record your own sound effects, essentially becoming a **Foley** artist. In Chapter 10, *Composing Music*, we will look at some techniques to create some unique sound effects in software.

Foley artists are traditionally people who create sound effects for film, television, and now games. The term Foley was coined from the originator, Jack Foley, who created real-time sound effects for early motion pictures. Today, the practice is no longer real time, but the name "Foley" is still synonymous with recording and creating sound effects.

- **Vocals**: The addition of vocals to games is a relatively new addition. Vocals were first introduced in cut or intro game scenes but now they are a main element in any AAA title. Furthermore, most AAA titles will enlist a well-known actor to provide vocals for further enhancement of the game. In Chapter 9, *Character Lip Syncing and Vocals,* we will cover some details about generating vocals. As well in several other chapters of this book, we will highlight the use of vocal cues in scenes.

While game audio design is similar to film and television, in many components, it differs primarily by its implementation. Audio for film follows a linear well-defined pattern, whereas in games audio is non-linear and may even be dynamic or adaptive. We will of course cover many aspects of how game audio is dynamic and adaptive in the Adaptive Sound and Music section.

Diegetic versus non-diegetic sound

If you have never heard of the term diegetic, you may just have gotten a queasy feeling in your stomach wondering what you got yourself into. Do not worry, the term diegetic refers to audio that is audible in the scene or screen as a part of the action or interaction. Conversely, non-diegetic refers to sounds that are added to the scene or screen and are not visible. Perhaps; it is more helpful if we look at some examples of diegetic and non-diegetic sounds, listed here:

- Diegetic sounds include:
  - **Sound effects**: Explosions, gun fire, car engine, or collisions
  - **Music**: Band playing, musical instruments onscreen playing, or car radio
  - **Vocals**: Character dialogue, voices, or crowds
- Non-diegetic sounds include:
  - **Sound effects**: Off screen sound effects such as coins entering a purse, tones to denote activity changes in a game, or footsteps
  - **Music**: Scary background theme music, a novelty theme, or boss theme music
  - **Vocals**: Narration, character vocal cues, or haunting voices

These terms may sound rather abstract right now, but be rest assured, we will get fairly intimate with the use of non-diegetic sounds in the adaptive sound and music section. As you will learn, one of the cornerstones of developing great game audio is building up good non-diegetic sounds.

 You may have already noticed that game audio borrows or shares a number of common film and television terms sound designers use. That, of course, is not by accident. Games have been using the same principals of audio design established for movies and television for many years. In fact, later on in this book, we will explore the use of various commercial **Digital Audio Workstations (DAW)** traditionally used for film or television and now plugins to Unity.

Audio layers or groups

In virtually all digital games, the three base audio components we defined earlier may also include effects that will be broken into distinct layers or groups. This not only simplifies audio composition and development, which can become quickly complex as we will see, but also separates out critical audio elements. While you can think of each layer of audio playing separately during the game, from the player's perspective they will hear all the layers mixed together. The following list defines a set of basic layers we will use to group our audio:

- **Ambient and environmental audio**: This includes both diegetic and non-diegetic audio such as waterfalls, ocean waves, birds chirping, a rowdy tavern, crowds, a humming power plant, or a band playing music. This group is not just limited to audio sound clips but may also include effects such as reverb, echo, distortion, or other environmental audio effects. We will cover ambient audio effects in more detail starting in Chapter 2, *Scripting Audio.*
- **Direct feedback audio**: This will include any sound elements that that need to react directly to player input in a scene or on the interface. Diegetic examples of this would be shooting/reloading a gun, throwing a grenade, or watching something explode. Non-diegetic examples of this would be the sound of character getting shot, boss music playing, vocal cues, or dialog. Starting in a Chapter 2, *Scripting Audio*, we will cover several examples of this type of audio.

- **Interface audio**: This includes sounds activated as part of the game interface. This typically would include items such as button clicks or notifications. We really won't go into too much depth in this area, as interface sounds are fairly standard and use the same principals you learn to manage other audio that is easily transferable to the interface.
- **Background or theme music**: This area is relatively self-explanatory and immediately conjures up your favorite game theme music. However, background music can be used to dynamically change and thus alter the tone of a game during various conditions. This form of audio change is known as adaptive music and is something we will spend a great deal of time on, starting in the Adaptive sound and music section. In Chapter 2, *Scripting Audio*, we will introduce the use of background music in a scene.

Remember, this is only a basic definition of layers we have grouped our basic audio components into. As you will see through the rest of this book, there are a number of other ways we can group or layer audio. In Chapter 3, *Introduction to the Unity Audio Mixer*, we will cover the use and definition of audio groups in more detail.

Now that we have some very basic audio terminology defined, let's get into putting some of this knowledge to use in Unity. In the next section, we will look at downloading and setting up Unity.

Getting started with unity

This section assumes that you have never installed Unity before and will take you through a step-by-step exercise on download and installation. If you have installed Unity before, you may still want to quickly review this section, just to confirm you have installed the required components.

Downloading unity

Follow the instructions to download Unity:

1. Enter the following URL, `https://store.unity.com/`, into your favorite web browser or just click on the link.

2. After the page loads, you will see several licensing options. For the purposes of this book, all you need is the **Personal** Unity license. So, just click on the **Download now** button on the **Personal** license as shown in the following screenshot:

Screenshot from Unity store showing Personal license Download now button

3. A new page will load, showing a big green button labeled **Download Installer**. Click on the button to download the Unity Download Assistant with your web browser.

4. After the package has completed downloading, open it as you would any other program. The Unity Download Assistant is relatively small so it should download quite quickly.

5. Agree to any security notifications or notifications you normally encounter when installing new software on your computer. After the installer launches, you will see a screen similar to the following screenshot:

Unity Download Assistant starting

If you are unable to install software on your computer due to security restrictions or other account settings, be sure to contact your administrator and ask them to give you access or have them install the software. During the course of this book, we will be downloading several software packages so it is advisable that you have the ability to install new software on your machine in order to complete all the exercises in the book.

6. Click on the **Next** button to continue. Then on the next page, select the checkbox to agree to the Unity license as shown in the following screenshot:

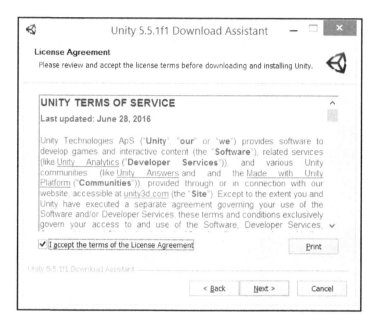

Unity terms of service page

7. Click on the **Next** button to continue. The next page will likely offer you an option to choose between 32 and 64-bit architecture. It is usually best to take the default (64 bit in most cases) and click on the **Next** button to continue.

8. The next page will allow you to choose the Unity components you want to install. This page allows you to choose from a number of components to install along with Unity. For the purposes of this book, you only need to install the default components. However, if you feel you may need or want other components, such as Android or iOS, feel free to select those as well. Just be sure to have the three main components selected as shown in the following screenshot:

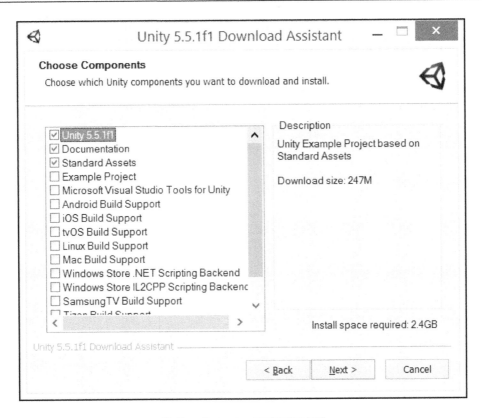

The Choose Components section of the Unity install

9. After you have made your component selections, click on the **Next** button to continue. For the next couple of dialog pages, just keep the defaults and let the installation download and install Unity. Since this can take a while, feel free to grab your beverage of choice while you wait for the installation to complete.

The Unity installation will generally run very smoothly, but if you do encounter some issues, it is best to follow the recovery instructions the installer may provide. If that doesn't fix the issue, just do a quick search and check the Unity forums. Unity has a huge community of developers that are very eager to assist newcomers with any issues, and it is almost certainly likely someone has already encountered a similar issue to yours.

Once the Unity installer has finished installing Unity, follow the instructions here:

1. On the last page of the installer, you will usually be prompted with an option to launch Unity right away. Be sure that option is selected and then exit the installer.

2. As the program launches, you may get a notice to provide an exception in your firewall; be sure to allow this. After Unity launches, you will be welcomed by a login screen as shown in the following screenshot:

Unity login or welcome screen

3. If you have never installed Unity before, you will need to create a Unity Account. Just click on the blue **create one** text as shown in the preceding screenshot. This will take you to a registration area of the Unity site. From there, complete that account setup, and when you are done, return to this item.

4. Now that you have a Unity account created, enter your email and password in the dialog and then click on the **Sign In** button. After you sign in, you will be directed to the project page.

That completes your first step to becoming a Unity developer. In the next section, we will create a new project and explore the Unity interface.

An introduction to unity

Now that we have Unity installed, let's dive right in and create a project and then take a quick overview of the interface. Perform the following directions to create a new Unity project:

1. If this is your first time running Unity, at this stage, you will have a dialog with a button allowing you to create a new project; click on the **NEW**. For those of you who have jumped here from another section in the book, be sure to launch Unity and make sure you are logged in with your Unity account. From there select the **NEW** project button at the top of the Unity start page.

2. The project dialog will open. Enter the project name as `GameAudioBasics` and then keep the defaults for all the other settings as shown in the following screenshot:

Creating a new project in Unity

3. After you fill in the Project name, click on the **Create Project** button.

4. Unity will close the dialog, and you will see a progress dialog flash as the project is initialized and the interface loads. When Unity is done loading, you will see a screen that looks similar to the following window:

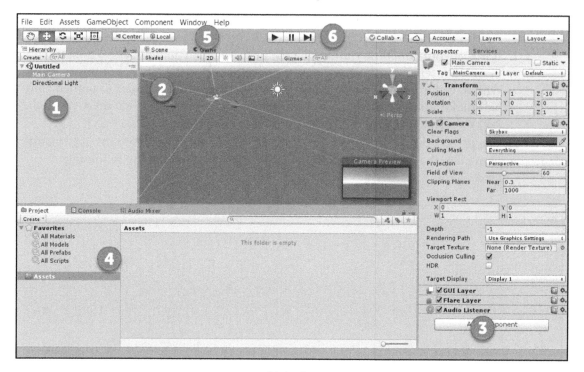

Unity interface

 If you have run Unity before or if you are using a different license, such as pro, your screen may appear to be quite different. Aside from any themes applied, you can return to the default layout by selecting from the menu **Window** | **Layouts** | **Default**.

Now that we have Unity running, let's review what each of the main windows or elements are for. You can follow along using the reference numbers shown in the preceding window screenshot to match the items in the list here:

- **Hierarchy window (1)**: This window shows the currently displayed scenes and scene elements called a **GameObject** in Unity. Currently, there should be a scene labeled **Untitled** in the window. Click on the arrow beside the scene to expand it and then click on the items beneath the scene. Notice how the other windows change depending on your selection.

- **Scene view (2)**: You can think of the scene window or the view as the design canvas for your game project. In this view, you can select and move objects around using the mouse or the principal direction arrows (the colored arrows). Feel free to select objects in the view and move them around. Don't worry about moving things out of place or getting lost as we are creating a new scene before we start building anything of importance.
- **Inspector window (3)**: This window exposes and allows you to edit the properties and components of the currently selected GameObject. A lot of the time you spend working in Unity will be editing values in this window. Again, feel free to explore this window by editing some properties of a GameObject.
- **Project window (4)**: This window shows all the resources or assets you have in the entire Unity project. As you can, see the project is currently quite bare. Not to worry, we will be quickly adding new assets.
- **Game view (5)**: This window or view shows how the game will look to the player. It differs from the **Scene** view because it only shows what the player sees. If you click on the game window tab, you will see a sparse view of the ground layer and sky. Again, this is because we have yet to add anything interesting.
- **Play mode (6)**: This is the set of buttons at the top of the Unity interface control running the game in the editor. The buttons allow you to play and pause the game play. If you click on the play button right now, not much will happen other than the **Game** view will present itself.

At an advanced level, that covers the main elements of the Unity interface without getting bogged down in too many details. It could very well take you months or years to become an expert in using all the features of Unity. So, in order to not overwhelm you, we will only focus on the relevant information you need to complete an exercise.

So far we have been looking at an empty project and scene. In the next section, we will import a project from the Unity Asset Store.

Downloading and importing project assets

One of the really great features of Unity is the Unity Asset Store. Game development is a complex process that requires many artistic skills in multiple areas to develop quality assets, such as 3D models, animation, textures, sound, music, shaders, and more. Chances are, if your development team is just you or a small group of developers and artists, your team will lack the skillset or time to develop all the assets for your project. Fortunately, the Unity Asset Store provides professional game quality assets at very competitive pricing or in some cases for free. Unity itself also provides a number of high-quality sample projects free of charge on the store. We will be using a couple of those projects in this book as the base for our exercises in audio development.

Follow the instructions here to download and import the project we will use for the rest of the exercises in this chapter:

1. From the menu select **Window** | **Asset Store**. This will open a new tab beside the **Scene** and **Game** views called **Asset Store**.
2. After the page loads in the window, there should be a search box visible at the top of the window. Enter the text unity viking village in the search box and click on the search button as shown in the following screenshot:

Searching in the Unity Asset Store

3. When the search completes, there will be a list of search results. The first result in the list should match *Viking Village* from Unity Technologies. Click on this item, and you should see the asset page as shown in the following screenshot:

Viking Village asset page

4. Click on the blue button labeled **Download**, as shown in the screenshot to start downloading the asset.

5. As the asset downloads, the button will show the progress. The download may take a while, so be patient and of course feel free to grab another one of your favorite beverages.

6. When the download completes, the button will read **Import**. Click on the button to import the project into Unity. You will be immediately prompted by a dialog informing you that this is a complete project, as shown here:

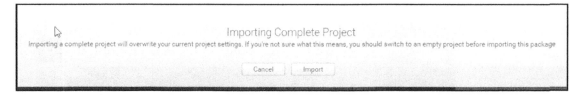

Project import warning

7. Click on the **Import** button on the dialog to continue the project import. Importing a new project over our project is entirely okay since we have nothing we wanted to save at this point.

8. A dialog will appear showing you the progress of the import. This take a couple minutes after which you will be prompted with the **Import Unity Package** dialog, as shown here:

Import Unity Package dialog

9. The **Import Unity Package** dialog shows all the assets to be imported as a part of the project. Feel free to scroll through the list and review the items being imported. Then, click on the **Import** button on the dialog to complete the project import.

10. Yet another dialog will open showing you the progress of the last stage of the import. Just be patient and enjoy that beverage or grab another, the asset will load in several more minutes.

> This project asset we are importing is on the large side, at around 900 MB. Fortunately, we will only need to do this once. As we will continue to reuse this project throughout the book. Generally, the assets you download from the Asset Store will often be under 100 MB.
>
> The amount of time to import a project will be determined by the size of the asset and the content. Assets such as textures, for instance, will be compressed and often take extra time to load. Unfortunately, the sample project we are loading is composed of several compressed assets.

11. When the import is complete, you will now find that the **Project** window is now showing several new asset folders.

Now, that we have our base project imported, in the next section, we take a quick look at the main scene and several features that will help us going forward.

A tour of the village

After doing all that work getting the project loaded; okay, perhaps not so much work as waiting, let's load the project scene and take a quick tour of the asset by following the directions here:

1. Click on the `Scenes` folder in the **Project** window and then double-click on the `The_Viking_Village.unity` file to open the scene. The screenshot here shows the **Project** window:

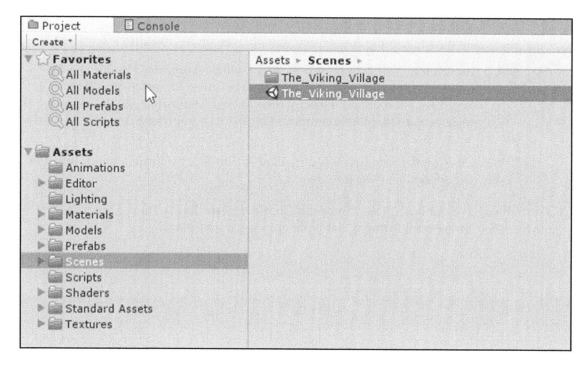

Opening the project scene

2. After the scene loads, you will notice that the **Hierarchy** window is now filled with objects. Click on the **Scene** view tab to open the view and you should now see something very similar to what is shown in the following screenshot:

Hierarchy window and Scene view

3. Press the editor play button, as shown in the preceding screenshot to start the scene and run the game.

4. As the game is running, the **Game** view will automatically present itself. Use the following commands to move around the game and explore the environment and features:

   - **W, A, S, D**: The standard first person movement commands. Use these keys or the arrow keys to move around the scene.
   - **Mouse**: This controls the look direction.
   - **Spacebar**: This is used to jump up. Quickly taping the Spacebar key will cause the camera to hover/fly while in manual mode.
   - **C**: This toggles between a controlled camera walkthrough and the manual or keyboard movement (first person).
   - **Esc**: This exits the mouse lock and makes the mouse visible in the editor again.

5. Take your time to explore the environment and feel free to move around as much as you like. When you are ready to move on, press the *Esc* key to make the mouse visible again and then press the play button again to stop the game running.

6. Hopefully, you noticed, as you were moving around the game, how quiet everything was. Fortunately, that makes this scene the perfect canvas for us to develop our own game audio. This is exactly what we will do for the next several chapters in this book.

Installing Unity and getting your first project loaded is a great first step to becoming a Unity game developer. Congratulate yourself for your patience in spending the time to work through this section. In the next section, we will get back to more audio development basics.

Importing audio into unity

Aside from downloading content from the Asset Store, there are a number of ways of introducing content into a Unity project. Most often, the simplest way of adding content to your project is placing the appropriate files into the relevant project folders. Unity is then smart enough to inspect the new files, provided the file type is supported by Unity, and determine the asset type to automatically import the content. Since there are a number of audio file types out there, let's take a look at the audio file format Unity currently supports in the following list:

- `.wav` / `.aif`: Both of these formats are uncompressed, lossless formats, which means they are exact copies of the original audio. The `.aif` originated on the Mac, while `.wav` came from the PC. Now both formats are supported by either operating system.

 Compressing audio or other forms of media is done in order to reduce the file size for easy transport or download. Since media compression will cause a loss of quality to the media, the term lossy is used to denote a compressed media format. Whereas, lossless or no loss, denotes a media format with no compression and thus no loss in quality.

- `.mp3`: This is the most common compressed or lossy format for audio. This format became very popular for transferring/downloading music.
- `.ogg`: This, also known as **Ogg Vorbis**, was developed as a patent free alternative to mp3. The standard format is lossy but it can support lossless as well.

 Unity can also import tracker module formats such as impulse tracker (`.it`), scream tracker (`.s3m`), extended module file format (`.xm`), and the original module file format (`.mod`). We won't cover these file types until later, in `Chapter 10`, *Composing Music*.

Now that you have a better understanding of the supported audio files types, let's import a couple of files into our project in the following exercise here:

1. Before importing any content, we will create a new set of folders in the project. This will help us organize and find this content later. As you can see, by just taking a quick look through the **Project** window, a game project may contain numerous assets in multiple areas.

2. Right-click (*control* + Click on Mac) on the root `Assets` folder in the **Project** window. Then, select **Create | Folder** from the context menu.

3. A new folder will be created under the `Assets` folder with the cursor prompting for input. Name the new folder `Audio`.

4. Right-click (*control* + Click on Mac) on the new `Audio` folder and select **Create | Folder** from the context menu. Name the folder `Ambient` and your **Project** window now look like the following screenshot:

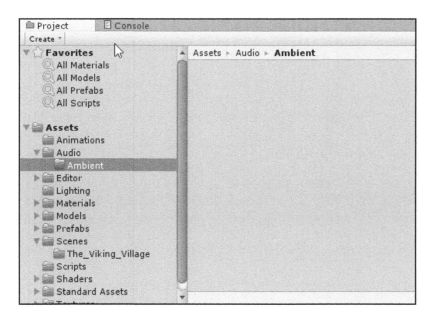

New Audio and Ambient folders created in Project window

5. Right-click [*control* + Click on Mac] on the `Ambient` folder and select **Show in Explorer** from the context menu. This will open a file explorer on your desktop. Double-click on on the `Ambient` folder to open it; the folder should be empty.

6. Go to your desktop and open the books downloaded source code `Chapter_1_Audio` folder in another file explorer window. Drag the folders so that they are adjacent to each other and both visible. A sample screenshot is shown here:

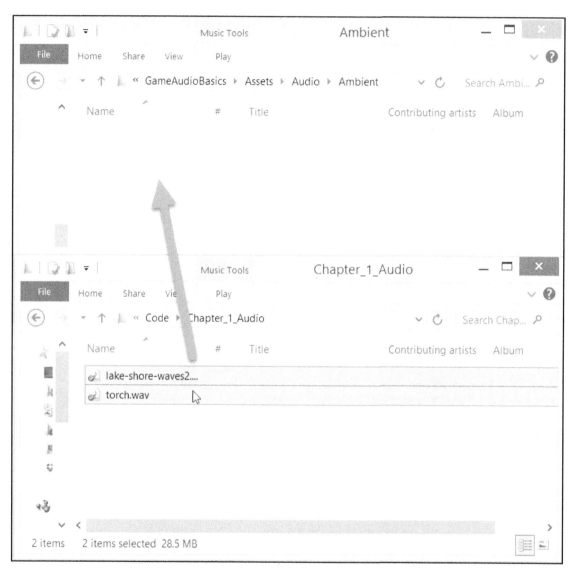

Ambient and source code folder: Chapter_1_Audio side by side

7. Drag and drop all the files from the `Chapter_1_Audio` folder into the `Ambient` folder. Then, switch back to the Unity editor. After a couple seconds, you should see the `Ambient` folder in the **Project** window update with the imported audio files, as shown here:

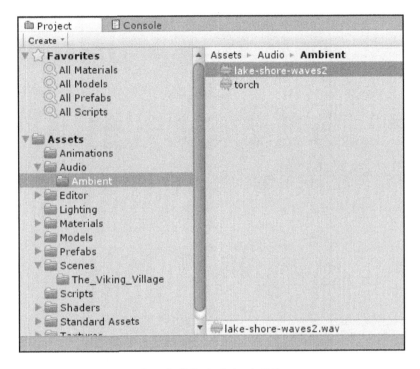

Imported audio files showing in project folder

8. Select the `lake-shore-waves2.wav` audio clip in the folder and then divert your attention to the **Inspector** window. You should see something similar to what is shown here:

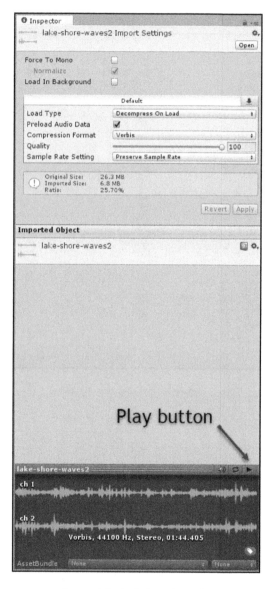

Inspector window showing imported audio clip

9. Click on the asset play button, as shown in the preceding screenshot, and enjoy the soothing sounds of waves hitting the lake shore. We will get into more details about what those other properties are in the next section.

Inspecting the imported audio files

Now that we have imported some new audio files into our project, let's take a more detailed look at how Unity handles them by following the exercise here:

1. Focus your attention to the bottom of the Inspector window showing the audio file import settings. The following is a labeled screenshot of the details we want to pay attention to:

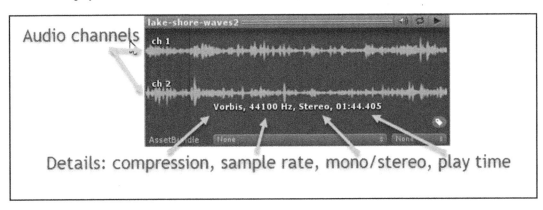

Examining the audio file details

2. The following is a definition of what each of those sections/terms mean:
   - **Audio channels**: This shows the various audio channels composed into the file. Unity can support up to eight channels of audio. The file we are showing has two channels in order to support stereo.
   - **Compression**: Unity will automatically apply compression against imported audio files. Very often you will want to stay with the defaults, but we will look at ways of altering the compression method here. Vorbis, the compression type shown, is similar to mp3. The compression formats supported by Unity are: Vorbis, PCM, and ADPCM.

- **Sample rate**: This represents the frequency at which the audio sample was recorded, displayed as the samples per second. Most audio will be recorded in the range of 44100 and 48000 Hz. Generally, the higher the sample rate, the better quality the audio will be and Unity supports up to 192000 Hz.
- **Mono/Stereo**: This stipulates if the audio will play in stereo or mono. This setting will be honored if a sound is played in 2D space. However, if the sound is played in 3D, this will change. We will explore 3D sound in more detail at the end of this chapter.
- **Play time**: This displays the minutes and seconds an audio file will play for.

3. Now that we have those definitions under our belt, we will take a look at how to alter some of the import settings. Switch your attention to the top of the **Inspector** window as shown in the following screenshot:

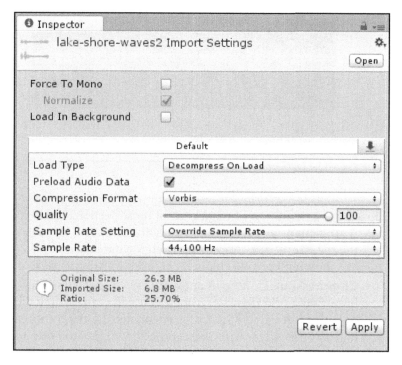

Inspector window audio import settings panel

4. Since we will be importing a number of audio files into Unity, it is important we review each of these settings in more detail here:

- **Force To Mono**: This setting allows you to force Unity to down sample the file into a single channel, which is useful for sounds be played in 3D or you just don't want to play in stereo.

- **Normalize**: This setting won't activate unless you force mono. Normalize refers to the down sampling process of converting a multichannel sound to a single channel. Normalize all the channels to be sampled at an equalized volume.

- **Load In Background**: This sets the clip to load in a background while the game is running. If you have a large audio file, you will certainly want to check this setting.

- **Load Type**: This tells Unity how to load the clip into memory and supports the following settings:

  - **Decompress On Load**: This works well for small to medium size files. The files will be decompressed into memory on load and not suffer any CPU performance when playing.

  - **Compress in memory**: This is best for large files played less frequently. Files will need to be decompressed before playing but the savings in memory may make this a preferred option.

  - **Streaming**: This plays the file directly from the disk. It is a great option for media played infrequently or memory management is an issue.

- **Preload Audio Data**: By default, the audio clip will be loaded unless this option is unchecked. Again, this is another good option for less frequently played files.

- **Compression Format**: This is the format used to compress the clip and is dependent on the game build settings. The format will match one of the following settings:

  - **PCM**: The pulse-code modulation is a format best used for smaller file sizes.

  - **ADPCM**: This is the format best used for short sounds with a lot of noise such as footsteps and weapons.

  - **Vorbis/MP3**: This is best used to compress larger files such as our sample file. The quality of compression can be set by the quality slider.

  - **HEVAG**: This is similar to ADPCM.

- **Quality:** This is a slider that allows you to downgrade the quality of a clip with the benefit of reducing the file size.
- **Sample Rate Setting**: This sets how the sample rate of the clip should be handled and will be one of the following:
    - **Preserve Sample Rate**: This prevents the sample rate from being modified.
    - **Optimize Sample Rate**: This will select the highest rate sampled within the file and apply that.
    - **Override Sample Rate**: This allows the sample rate of the file to be downgraded. This will generally reduce the audio quality but for some large files or specific audio effects this may be preferred. This setting can never be used to artificially increase the quality or sample rate of a clip.
- **Sample Rate**: This value can only be changed if the Override Sample Rate setting was selected. Again, a sample can easily be downgraded to reduce the file size and quality but this setting cannot be used to upgrade a file beyond what it was originally recorded at.

5. As you can see, there is a lot going on in this panel and initially it may be difficult to grasp all the terminology used. Fortunately, this panel is something we will come back to several times over the course of this book and you will get to become quite familiar with the terms and settings.

Let's use some of that new knowledge to tweak the settings on that `torch.wav` file we just imported by conducting the following exercise:

1. Select the `torch.wav` file in the **Project** window `Assets/Audio/Ambient` folder.
2. In the Inspector window, check the **Force To Mono** setting. The torch clip will be used as a full 3D sound and does not need two channels or stereo. Be sure the **Normalize** box is also checked.
3. Click on the **Apply** button at the bottom of the panel. After a few seconds, this will apply the changes to the audio clip; Notice at the bottom of the Inspector window how the audio is now using only a single channel. Click on the play button to play the clip, you will most likely not hear much difference.
4. Click on the **Sample Rate Setting** drop down-list and select the **Override Sample Rate** option. Then, open the **Sample Rate** list and select **22050 Hz** from the list and then click on the **Apply** button. After the settings are applied, the preview clip should match the following screenshot:

Preview showing modified audio clip settings

5. The reason we downgraded the clip is to reduce some of the harsher tones. Feel free to downgrade or adjust the sample further to see the effects it has on the sound quality. Be sure to reset the clip to the settings shown in the preceding screenshot as we will be using this sound later in the chapter.

Downgrading the torch clip to balance the tones may not be an optimal solution in some cases and in fact there are many other ways of equalizing a clip, as we will see. However, optimizing a clip at the source, as we did here, will always be in your best interest. In fact, if your game becomes bogged down due to overuse of audio, one of the core solutions is to optimize the imported file settings first. Audio performance and optimization is something we will cover in more detail in Chapter 11, *Audio Performance and Troubleshooting*.

6. After you are done editing the audio clip settings, select **File | Save Project** from the menu. This will save the project and allow us to close the editor now if we need to.

That completes our introduction to importing audio content into Unity. In the next section, we will look at how these clips can be added to our village scene.

Audio sources and listeners

Before we add audio to our scene, we need to cover a few more basic concepts within Unity.

Of course, the best way to do that is to get hands on and explore more of the scene objects with the following exercise:

1. If you have taken a break, open back up Unity and reload the `GameAudioBasics` project, which we saved at the end of the last section. Of course, if you haven't taken a break, good for you, and just continue as you were.

2. Now, divert your attention to the **Hierarchy** window and specifically the search field at the top of the window. Click on the down arrow at the left of the search field, to select the form of the search as shown in the following screenshot:

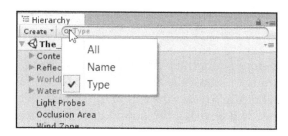

Setting the search type

3. Now, enter `AudioListener`; make sure to use the same case in the search field. This will filter the GameObject in the **Hierarchy** window with an AudioListener component attached, as shown in the following screenshot:

Hierarchy window showing filtered list of game objects with AudioListener

4. As you can see, this filtered list of objects is showing us the various scene cameras. A camera in Unity is what captures the rendered view of the scene. As such, you can think of a camera as the player's eyes to the game world. Therefore, it only makes sense that we also make the camera be able to listen to the world using the AudioListener component. That way, as the camera moves around the scene, the ears or Audio Listener, will also be tightly coupled.

A GameObject in Unity is the base scene object. What differentiates one object from another is the components attached to the GameObject. A component is a script that applies specialized functionality to a GameObject. A component could include everything from a camera, audio listener, audio source, mesh renderer, and so much more. The Inspector window allows you to view, modify, add, and remove components on a GameObject.

5. Select **Camera_high** at the top of the list in the **Hierarchy** window and take a look at the **Inspector** window and bottom-right corner of the **Scene** view as shown in the following screenshot:

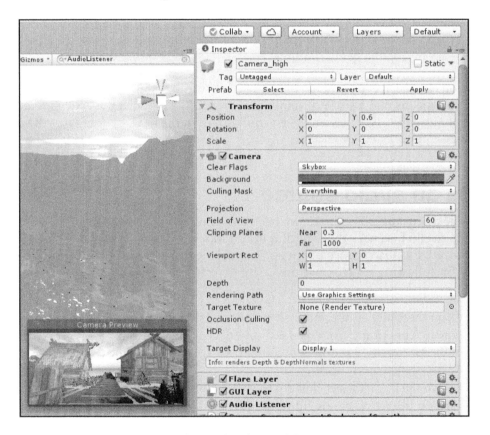

Camera preview and Inspector window

6. As you can see, there are a number of components attached to the **Camera_high** object in the **Inspector** window. We won't get into the details of all the components but just take notice of the **Camera** and **Audio Listener**. Remember that these two components equate to the scene's eyes and ears. Select the **Camera_high** object selected and press the **Play** button to run the scene.

7. After the scene starts running and switches to the **Game** view, press the *Esc* key to unlock the mouse. Then, go to the **Inspector** window and scroll through the components. Feel free to turn off and on components by unchecking the checkbox beside the component name. You can even alter the component settings if you like. Notice how the **Game** view changes as you make those changes. Don't be afraid to change several things; as long as you are in play mode, nothing will be saved.

8. When you are done with exploring the **Inspector** window, press the Play button again to stop the game running.

Good. As you can see, we already have a number of Audio Listener components set up on the scene. This means that we can certainly hear any audio. However, we are still missing the source of our audio, which hasn't been configured. In the next section, we will add an Audio Source component to our scene.

Adding an audio source

In order to hear any audio in a scene, we need two components added to game objects. They are the Audio Listener - the ears, and the Audio Source - the noise. As you probably already realized, the dead silence of our scene must mean there are no configured Audio Sources. In the following exercise, we are going to rectify that issue by adding an Audio Source:

1. Open the Unity editor and make sure the `Viking Village` scene is loaded. If you are continuing from the last section, be sure to click on the **X** on the right side of the **Hierarchy** window search field. This will remove the type filter and show all the scene objects again.

2. Locate the GameObject called **AccessibleVolume** in the **Hierarchy** window and click on the arrow beside it to expand and show its child objects. Select the **Capsule 5** object and press *F*, to frame select the object as shown in the following screenshot:

Frame selecting the Capsule 5 GameObject

3. What we want to do is use the **Capsule 5** object as an Audio Source for our `lake-shore-waves` ambient sound we imported earlier. We will use this object as it is conveniently situated close to where we want our Audio Source. Before adding the audio though, let's make a couple changes to the capsule.

 We are going to add the audio to the scene following the audio layers and groups we defined earlier. Therefore, the first layer we will be adding the audio to is for the ambient and environmental background noises.

4. With the capsule object still selected, rename the object `Ambient_lake-shore-waves` and then set the **Z** position on the **Transform** component to `60` as shown in the following screenshot:

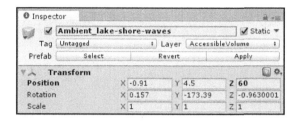

Renaming and altering the position of the Capsule 5 GameObject

Giving your game objects an appropriate name is essential, especially as your scene becomes more complex. Notice how we prefixed the object name with our layer name and then followed that with the audio clip name.

5. After you changed the **Z** position of the **Transform,** you will notice that the object moves to shore of the lake in the **Scene** view. This is exactly what we want, as this capsule object will be the source for the lake-shore-waves ambient sound.

6. Next, click on the button **Add Component** button at the bottom of the **Inspector** window. Type `audio` in the search text and notice how the list filters to components with audio in the name. Select the Audio Listener component as shown in the following screenshot:

Adding the Audio Source component

7. We now have an empty **Audio Source** component on our object. Click on the target icon located next to the **AudioClip** property. This will open the **Select AudioClip** dialog. Select the **lake-shore-waves2** clip from the list as shown in the following screenshot:

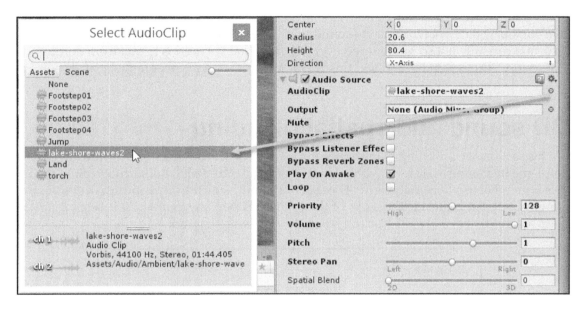

Setting the AudioClip on the component

8. Close the dialog after selecting the clip. We won't worry about all the other settings on the component right now. However, we do want to make sure the clip loops, since, after all, it is ambient sound that should keep playing over and over again. Click on the checkbox next to the **Loop** setting to make sure the audio loops.

 Audio clips will typically be designed to either play forever, called a loop, or play just once, called a single shot. In most cases, you will want your ambient sounds to loop, but not always. Whereas, audio-like weapons or footsteps will generally be a single shot. A looping audio clip is one that is designed to play over and over again with no noticeable break or change when the clip plays over.

9. With the Audio Source is added to the scene, press the Play button. Explore the scene by moving around and listening to the audio as you move. When you are done exploring, press Ctrl+P (*command* + P on Mac) to stop the scene running.

10. Select **File | Save Scene** from the menu, to save the changes we made to the scene. It is a good habit to save your scene often in Unity and especially when you are working with large scenes.

Good, we now have an ambient Audio Source in our scene. Of course, most likely, the first thing you noticed is that the sound was everywhere and that certainly is not what we want. We obviously only want our waves sound to be more audible when we get closer to the lake and certainly not so pronounced everywhere. What we need is to make our Audio Source use 3D or spatial sound and this is exactly what we will cover in the next section.

3D sound and spatial blending

In this section, we are going to introduce the concept of 3D sound and show how this is implemented at the basic level within Unity. Since the introduction of virtual reality, there has been other implementations of 3D or spatial sound, which Unity can support through plugins, but that is outside the scope of this section. Either way, perhaps it is best to start with a definition of 2D and 3D sound using the following diagram:

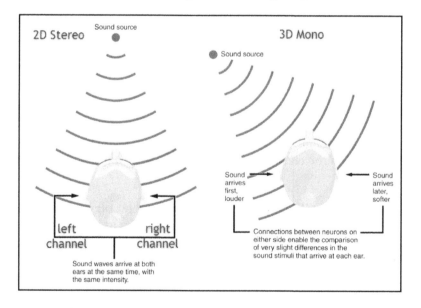

Representation of 2D stereo versus 3D mono or spatial audio (see: https://icodelikeagirl.com)

In Unity, the basic simulation of 3D sound is achieved by reducing the audio to a single channel and then attenuating (altering the volume), depending on the distance and location to the listener. There are several variables that allow us to customize how an Audio Source is spatialized in Unity, which we will cover when we convert our lake waves 2D ambient sound to 3D in the exercise here:

1. Continuing from the last section, be sure the `Ambient_lake-shore-waves` object is selected in the **Hierarchy** window.
2. Go to the **Inspector** window and scroll the component list to the bottom so that all of the **Audio Source** component is visible.
3. Drag the **Spatial Blend** slider all the way to the right in order to make the sound entirely 3D as shown in the following screenshot:

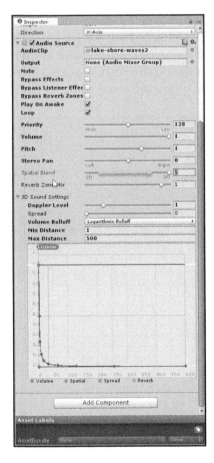

Setting the spatial blend on an Audio Source

Depending on the audio effect you are after, you may not want a full 2D or 3D Audio Source. Fortunately, with the Spatial Blend slider, you can select a mixture of both 2D and 3D sound. An example of an Audio Source that may use both 2D and 3D is an audio effect that needs to be heard everywhere but also has an obvious source.

4. At this point, we won't make any other changes to the **Audio Source** but take note of the 3D sound settings and especially the graph at the bottom of the component. Observe the line representing the listener position on the graph. Pay particular attention to that line, and press the Play button to run the game.

5. Move around the scene and move to the water down the boardwalk. Notice how the sound does get louder as you approach the water or if you turn the direction will also change to represent where the Audio Source is. However, the sound probably isn't quite as loud as we want and the falloff is just too gradual.

6. Stop the scene from running by pressing *Ctrl+P* (*command* + P on Mac).

7. Let's alter the 3D settings on our Audio Source. Change the **Max Distance** on the **3D Sound Settings** of the Audio Source to 100. Notice how this changes the graph as shown in the following screenshot:

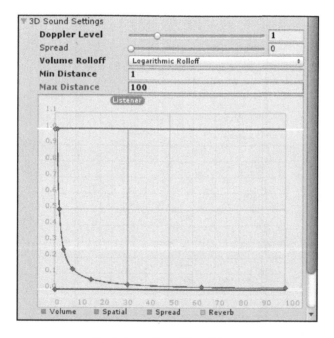

Changing the max distance of the Audio Source

8. Press play and move around the scene again. Notice how the sound now attenuates better as you move close to the shore. Feel free to change the various 3D sound settings and see what effect they have on the audio playback.

The **3D Sound Settings** volume/distance graph curves and lines can also be altered by clicking on them and dragging the line or keys to alter their position and shape. Double clicking on a curve or line will introduce a new key which will allow you to alter the shape of the curve even further. With this ability to alter an audio sources volume, spatial, spread, and reverb over distance is very powerful and can allow you to create some very interesting effects.

9. When you are finished altering the Audio Source settings stop the scene. At this point, if you find a combination of different audio settings, you think, might work better, feel free to set those values now. After you are done making the changes, be sure to save the scene by selecting **File - Save Scene** from the menu.

As you can appreciate, now there are numerous ways to configure a sound to be 2D, 3D, or some mixture of both. How about we add another ambient sound for all the torches in our village by following this exercise:

1. Switch your attention to the **Hierarchy** window and click on the search type dropdown on the left of search field. Then, be sure to select by **Name** as shown in the following screenshot:

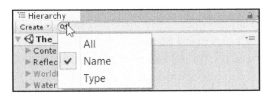

Changing search filter type to by Name

2. Enter `prop_torch` in the search field. Notice how the **Hierarchy** window filters the objects to just display those with the matching name. Select all the objects in the window by clicking on the top item and then while holding the Shift key, select each of the remaining items in the list. So, all the torch items are selected as shown in the following screenshot:

Selecting all the torch objects

3. Making sure that all the objects are still selected, go to the **Inspector** window and click on the **Add Component** button at the bottom of the window. Then, as you did before, type `audio` in the search field to filter the list to audio components. Select the Audio Source component from the list to add it to all the `prop_torch` GameObjects.

In our example, we are modifying several copies of the same object, the torch. Yet that doesn't have to be the case. You can use this same technique to modify several different objects as long as they share a common component.

4. After the **Audio Source** is added to the objects, set the properties on the component to match those in the following screenshot:

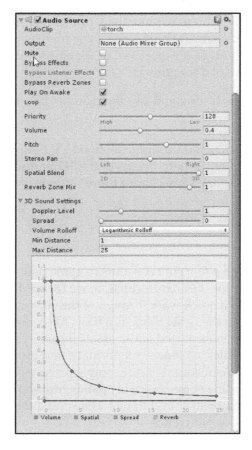

Torch Audio Source properties

5. If you find yourself struggling to set any of the properties on the Audio Source component, refer to the preceding sections in this chapter. After you are done making the edits, press the Play button to run the scene.

6. Be sure to explore the scene and be sure to move close to the water and around the torches. Feel free to make changes to the Audio Source settings as you explore. As always, if you find some settings sound better, remember those and make those edits again after you exit the play mode.

Have you noticed that the exercise instructions become less specific as you move through the exercises? Well, of course that is intentional and not only will it test your knowledge and make sure you are paying attention, but it also forces you to explore the Unity editor and find your own way to do something. There are numerous ways to do even the simplest tasks in Unity, and as you gain experience in the editor, you will find your own preferred ways of doing things.

7. When you are done testing and tweaking audio, be sure to the save the scene and project.

Well, that completes this section and our introduction to 3D sound in Unity. We covered this material quickly and did not go into details of the **3D Sound Settings**. There will be plenty of time to cover additional details about those settings in upcoming chapters.

Summary

In this chapter, we introduced a few core concepts in game audio, which we will expand on in successive chapters. After the audio introduction, we focused on downloading and installing Unity, followed by a quick walk through of the editor. From there, we imported a complete sample project from the Asset Store as a basis for completing the exercises in this and the later chapters. We then imported audio assets into the sample project and learned about compression, sample rates, channels, file formats, and more. With those new audio assets, we configured an ambient sound in our sample project, deciding later to convert that sound to 3D after understanding some basics of spatializing sound. Finally, we finished the chapter by adding another ambient sound to our scene and altering the various Audio Source settings to our auditory preference.

With this introductory chapter done, in the next chapter we will again dive into new areas of game audio and Unity development, which will include an introduction to Unity scripting, audio triggers, physics, and weapons sounds and music.

2
Scripting Audio

Unity is a powerful game engine that provides an excellent editor interface that allows you to develop games without any coding skills using various predeveloped assets. However, while it is possible to build games without code, it is less practical and will just restrict your creativity in the end. The scripting engine in Unity is powerful and relatively easy to use, especially if you have any experience or knowledge of using a C style language (JavaScript, C, C++, Java, and C#). Even if you are here as a sound designer looking for tips on how to work with audio in Unity, you will benefit greatly from learning some scripting. For those of you who are quite familiar with scripting in Unity, don't run off to the next chapter. While this chapter will cover scripting at a basic level, it still will focus primarily on working with audio components.

 This chapter will only teach you some basic Unity scripts in C# focused on using audio components. We will not go into details of syntax or language structure and it is intended as a phrase book for reuse. If you are interested in learning more about C# scripting in Unity, there are plenty of free online resources available, just a search away.

For this chapter, we will start with a very quick introduction into Unity scripting and then quickly dive into writing scripts. While a good part of this chapter will start with scripting in Unity, our primary focus will be to continue working with the various audio components, understanding good sound design principals, weapons, and physics as well as other audio techniques. The following list summarizes what we will cover in this chapter:

- Introduction to scripting in Unity
- Building a musical keyboard
- Weapons and sound
- Randomizing audio
- Background music

For those of you continuing from the last chapter, you should have everything you need already. If you have jumped ahead to this chapter from the earlier one in this book, be sure you have Unity downloaded, installed, and configured. You will also need to download the book's source code from the Packt website and the Unity `Viking Village` sample project from the Asset Store. Refer back to `Chapter 1`, *Introducing Game Audio in Unity*, if you are unsure on how to locate and download this asset from the Asset Store.

As always, unless you are a Unity master, it will most certainly benefit you to complete the exercises as you read through the material in this chapter. There really is no better way to learn than to do.

Introduction to scripting in Unity

In this section, our goal is to understand how Unity scripts integrate as components on top of GameObjects. If you recall from `Chapter 1`, *Introducing Game Audio in Unity*, all the functionality built into Unity is in the form of components and components are just scripts and code. Take a look at the following diagram, which should demonstrate the basic concepts of a **GameObject** and **Component:**

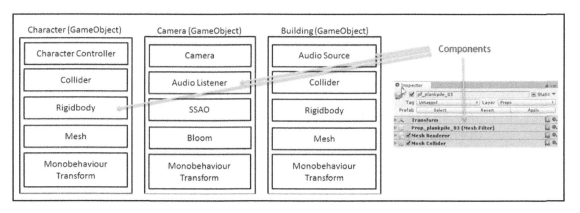

A simplistic view of how components combine to create various game objects

As the diagram shows, all objects are derived from GameObject, which means, they all essentially share the same base level object. If you look at the bottom of the objects in the diagram, you will see a component called `MonoBehaviour` with `Transform`. As we will see, `MonoBehaviour` is the base component, that we will generally derive other components or scripts from.

Not all components have to be attached to a single GameObject. In fact, in most cases, a complex object will be made of multiple GameObjects with numerous components attached to each child GameObject.

Perhaps, it will be helpful if we took a look at what the basic structure of one of these scripts looks like, as follows:

```
Example.cs                          ○
No selection
  1 using UnityEngine;          ←——————   using library
  2
  3 public class Example : MonoBehaviour {
  4                                        class called Example derived
  5    // Use this for initialization         from MonoBehaviour
  6    void Start () {
  7
  8    }                          ←——————   initialization code goes here
  9
 10    // Update is called once per frame
 11    void Update () {
 12
 13    }
 14 }                            ←——————   game code goes here
 15
```

Screenshot from MonoDevelop showing framework of starting script

The preceding screenshot shows a starting Unity C# script in the MonoDevelop editor. It is the default scripting editor for Unity. We will see how to launch MonoDevelop or other script editors later, when we get our hands on scripting.

From the `Example.cs` script, you can see that there are four main sections in the starting script. At the top, we define any external libraries the script may need to import. The `UnityEngine` library, for instance, covers most of the core game engines functionality and will almost always be a requirement.

Next, we have the class definition. You can think of a class as a template or the blueprint of a component. As we mentioned before, a GameObject may use multiple components or scripts to describe its functionality. The naming syntax of `Example : MonoBehaviour` denotes that the class is called `Example` and it derives from `MonoBehaviour`. In most cases, your scripts will derive from `MonoBehaviour`.

After that, we have a couple of methods defined. One for carrying out object initialization (Start) and the other for running every frame (Update). There are several other methods Unity provides for interacting with the game engine but certainly the most common are Start and Update.

Let's carry out an exercise which should help demonstrate some of the preceding concepts further and get us prepared to write a simple script. Follow the instructions to get started:

1. Open up the Unity editor to the GameAudioBasics project we created in the last chapter or create a new project called GameAudioBasics. If you are unsure on how to create a new project, you should refer back to Chapter 1, *Introducing Game Audio in Unity*.

2. Create a new scene by selecting **File** | **New Scene** from the menu. If you are prompted to save the scene, then go ahead and do so.

3. The new scene should only have a **Main Camera** and **Directional Light**, as shown in the screenshot of the **Hierarchy** window as follows:

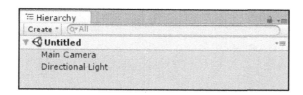

New scene contents

4. Create a new GameObject by selecting **GameObject** | **Create New** from the menu. Rename the new object VirtualKeyboard and reset the **Transform Position** to 0, 0, 0 as shown in the screenshot of the **Inspector** window here:

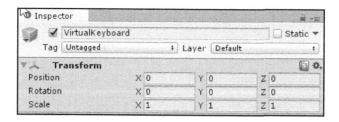

Setting Transform position to 0,0,0 or 0 Transform

5. At this point, if you look in the **Scene** or **Game** view, the new object will not be visible and that is expected. After all, the object is empty and does not contain any component to render a mesh.

6. Click on the **Add Component** button at the bottom of the **Inspector** window. Type `audio source` in the search textbox. This will filter the list to just show the **Audio Source** component. Select that component to add it to the object.

7. Click on the **Add Component** button at the bottom of the **Inspector** window, again. This time, type `New Script` in the search field. Select the arrow icon beside the **New Script** option to open the **New Script** panel as shown here:

Creating a new script called Keyboard

8. Enter the name of `Keyboard` as shown in the preceding screenshot. When you are done editing, click on the **Create and Add** button at the bottom of the panel.

9. Click on the gear icon beside the new Keyboard component, and from the context menu, select the **Edit Script** option as shown in the following screenshot:

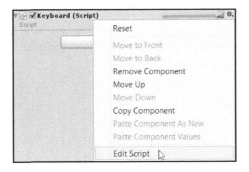

Editing the Keyboard component script

10. If you are new to Unity, then MonoDevelop; the default script editor will open with the new Keyboard (script). This script, aside from the name, will resemble the example script we already saw earlier.

 There are a number of different editors available for developing scripts in Unity. Visual Studio or Visual Studio Code are great editors that provide many additional features over MonoDevelop. For this book, we will continue to use MonoDevelop for the few exercises we will be carrying out scripting with. If you are working with more than a couple of scripts, you will certainly want to upgrade to a fully-featured editor.

11. Take a quick look around the MonoDevelop editor. The editor is like any other text editor you may have used before but with a number of added coding features. If you are new to scripting, don't be intimated. For the most part, we are only going to use this editor to write and edit a few lines of code.

That completes our very brief introduction to Unity scripting. In the next section, we are going to get hands-on and write a script to control audio playback in an interesting manner.

Building a musical keyboard

Now that we have looked at how quickly we can create a simple empty script, let's explore the possibilities of scripting audio components. As we already saw in the last chapter, it is possible to use audio components without writing any scripts. However, scripting gives you more control over an audio source with only a few lines of code.

In this section, we are going to use scripting to build a simple keyboard that you will be able to play multiple instruments with. We will even allow the keyboard to record and play back sessions. All in less than 30 lines of code. Follow the instructions here, to start creating this script:

1. We will continue where we left off from the last time by jumping back into MonoDevelop. Be sure the tab showing the `Keyboard` script is open and the script shell has not been modified.

2. At the top of the file, just below the `Keyboard` class definition, enter the following lines of code:

```
private AudioSource audioSource;
public int transpose = 0;
```

As you type within MonoDevelop, you will notice the editor helps you complete words by making suggestions. This feature is called **intellisense** and almost all code editors provide it at some level. To accept the top suggested word at any time just tap the *Tab* key.

3. Those couple of lines just store the objects `audioSource` and an integer variable called `transpose`. The keyword at the start of each line denotes whether the variable is `public` or `private`. A `private` variable is only accessible within the class, while a `public` variable is visible outside the class and exposed in the editor interface. There is a way to expose `private` variables in the editor interface but we will leave that for another time.

4. Next, enter the following line inside the `Start` method:

```
audioSource = GetComponent<AudioSource>();
```

5. That line just finds an `AudioSource` component attached to the GameObject and stores the value in that `private` variable we declared earlier. `GetComponent` is a special method that searches the GameObject that the script is attached to and looks for a specific component denoted within <> tags. If there is no matching component, the method will return nothing or `null`.

Be sure that you always match the character case of any variable names or keywords. For instance, `audioSource` is completely different from `AudioSource`. You will also generally want to match the white space (spaces and new lines) in the code as well. While you can get away with omitting a lot of white space, it just makes the code more readable.

6. Pay attention when you are entering the next section of code in the `Update` method, as it is the longest piece of code you will need to enter:

```
var note = -1; // invalid value to detect when note is pressed
if (Input.GetKeyDown ("a")) note = 0;  // C
if (Input.GetKeyDown ("s")) note = 2;  // D
if (Input.GetKeyDown ("d")) note = 4;  // E
if (Input.GetKeyDown ("f")) note = 5;  // F
if (Input.GetKeyDown ("g")) note = 7;  // G
if (Input.GetKeyDown ("h")) note = 9;  // A
if (Input.GetKeyDown ("j")) note = 11; // B
if (Input.GetKeyDown ("k")) note = 12; // C
if (Input.GetKeyDown ("l")) note = 14; // D

if (note >= 0 && audioSource != null)
{ // if some key pressed...
    audioSource.pitch = Mathf.Pow(2, (note+transpose) / 12.0f);
```

```
        audioSource.Play();
    }
```

7. This section of code within the `Update` method is run every frame of the game. Generally, our game will run from 30-60 frames per second, which put another way, means that the section of code will run 30-60 times per second or more. The first line creates a variable with the `var` keyword called `note` and sets the value to `-1`. After that, it does several `if` tests to determine what the currently typed keyboard key is using a special object called `Input`. `Input.GetKeyDown("")` returns true or false depending on whether the key is pressed. If the key is pressed (true) the value for `note` is set depending on the key pressed. `note` is set to a value that matches the pitch of the key, you can see in the end of line comments which key matches which note. The last test or `if` statement is a test to see if the value for `note` is greater than or equal to zero **and** (represented with `&&`) the `audioSource` is not equal to null. In order for the script to execute the code inside the if statement, both conditions must be true, hence the use of the and (`&&`). Finally, if a key is pressed and our `audioSource` has been found, we set the pitch using some math, based on the key pressed (`audioSource.pitch =`). Then, we play the sound by calling the `Play` method on the audio source using `audioSource.Play()`.

    The math function expressed by `Mathf.Pow(2, (note+transpose)/12.0f)` is used to calculate the frequency or pitch of a note using the 12-**tone equal temperament** (**TET**) method or 12-TET. It is a way of tuning a musical instrument to match a 12 note octave scale, or in our case, a virtual musical instrument. This allows us to tune a single note of an instrument into a full virtual instrument. In `Chapter 10`, *Composing Music*, we use other methods to play and create virtual musical instruments.

8. After you are done entering all the code in the editor, your script should match what is shown in the screenshot here:

```
Keyboard ▸ No selection
1 using System.Collections;
2 using System.Collections.Generic;
3 using UnityEngine;
4
5 public class Keyboard : MonoBehaviour {
6     private AudioSource audioSource;
7     public int transpose = 0;
8
9     // Use this for initialization
10    void Start () {
11        audioSource = GetComponent<AudioSource>();
12    }
13
14    // Update is called once per frame
15    void Update () {
16        var note = -1; // invalid value to detect when note is pressed
17        if (Input.GetKeyDown ("a")) note = 0;  // C
18        if (Input.GetKeyDown ("s")) note = 2;  // D
19        if (Input.GetKeyDown ("d")) note = 4;  // E
20        if (Input.GetKeyDown ("f")) note = 5;  // F
21        if (Input.GetKeyDown ("g")) note = 7;  // G
22        if (Input.GetKeyDown ("h")) note = 9;  // A
23        if (Input.GetKeyDown ("j")) note = 11; // B
24        if (Input.GetKeyDown ("k")) note = 12; // C
25        if (Input.GetKeyDown ("l")) note = 14; // D
26
27        if (note >= 0 && audioSource != null)
28        { // if some key pressed...
29            audioSource.pitch = Mathf.Pow(2, (note+transpose) / 12.0f);
30            audioSource.Play();
31        }
32    }
33 }
```

Completed script in editor.

9. Now that we have our script written from the menu, select **File** | **Save** to save the script. After the file is saved, return it to the Unity editor and wait while the script compiles, which should only take a few seconds. At this point, you will want to open the **Console** window and make sure no red compiler errors appear. An example of a compiler error is shown in the following screenshot:

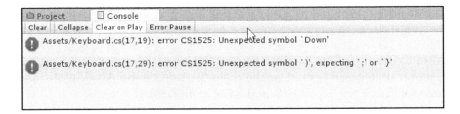

Compiler errors shown in the Console window

The compiler errors will often be the result of typos, incorrect case, or missing semicolons and/or braces. Try to take your time when entering a script for the first time in order to avoid these simple but frustrating mistakes.

10. Unity is generally very helpful in locating the script error, showing the line and position. However, you can also double-click on the error in the **Console** window and your code editor will open automatically with the cursor set on the offending line.

11. Be sure that your script is clean of any errors, you may see some warnings (yellow yield sign), but just ignore those and then click on the play button. The scene will run empty; this is because we have yet to set or even import our instrumental notes.

If you are unable to play the scene, it likely means you have a script compilation error. Verify that the console window has no errors, and if you made any changes to the script, be sure they are saved.

Well, hopefully you managed to get that script entered without any compiler errors. If you entered the script without any errors, give yourself a pat on the back. For those of you that had a few errors, don't get frustrated, it happens to the best of us.

If you feel that you just can't figure out this scripting thing and are completely stuck, not to worry. The completed version of the script is provided in the source code download folder called Scripts for this chapter.

Importing and playing notes

Of course, in order to use our new Keyboard script, we are going to need some notes recorded for at least one instrument. Let's get back into Unity and import some tunes by following the following exercise:

1. From the menu, select **Assets | Import Package | Custom Package....** A file explorer dialog will open. Use the dialog to find the book's downloaded source code for Chapter_2_Assets and a file inside called Chapter_2_Keyboard_Tunes.unitypackage. Select the file and click on the **Open** button to begin importing the asset.

2. A progress dialog will quickly flash showing the asset being decompressed and then the **Import Unity Package** dialog will be shown as follows:

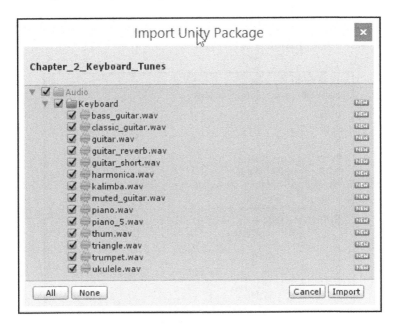

Import Unity Package importing keyboard tunes

3. Click on the **Import** button on the dialog to import all the tunes into the project. Again, you will see another progress dialog quickly flash and the assets will be imported.

4. Select the `VirtualKeyboard` object in the **Hierarchy** window. In the **Inspector** window, expand the **Audio Source** component we added earlier. Set the component's **AudioClip** source to the `ukulele` clip by clicking on the target icon beside the setting and then selecting the item from **Select AudioClip** dialog, as shown in the screenshot here:

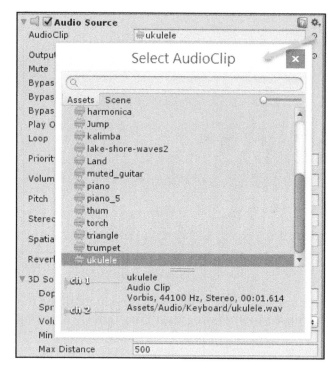

Setting the AudioClip source

5. Close the dialog after you make the selection. Keep all the defaults for the **Audio Source** component. No need to set 3D sound or other fancy audio settings.

6. Click on the play button to start the scene running. After the scene starts running, type some notes by typing any of the following keys a,s,d,f,g,h,j,k, or l.

7. Depending on your musical skills, you may be able to play notes or something that sounds like music. You can change the type of instrument anytime while the scene is running. Just be sure if you change an instrument to click back in the **Game** view, otherwise the keyboard strokes won't register.

8. The audio sounds provided in the imported asset will generally be recorded from instruments playing a C4 note or middle C. However, not all the audio is recorded at the middle C, some of it may be other notes. If you have a musical ear you can alter the instrument so it starts from middle C by setting the `transpose` on the `Keyboard` component. A `transpose` value of +12 or -12 will increase/decrease the note by a full octave. While a transpose value of +1/-1 will tune the note up or down the scale to D (+1) or B (-1) for instance. The following chart shows how the notes are arranged and written on sheet music, with corresponding matching keyboard keys shown underneath:

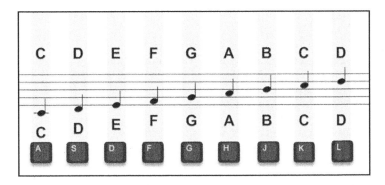

Notes matching keyboard keys

9. When you are done playing the keyboard, click on the play button to stop the scene. Be sure to save the scene by selecting from the menu **File | Save scene as....** This will open a **Save Scene** dialog, keep the default path, name the scene `VirtualKeyboard`, and click on **Save**.

As you can see, with just a small amount of code, we were able to control playing an audio source into a virtual instrument. While the keyboard is not perfect, it certainly demonstrates the power and ease of scripting audio. In the next section, we are going to make some improvements to the `Keyboard` script in order to demonstrate other scripting and audio concepts.

Enhancing the virtual keyboard

Our Keyboard script allows us to play an audio source like an instrument. In order to demonstrate a couple of other scripting concepts with audio sources, let's add a couple of features to our script by following the following exercise:

1. The first set of features that we will add is the ability to record a session and then play the audio back. This may sound like an incredibly complex task, but it is something we can accomplish with just a few more lines of code.

2. Open back up MonoDevelop or your favorite script editor and add the following lines just after the declaration of the transpose variable, as shown here:

```
public int transpose = 0; //after this line
private List<int> notes = new List<int>();
private int index = 0;
public bool record;
public bool playback;
```

3. The first new variable is marked private and is used to store the notes played as we record. The variable is a List that stores a specific type, in this case, integers or note values. Next, is a variable called index, which will be used to indicate the playback position. After that, we have two Boolean variables marked public, which will allow us to control if the script is recording or playing.

4. Make your way down to the middle of the Update method, the empty line between the top section of if's and the bottom if statement and insert the following section of code:

```
if (record) {
   notes.Add (note);
} else if (playback) {
   index = index + 1;
   if (index > notes.Count - 1)
       index = 0;
   note = notes [index];
}
```

5. That piece of code may be a little tricky as you have to be careful to get all the braces (`{ }`) in the right place. Apart from that, the code is fairly simple. The first `if` statement checks if the script is set to `record`, if so, then it adds the currently played note to that List, called `notes`. Next, comes a second `if` statement prefixed with an `else`. The `else` ensures that if the first test fails, then the second `if` statement will be tested. However, unlike the aforementioned multiple if statements, the first condition must fail. This if/else statement, therefore, adds two additional states or modes to our keyboard, which already had a default play state. Inside the `else if` statement, if the `playback` value is `true`, then it does a test to make sure that the incremented index value is not greater than the number of items in the list subtracted by one. We subtract by one to make sure the index value is never greater than the number of items in the list. If the value of the index is greater than the list count, we reset the index to zero in the next line. In the last line of the code `note = notes[index];`, we index or select into the list by a value represented by the `index` variable. Just remember, that while the script is in playback mode, the index value will keep looping over the values in the list. Thus, any session you record will keep looping until you stop playback.

6. After you are done entering those few lines, save the file and go back to the Unity editor. As mentioned earlier, make sure the script compiles with no compiler errors. If you have no compiler errors, press play. Otherwise, go back and fix the compiler errors.

7. As the scene is running, be sure to select the `VirtualKeyboard` object in the **Hierarchy** window, so you can look at the components in the **Inspector** window, as shown here:

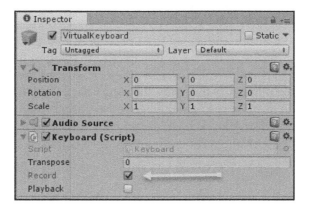

Keyboard script running in the Record mode

8. Click on the checkbox next to the **Record** setting on the **Keyboard** component. Click on the mouse in the **Game** view and then type some keys to play the virtual instrument. After a 15-30 seconds of playing, click on the **Record** checkbox to stop recording. Then click on the **Playback** checkbox to play the session you just recorded.

If you are trying to find or think of something to play, the following score is always a good starting place:

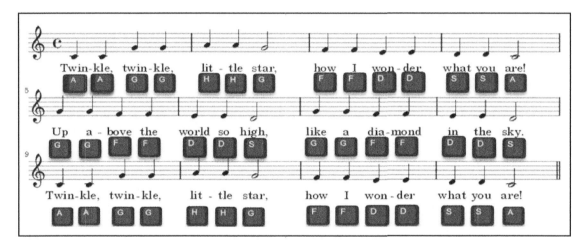

Play the song by typing the respective keys as shown, on your keyboard.

9. Let the session play for a couple of loops. When you are finished testing the new features, click on the play button to stop the scene.

As you can see, with just a dozen additional lines of code, we added a couple of significant features to our simple example. Of course, there are plenty of other features you could add to this example in order to create a full-blown synthetic keyboard, perhaps, even allowing you to create musical scores in Unity and play the songs back later in a game, similar to an **MIDI** track. For now, that is all we are going to cover with this script, but feel free to add any additional features on your own. We will reuse this `Keyboard` script later in `Chapter 8,` *Visualizing Audio in Games*, syncing audio with graphics to demonstrate how audio can be synced with graphics.

If you are still feeling uncomfortable with scripting, that certainly is expected. The preceding exercise was really only intended to introduce you to a few core concepts that you can apply for the rest of the scripting examples in this chapter and the book. In the next section, we will look at another example that demonstrates more audio scripting concepts and is more practical for an actual game.

Weapons and sound

In the last couple of sections of the last chapter, we introduced ambient sounds as the first layer or group of audio to our `Viking Village`. For this section, we are going to introduce a new layer of audio, the direct feedback group. If you recall from the introduction in the first chapter, this is the layer of audio that covers sounds activated by a player action or reaction within the game, which may include audio such as explosions, weapons, character dialog, or boss music.

Back in `Chapter 1`, *Introducing Game Audio with Unity*, we introduced the terms diegetic and non-diegetic. Are you able to categorize the audio we have used thus far or in the next examples as diegetic or non-diegetic? A quiz will be provided at the end of this section.

What better way to introduce direct feedback audio than by adding a weapon and the sounds associated with a weapon. For the example in this section and following with our theme of a `Viking village`, the weapon we will use is a throwing ax. Since we are basically constructing a projectile weapon, the same concepts could be easily applied to other games for weapons such as grenades, cannons, and knives.

Jump back into Unity and follow the instructions here to start the next exercise:

1. Make sure that you have the `Viking Village` sample project from Unity loaded into the project you are using. If you need to download and install the village project, refer back to `Chapter 1`, *Introducing Game Audio with Unity*, in the section *Downloading and Importing Project Assets*.
2. From the menu, select **Assets** | **Import Package** | **Custom Package...**. This will open a file open dialog. Use the dialog to go to the place you downloaded the books, source code and open the `Chapter_2_Assets` folder. Select the file called `Chapter_2_Viking_Village_Start.unitypackage` and then click on the Open button to begin importing the file.

3. From the **Project** window, open the `Assets/GameAudio/Scenes` folder and double-click on the `The_Viking_Village_Chapter2_Start` scene to open it in the editor as shown here:

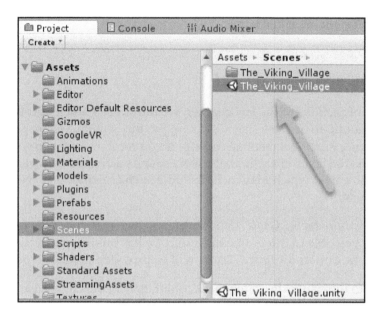

Opening starting scene

4. Wait a few seconds for the scene to open. After the scene loads, press play. Move around the scene and confirm that the torch and shore wave's ambient sounds can be heard. If you missed `Chapter 1`, *Introducing Game Audio with Unity*, you may want to skim back over the chapter sections where those audio sounds were set up.

5. Press the play button again to stop the scene. Locate the **Camera_high** object in the **Hierarchy** window by typing `Camera_high` in the search field. Then, select the object and confirm the camera preview matches as shown in the screenshot here:

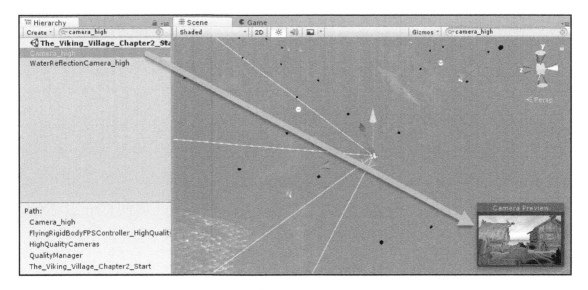

Selecting the Camera_high object in the Hierarchy window

6. Click on the **x** inside the search field to remove the filter. The `Camera_high` object should remain selected and visible in the scene. Right-click (*control* + click on Mac) to open the context menu and select **Create Empty**. This will create an empty child game object. Rename the new object `axController`.

7. Open the `Assets/GameAudio/Scripts` folder in the **Project** window and locate the `axController` script. Drag and drop the script from the **Project** window onto the new `axController` object in the **Hierarchy** window as shown in the screenshot:

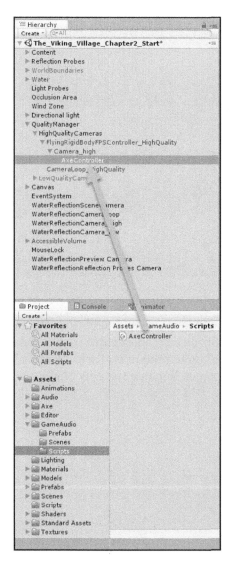

Dragging script onto axController object

8. With the `axController` object selected in the **Hierarchy** window, notice in the **Inspector** window that we now have a new **axe Controller** component. In the new component, there is an open slot for a GameObject called **axe Prefab**. Open the `Assets/GameAudio/Prefabs` folder in the **Project** window and drag the `axPrefab` prefab onto the empty slot in **axe Controller** component as shown here:

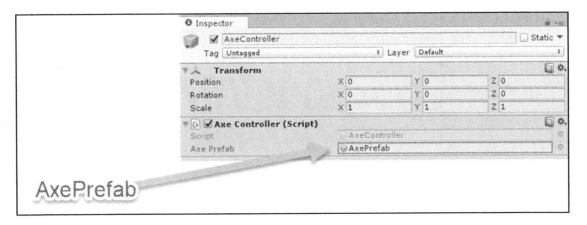

Dragging axPrefab prefab into the empty GameObject slot

 A Prefab is GameObject that has been saved outside of a scene as a reusable object as a Project asset. They are an essential item in Unity and used everywhere. You will learn more about Prefabs as we progress through the book.

9. Press play to start the scene again. This time, as you are moving around, click on the mouse button. Now, your player throws an axe as shown in the screenshot here:

An axe being thrown in the scene

10. When you are done throwing your fair share of axs, press the play button to stop the scene. Be sure to save the scene and your hard work by selecting **File** | **Save Scenes** from the menu.

Certainly, at this stage of the book, you noticed the missing audio of the axe being thrown and hitting objects right away. Fortunately, we will look at correcting these omissions in the next sections.

Throwing the ax

When the player throws the ax, we want our audio to describe a couple of things. First, we want the player to know they are throwing something, so we certainly need to add a sound for throwing. Second, that axe looks big and heavy, which means we probably also want to describe that with perhaps a grunting sound.

Remember, as a sound designer, your job is not just to drop in audio effects that seem to match an action or environment. You also want to add sounds that invoke emotion, mood, and enhance the players connection with their character or the world, which takes us back to diegetic and non-diegetic sounds. Are you keeping track and ready for the quiz at the end of the chapter?

Open back up Unity to where we left off from the last section and follow the exercise to add those sounds:

1. Be sure to locate the `axController` object in the **Hierarchy** window and select it.

2. Click on the **Add Component** button in the **Inspector** window, this will open the component list drop down. Type `audio source` in the search field. Then, select the **Audio Source** component from the filtered list as shown in the screenshot here:

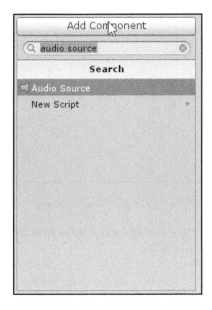

Selecting Audio Source component from component list

3. This will add an **Audio Source** component to the `axController` object. Add another **Audio Source** just as you just did. That's right, we want two audio sources.

After you have added both audio sources, open the first one and uncheck the **Play on Awake** setting. Then, click on the bullseye icon besides the **AudioClip** setting to open the **Select AudioClip** dialog. Type `throw` in the search field and then select the clip from the filtered list as shown in the following screenshot:

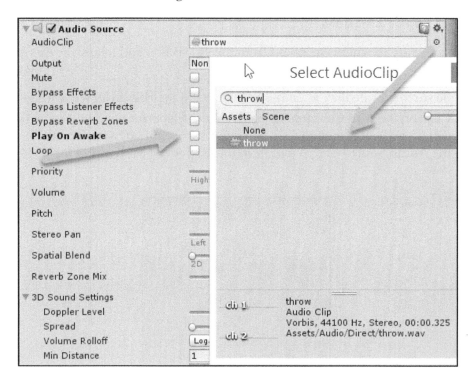

Setting the AudioClip for the Audio Source

1. Follow the same steps for the second **Audio Source**. However, this time look for and add the `grunt` audio clip.

In this example, we use two audio clips for the throw sound and grunt. The reason we don't combine these sounds into a single audio clip is to allow us more control. This control of playback will be demonstrated in the next section.

2. After you are done editing, press the play button. Feel free to move around the scene and throw some axs by clicking on the mouse button. When you are ready to stop playing, click on the play button to stop the scene.

As you can hear, by playing the scene, those simple additions of sound provided an extra level of direct auditory feedback to the player. Now, the player not only sees the axe being thrown, but they can hear it as well. There is the sound of the throw, a swooshing noise, overlaid with a vocal grunt. We added the grunt in order to let the player know there was considerable effort used in throwing the ax. If we omit the vocal grunt sound, a player feels disconnected about the effort the character is making. Let's try this, open up Unity and follow the exercise here:

1. Locate the `axController` object in the **Hierarchy** window and select it.
2. In the **Inspector** window, disable the second audio source (`grunt` audio clip) by unchecking the box beside the component name, as shown here:

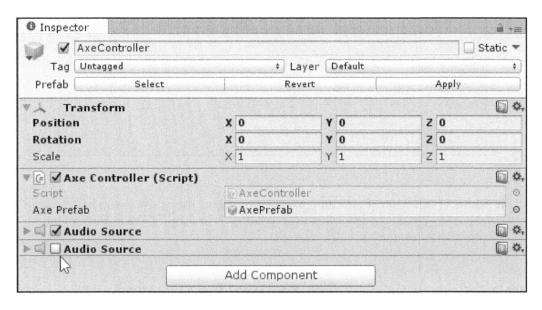

Turning off the second Audio Source

3. Press the play button to run the scene. Move around and throw several axs. Think about the mood or emotion you have toward the character as you throw the ax.
4. After you have played the scene for a while without the grunt sound, click on the checkbox on the second audio source to enable it again. Now, throw some more axs. Think again about how the connection to the character changes.

5. Next, expand the second audio source and lower the volume on the grunt audio clip, as shown here:

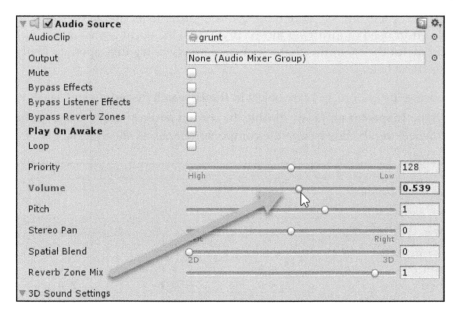

Changing the Audio Source volume

6. Think about what effect changing the volume of the grunt sound has or says about the character. Does a louder or softer grunt sound say something about the physical condition of the character?

7. When you are done experimenting, press the play button again to stop the scene.

Hopefully the preceding little exercise increased your appreciation for the subtlety of good sound design. We also started to introduce some other aspects of sound design known as adaptive sound. Adaptive sound and music is a dynamic way of altering game audio depending on the player's circumstances. Adaptive audio is prevalent in most games these days and a whole section of this book is devoted to it.

Of course, our scene is still missing the impact audio of the axe hitting things. Before we add those audio elements and since this chapter is about scripting, we will inspect the inner workings of the axController script in the next section.

Understanding the axController script

As you may have noticed, we avoided the tough work of manually entering the axController script. Instead, the script was provided as part of the chapter assets, not because the script is complicated, but because we wanted to focus on understanding audio rather than improving your typing skills. Although, we do still want to take the time to look over the script and understand the inner workings.

Open up Unity and follow the steps given to open the script in the editor:

1. Go to the **Project** window, and in the search field, type axcontroller. This will filter the contents of the **Project** window to show you the axController script. The file is shown in the screenshot here:

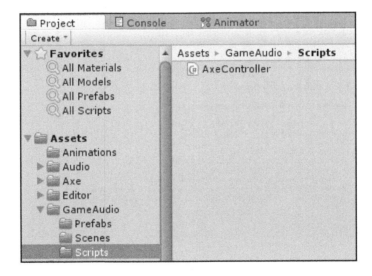

Finding and selecting the axController script

2. Select the script to display the file in the **Inspector** window as shown here:

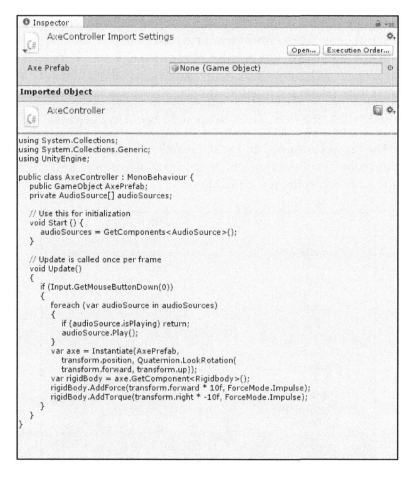

axController script shown in the Inspector window

3. Take a look at the script and notice that it is broken down into the same sections we used in our `Keyboard` script.

4. At the top of the script is the first section, the variable declarations. Again we have a mix of `public` and `private` variables as shown here:

```
public GameObject axPrefab;
private AudioSource[] audioSources;
```

5. The `public` variable `axPrefab` is used to hold the prefab we set as the thrown object. Remember how we set it by dragging the premade prefab into the open slot. Notice that it is of type GameObject, which means we could allow for almost any object to be thrown. Next, the `audioSources` variable is an array (denoted by `[]`) of audio sources. The variable is marked private, which means it will be set internally in the class.

6. The next section is the `Start` method. Remember the `Start` method is used to initialize variables and perform start-up tasks. True to form, inside the method the `audioSources` variable is initialized by calling `GetComponents`. It is just like the `GetComponent` method, but it returns all the components that match a type and not just one. Here is that line of code for review:

```
audioSources = GetComponents<AudioSource>();
```

7. The last section of our script is the `Update` method, which, as we recall, is executed for every frame of the game. Here is the code inside the `Update` method:

```
if (Input.GetMouseButtonDown(0))
{
    foreach (var audioSource in audioSources)
    {
        if (audioSource.isPlaying) return;
        audioSource.Play();
    }
    var axe = Instantiate(axPrefab,
        transform.position, Quaternion.LookRotation(
        transform.forward,transform.up));
    var rigidBody = ax.GetComponent<Rigidbody>();
    rigidBody.AddForce(transform.forward * 10f,
ForceMode.Impulse);
    rigidBody.AddTorque(transform.right * -10f,
ForceMode.Impulse);
}
```

8. The first thing to notice about this code it is that is all controlled by the first `if` statement, which is used to determine if the mouse button is pressed. This is done using the `Input` object, which allows us to inspect the keyboard and mouse state. The statement `Input.GetMouseButtonDown(0)` returns true/false depending on if the button is pressed. If the mouse button is pressed, then the code is executed inside the `if` statement. The next line of code starting with `foreach` is used to loop through `audioSources`, initialized earlier. The line: `foreach(var audioSource in audioSources)` is read as; for each audio source, we call a in `audioSources` do the following. Inside the `foreach`, the first statement determines if the audio source, `a`, is playing using the `isPlaying` property. If the audio source is playing, the return method is called, which exists of the entire `Update` method. This is done so that if an audio clip is playing, it can play to finish and to prevent rapid fire axe throwing. If the source is not playing we execute the next line, which uses the `Play` method to play the clip. This section of code will be executed for every audio source in the `audioSources` variable. The last part of code is the most complicated and is best left for readers wanting a broader discussion on using the Unity physics engine. Since our focus is primarily on audio scripting, just know that this section of code creates a new ax, with the `Instantiate` method, and then throws the object with the `AddForce` and `AddTorque` methods of the attached `Rigidbody`.

9. Notice that although we call some variables `axe` or `axePrefab`, this script could be used to throw any object.

Now, we have added the audio to provide direct feedback to the player when they throw that heavy ax. Yet, we are still missing one last piece of audio in the scene and that is the sound of the axe hitting objects. In the next section, we will add the audio effects of the axe hitting or colliding with other scene objects.

Playing sounds on collision

As we mentioned, the last missing element of our scene so far is the sound the axe makes when it hits something. Now, this may seem like it could be quite complicated, and in fact it can be. For instance, you may want to have different objects sound different when getting hit or even perhaps break and make more noise. While that level of detail is entirely possible in Unity, it is a bit overkill for our simple audio demonstration. Instead, we are going to add audio effects to just the axe by following the exercise here:

1. Enter the search text `axprefab` in the search field of the **Project** window. Select the prefab in the folder so the components are shown in the **Inspector** window.

2. Click on the **Add Component** button at the bottom of the Inspector window and then type audiosource in the search field. Select the **Audio Source** from the filtered list to add the component to the object.

3. Open the **Audio Source** component and set the properties to match what is shown in the screenshot here:

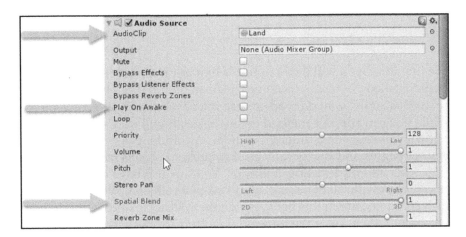

Setting Audio Source properties on axPrefab

4. Click on the **Add Component** button again and this time type axaudio in the search field. Select the **axe Audio Controller** component from the list to add it to the object.

5. Press play to start the scene running. Move around and of course throw those axs. Notice how the axe now makes a sound when it hits an object. When you are done testing, press play to stop the scene.

Did you notice as you were running the scene how the axe sounds were obviously not only 3D but they matched well to how much force the axe hit or landed with? That is because we modified the playback of the audio depending on the force of the collision. Let's examine what is happening in the axAudioCollider script here:

1. Locate the axAudioCollider script and open it in the **Inspector** window or your script editor. Either will work because we are only reviewing the script and not editing anything.

2. There is only one section of code we are interested in and that is shown here for review:

```
void OnCollisionEnter(Collision collision)
{
```

```
if (collision.relativeVelocity.magnitude > 2)
    {
        var magnitude = collision.relativeVelocity.magnitude;
        var volume = Mathf.Clamp01(magnitude / volumeRatio);
        var pitch = magnitude / pitchRatio;
        audioSource.volume = volume;
        audioSource.pitch = pitch;
        audioSource.Play();
    }
}
```

3. The first thing you will likely notice is that our main working code is in a new method called `OnCollisionEnter` instead of `Update`. The reason for this is because we only want our code to run if an event, such as a collision, is triggered. While you can add this method to any object, it will only trigger when the object's collider collides with a different collider. A collider is a core element to the Unity physics engine and is generally used to prevent objects from passing through each other and/or detecting collisions. You can also have colliders that allow objects to pass through but still alert you of a collision. We will explore the use of such colliders later in this book. Inside the collision event method, the first `if` statement tests to see if the force or magnitude of the event is large enough to warrant playing a sound. This eliminates the potential for a lot of additional noise if an object rolls around for a while after landing or gets hung up. After, set some temporary variables to hold the magnitude of the collision and the calculated alteration in volume and pitch. We calculate a volume and pitch change using a simple ratio formula of the collision magnitude over a constant. This attenuation based on collision force is natural, after all, the more forceful collision, the louder it is. That technique, combined with already setting the audio to use 3D gives a more natural quality to the impact of the ax. Finally, we set the volume and pitch change based on the calculations and then play the sound.

The `Mathf` static object is a library of useful math functions. The `Clamp01` function just makes sure the output value is always between the range 0 and 1.

4. After you take a look at the script, go back and select the `axPrefab` prefab so that it is visible in the **Inspector** window.

5. Press play to run the scene. Now, as the scene is running try changing the **Volume Ratio** and **Pitch Ratio** on the **axe Audio Collider** component as shown here:

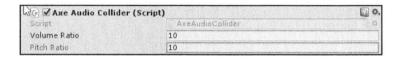

ax Audio Controller component settings

6. Notice how changing those values can alter the collision sounds of the ax, especially the pitch. Try to alter the ratios until you find a sound that sounds the most natural. When you are done testing, press play again to stop.

7. Be sure to save the scene and project.

Quiz time

Of the three audio effects, we used in this section can you identify if they were diegetic or non-diegetic?

ax throwing sound

Character grunt

ax colliding

The answers will be provided at the end of the end of the chapter.

Thus far, we have made good progress adding audio to our scene. Yet, as you continue testing over and over again are you starting to notice that all the audio becomes repetitive. In the next section, we are going to introduce techniques to break up that repetition.

Randomizing audio

Randomizing audio is the practice of tuning an audio source playback in a random manner to avoid exact repetition in your games audio. Of course, another way to avoid audio repetition is create multiple sound effects for the same noise, music or dialog, and then randomly select one each time the audio needs to be played. While using multiple variations of the same audio clip is preferred it does increase memory resource usage and asset management.

For this section, we are going to borrow a couple techniques we already used to slightly alter or randomize the playback of our audio without needing to provide multiple variations. Open up Unity and follow the following exercise to randomize the scene audio:

1. Locate the `axController` script in the **Project** window and then double-click on the script to open it in your editor.

2. Scroll down to around line 21 as shown here:

```
if (audioSource.isPlaying) return;
```

3. After that line, enter the following lines of code:

```
audioSource.pitch = 1.0f + Random.Range(-.1f, .1f);
audioSource.volume = 1.0f - Random.Range(0.0f, .25f);
```

4. Be sure the preceding code is entered before the `Play()` method is called. Those two lines of code alter the `pitch` and `volume` by a random amount determined by the `Range` method of the `Random` static object.

5. When you are done editing the script save the file and return to Unity. Be sure to wait for the script to compile and be sure there are no compilation errors. If there is you will need to fix them by correcting the errors in the script before proceeding.

6. Press the play button in Unity to test the scene. Move around and throw some axs, notice the slight variation in the audio now makes those sounds much less repetitive. Stop the scene when you are done testing.

As you can see with just a couple lines of scripting, we added variation to our audio effects. Providing your players with variation in audio and other effects reduces the repetitive nature of gameplay and extends their interest.

If you are interested, feel free to add variation to the other audio effects we currently have in the scene. With the `axAudioCollider` you could add a similar adjustment to the volume and pitch as we did with the preceding example. We will leave this exercise up to the reader to do on their own.

There is one other audio effect in the scene, which certainly benefit from some randomization and that is the torch audio. Follow the directions here to randomize the torch audio:

1. Get back into Unity and type `prop_torch` in the **Hierarchy** window search field. This will filter the list to just the torch props. Select all the torches in the window by selecting **Edit** | **Select All** from the menu. This will also select the scene but that is of no consequence. Your selection should match the following screenshot:

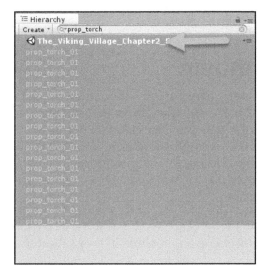

Selecting all objects in the Hierarchy window

2. Click on the **Add Component** button in the **Inspector** window and type `random` in the component search field. Select the **Random Audio Controller** component from the list to add it to torch objects.

The `RandomAudioController` script is essentially the same piece of randomization code, we used but in the `Start` method. Feel free to attach this script to any audio source you want to vary across multiple sources.

3. Press play to run the scene again. Are you blown away by the depth that one effect added to the scene? Now, you can hear multiple distinct torch sounds all around your character in the scene. Those minimal differences coupled with the 3D sound give the scene more depth or volume. You as the player, now feel as if you are in a much larger area which is a good thing.

4. Stop the scene and disable the **Random Audio Controller** then play the scene again. Note how the lack of audio variation makes the scene appear dull now.

5. When you are done testing, be sure the **Random Audio Controller** is enabled again and then save the scene and project.

Certainly, you can appreciate the value of giving your audio variation now. As you have seen the effects of audio randomization or variability can be quite astounding. Not to mention the effect it has on reducing game play repetitiveness. In the next section, we will look at one last example, scripting music.

Background music

In the last section of this chapter, we will introduce another layer of audio with background or theme music. This is an often overlooked layer that can really set the mood of the game or during the progression of a game. In later chapters of this book where we cover adaptive music we will get into detailed examples of altering music during gameplay. For now though, we are going to look at a simple use of scripting to set the looping behavior of some background music we want to use for our scene. Follow the instructions here to add background music to the scene:

1. Open up Unity to the `Viking Village` scene as we last left it. Create an empty `GameObject` in the scene and rename it `BackgroundMusic`.

2. Locate the `viking_music` audio clip in the **Project** window. Drag the clip onto the new `BackgroundMusic` object in the **Hierarchy** window. This will automatically add an audio source component with the audio clip set.

3. Locate the `MusicLooper` script in the **Project** window. Drag the script onto the `BackgroundMusic` object in the **Hierarchy** window. Set the properties of the **Music Looper** component to match those shown in the screenshot here:

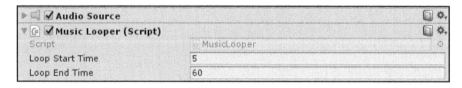

Music Looper component settings

4. Press play to start the scene. Let the scene run for at least a minute. Notice how the background music loops at roughly a minute. The `MusicLooper` script is used to extract sections from an audio file and play those over and over again. Press play again to stop the scene.

5. Open up the `MusicLooper` script in your script editor. As you can see the script is quite simple and the interesting section of code is shown here:

```
if (audioSource != null &&
    audioSource.isPlaying &&
    audioSource.time > loopEndTime)
{
    audioSource.time = loopStartTime;
}
```

6. This section of code, which is run in the `Update` method, checks every frame if the clip has played past the `loopEndTime`. If it has, the clip is reset back to the `loopStartTime`, which allows us to only play part of an audio clip.

The last example was short but surely showed you an effective way of playing only a part of audio clip with scripting. In later chapters, we will use other tools that provide far more control over a how a clip is played.

Quiz answers

ax throwing sound: diegetic, as you would expect to hear the axe as at is thrown

Character grunt: non-diegetic, this is an off screen sound that adds tone or mood to the scene

ax colliding: diegetic, you would expect the axe to make noise when it hits objects in the scene

Remember the importance of using non-diegetic sounds or music in a scene.

That completes this chapter on scripting. If you did not complete all the examples in the chapter the completed `Viking Village` scene is provided in the book's downloaded source code.

Summary

In this chapter, we introduced Unity scripting at a very high level. Even a basic understanding of scripting will be essential to sound designers or other artists working on Unity projects, as it provides them with the ability to make simple changes without interrupting a dedicated developer. From a basic scripting introduction, we worked our way into a more practical example of writing a simple musical keyboard. It not only introduced additional scripting concepts but also exposed how some of the essential audio source component properties can be altered to match an instrument. After that, we jumped back into the `Viking Village` project and looked at another good scripting example that showcased weapons. Through repeated testing of our scene we then realized our audio was becoming quite repetitive. The solution was to introduce volume and pitch randomization on our audio playback to introduce variation and make those sounds less repetitive. Finally, we looked at one last example with background music on our scene and controlling the looping play time.

Even this early in the book, we managed to cover many of the core audio components introduced in Unity 4.x and earlier. In the next chapter, we will jump into the new audio mixing features introduced in Unity 5 and start to explore a whole new world of audio development with Unity.

Introduction to the Audio Mixer

3

In the previous chapters, we introduced the core audio components within Unity and how to work with them through the editor and scripting. As you have seen, assuming that you worked through those chapters, we were able to introduce a number of audio elements into our basic scene with good results. Chances are, if you were building a simple game a couple of years ago, those techniques would have worked well for most of your needs. In fact, that was the case for the majority of Unity developers. However, the game industry is always pushing the limits in the production value, with advances in graphics and audio. It seems with every new graphics enhancement, game audio needs to increase realism and immersion. In order to keep up with the current and mainstream, Unity introduced a fully integrated Audio Mixer in the release of 5.0. The capabilities and features of the Unity Audio Mixer will be our main focus for the next few chapters in this book.

In this chapter, we are going to introduce the Audio Mixer, and elaborate on why it is such a game changer for audio development and how to convert our scene to use it. From there, we will look at the basics of grouping, signal routing, and various other audio affects we can apply with the mixer. Here are the main sections we will cover in the chapter:

- Introducing the Unity Audio mixer
- Shaping audio with effects
- The master mixer and controling signal flow
- Routing audio signals in the mixer to effects
- The duck volume effect

As with previous chapters, in order to complete the exercises in this chapter, you will need to have Unity installed on a computer, a downloaded copy of the book's source code, and the `Viking Village` Unity example project installed. All the instructions for downloading and installing these resources are provided in `Chapter 1`, *Introducing Game Audio with Unity*.

We will start from where we left off in the last chapter. For those of you who have jumped to here from another chapter, first install the `Viking Village` project and then import the `Chapter_2_Viking_Village_Start.unitypackage` from the `Chapter_2_Assets` folder. If you are unsure on how to install the required project or import an asset, then go back and start from `Chapter 1`, *Introducing Game Audio with Unity*.

Introducing the Unity Audio mixer

Released in Unity 5, the Audio Mixer provides the functionality of an embedded **Digital Audio Workstation (DAW)**. Previously, you would have used a DAW to mix or produce various sound effects or music into importable assets. Those assets would then be imported into Unity and used within various audio sources. Now, with the mixer, you can mix and produce various audio effects directly in Unity, thus eliminating the need for specialized external software and additional preprocessing by a sound designer. Not to mention that having a DAW within the game engine allows for additional specialized dynamic and adaptive audio effects.

 While the Audio Mixer is a great tool, it still has some shortcomings; therefore, we will also be looking at other DAW tools that can integrate directly with Unity in later chapters.

The best way for us to get in and understand the basics of the Audio Mixer is to get hands on and use it for our sample project. Open up Unity and follow the instructions to get started:

1. If you are continuing from the end of the last chapter, just continue to the next point. For those who just got here, open up the `Viking Village` project within Unity. Then import `Chapter_2_Viking_Village_Start.unitypackage` from the `Chapter_2_Assets` folder in the source code download folder. Next, locate the scene **The_Viking_Village_Chaper2_End** in the **Project** window and open it. Again, if you have any issues completing any of those tasks, reset yourself back to `chapter 1`, *Introducing Game Audio with Unity*, please.

2. Select the `Assets` folder in the **Project** window and right-click to open a context menu. From the menu, navigate to **Create** | **Folder**. Rename the folder `Mixes`.

3. Right click (or *control* + click on Mac) and then on the new `Mixes` folder. From the context menu, navigate to **Create** | **Audio Mixer**. Name the new mix, `Master`, and then double click to open it in a new Audio Mixer window as shown in the following screenshot:

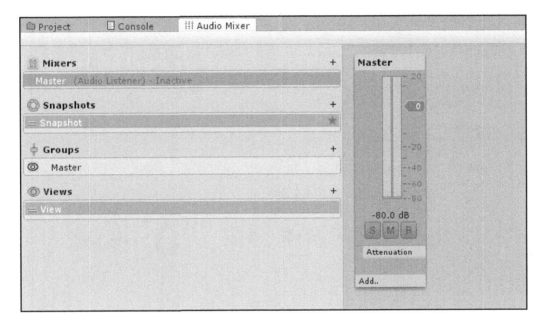

Audio Mixer window showing Master

4. The **Audio Mixer** window should line up with your **Project** window. If it doesn't, just drag it into place. We now have an empty `Master` or top mixer. By convention, we will use the word Master to refer to our root or top level mixer. Of course if you want to call your top level mixer something else later, that is entirely up to you.

5. Click on the plus icon on the same line as **Groups**. This will create a new child mixer of the **Master**. Rename the child `Music` as shown in the following screenshot:

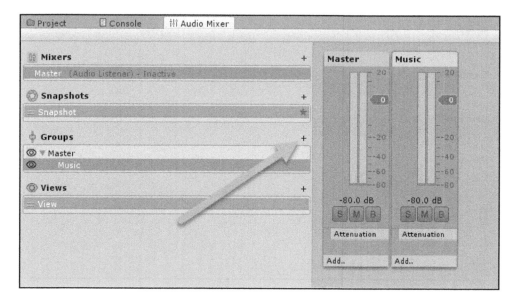

Creating a child mixer group called Music

6. Locate and select the **BackgroundMusic** object in the **Hierarchy** window. From the **Inspector** window, expand the **Audio Source** component and then click on the target icon beside the **Output** setting. This will open the **Select AudioMixerGroup** dialog. Select the **Music** mixer group as shown in the following screenshot:

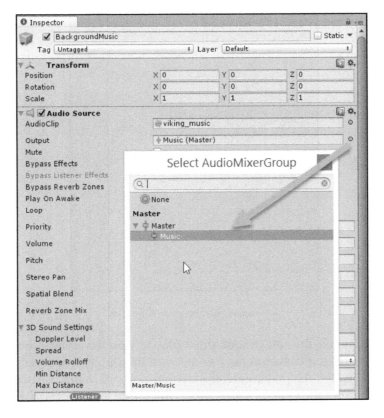

Setting the Output for the Audio Source to the Music mixer group

7. Click the play button to run the scene. Press the *Esc* key to unlock the mouse and then click on the **Edit in Play Mode** button at the top of the **Audio Mixer** window. Adjust the slider on the **Music** group to -21 as shown in the following screenshot:

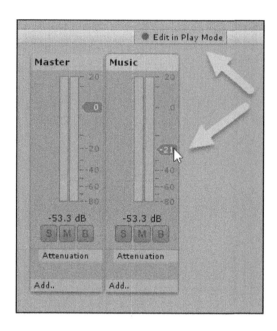

Adjusting mixing group volume during the play mode

8. After you make the adjustment, press play to stop the scene. Notice how you were able to control the music volume with the slider. You should also notice that after you exited the play mode, the change was still in place. This is different behavior from the general temporary editing you may perform during testing. Just be especially aware that any changes you make during the play mode in the Audio Mixer will be saved when you exit.

9. Feel free to run the scene again and change the slider back to your preference. Try changing the **Master** slider as well. When you are done setting the sliders, exit from the play mode.

We now have a single group or layer in our **Master** mixer. In the next section, we will create the other layers/groups we defined in Chapter 1, *Introducing Game Audio with Unity.*

Creating mixer groups

Before we move on to other features of the Audio Mixer, let's set up our additional audio layers or groups by following the exercise here:

1. Click on the **Master** node under the **Groups** list and then click on the plus icon again. This will create another child mixer. Rename this group `Direct`.

2. Follow the same procedure again to create another group called `Ambient`.

3. Do this yet again to create a last group called `Interface`.

4. Your **Audio Mixer** window should now look like the following screenshot:

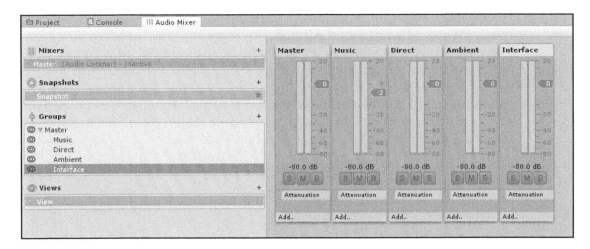

Audio Mixer window with all layers/groups created

In `Chapter 1`, *Introducing Game Audio with Unity*, we broke our audio into four layers: ambient, direct feedback, interface, and background music. As we mentioned before, this convention works well for us in this example. There may well be other times where it makes sense to break audio into different groups, perhaps by the location or area for instance. How you break up the audio for your scene or game is entirely at your discretion; do whatever works well for the situation at hand.

5. Locate the `AxeController` object in the **Hierarchy** window. Select the object in the window and then set both of the Audio Source component's output properties (throw and grunt) to the **Direct** mixer in the **Inspector** window.

You can quickly locate any Game Object or asset quickly by just typing the name into the window's search field. As you type, the window's contents will filter to match your search.

6. Locate the **AxePrefab** prefab in the **Project** window. Select the **Prefab** in the window and then set the **Audio Source** component's **Output** property to the **Direct** mixer in the **Inspector** window.

7. Locate the `Ambient_lake-shore-waves` object in the **Hierarchy** window. Select the object in the window and then set the **Audio Source : Output** property to the **Ambient** mixer in the **Inspector** window.

8. Finally, locate all the `prop_torch_01` objects in the **Hierarchy** window. From the menu, navigate to **Edit | Select All,** and select all the torches in the window. Then, in the **Inspector** window, set the **Audio Source : Output** property to the **Ambient** mixer.

9. After completing all that hard work, save your scene **File | Save Scene**. Then, click on the play button to run the scene. As the scene is running, click on the **Edit in Play Mode** button on the **Audio Mixer** window. Adjust the mixers to roughly match the settings in the following screenshot:

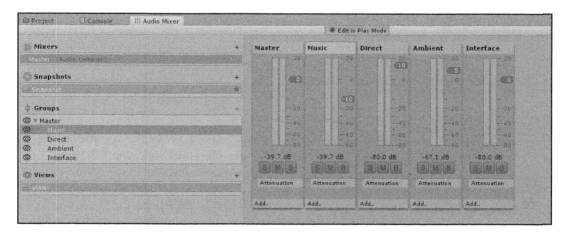

Audio Mixer settings adjustments by group (layer)

10. When you are done making changes, exit the play mode.

After completing these exercises and organizing our scene audio into mixers, you should have a basic understanding of the Audio Mixer and how audio can be broken into groups and remixed.

In the next section, we will dig deeper into controlling the tone and shape of audio with effects.

Shaping audio with effects

Thus far, we have used the mixer to group our audio sources into controllable groups or child mixers. This has allowed us to quickly balance the audio volume from various sources in our scene. While this is a great feature, it really is only the start of what is possible. The Audio Mixer not only allows you to mix or blend audio together, but you can apply numerous audio effects to each mix and even route the signal of a mix through other mixes. At this point, this may all sound a little abstract, so let's take a look at a simple hands-on example for adding audio effects:

1. Press play to run the scene. As the scene is running, switch your attention to the **Audio Mixer** window and click on the **Edit in Play Mode** button.

2. Isolate the mixer by clicking on the **S** button at the bottom of the group, if you want to apply an effect to the **Music** mixer. Then, turn the volume up on the mixer so it is equal or greater than **0** as shown in the following screenshot:

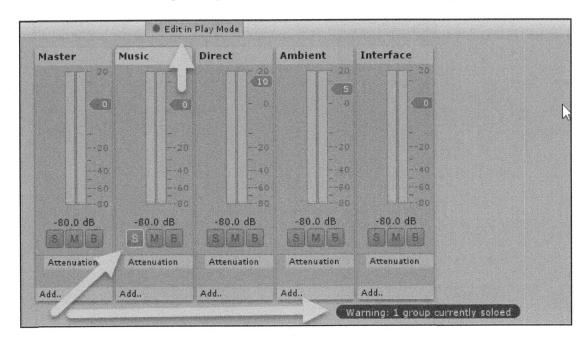

Setting the Music mixer to Solo mode and increasing the volume

The three buttons at the bottom of the mixer control the mode and are defined here: S = solo, only the single mixer is sent; M = mute, the mixer is muted; B = bypass, the mixer bypasses all audio effects

3. Now that the Music group is the only channel playing, we will be able to easily hear the impact of any effects we add. Make sure to select the **Music** mixer group and then switch to the **Inspector** window.

4. Click on the **Add Effect** button, and then from the context menu, select **Lowpass** as shown in the following screenshot:

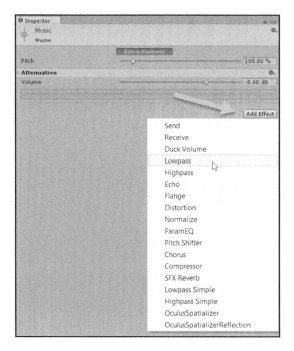

Adding a Lowpass effect to the Music mixer

5. Set the **Cutoff freq** to a value around 2000 using the slider or text entry field, as shown in the following screenshot:

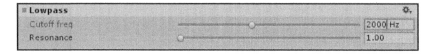

Setting the Lowpass effect cutoff frequency

The **Lowpass** effect or filter allow you to cut off sound above the threshold frequency. This can be useful for pulling out lower tones or softening an audio clip. It has also been used to great effect for quieting audio in pause menus or if a character experiences a temporary loss of hearing.

6. Notice how the sound of the music changes as you lower the cutoff frequency. Click on the **Add Effect** button again and select **Highpass** from the context menu. Set the **Cutoff freq** to a value around 1500 using the slider or text field, as shown in the following screenshot:

Setting the cutoff frequency on the Highpass effect

 The **Highpass** filter or effect is the opposite of the **Lowpass**. The effect cuts off all the frequencies below the threshold frequency. This effect can be useful for cutting off lower tones and enhancing or isolating higher frequency sounds, such as bagpipes for instance. It can also be used to intensify or give an audio element an eerie screeching tone.

7. The first thing you notice when you add the **Highpass** effect is the music volume drops to being barely audible. This is because the default cutoff frequency of the **Highpass** effect is cutting off those low tones before they even get to the **Lowpass** effect. As the arrow on the preceding screenshot shows, all audio effects are applied top to bottom. In our example, the effects are added in the following order: **Attenuation**, **Lowpass**, and then **Highpass**. When you lower the **Lowpass** cutoff frequency to around 2000, this allows for only those lower frequencies to pass through to the next effect. Since the **Highpass** effect; **Cutoff** is set to 2000, this allows a small band of around 500 Hz (1500-2000 Hz) of audio pass. If you listen to this, you will hear the music now sounds like it is playing from a can or a cheap speaker.

8. Hover your mouse to the top of the **Highpass** effect; notice how the cursor changes to a vertical arrow. Click on the effect bar, and while holding the mouse, drag the effect above the **Lowpass** and drop it into place. This will reorder the effects as shown in the following screenshot:

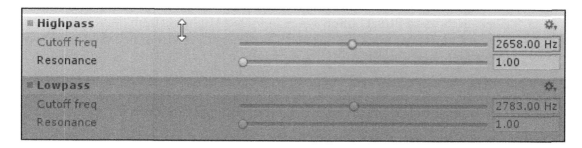

Moving the Highpass effect above the Lowpass effect

9. Adjust the cutoff frequency of the **Highpass** and **Lowpass** effects. Notice now, the combined effect sounds different with the order changed. When you are done testing, delete each of the effects by clicking on the gear icon and selecting **Remove this Effect** from the context menu. Then, stop the scene.

Now that we have explored how to add audio effects to a group and the importance of effect order, we will explore a more visual example of shaping audio in the next section.

Visualizing audio equalization

An excellent visual example of altering an audio signal is the parametric equalizer, which allows you to balance a range of tones visually. Follow the exercise to set up this effect:

1. From the **Audio Mixer** window, click on the **Add** button at the bottom of the `Music` group to open the effects context menu. Then, select the **ParamEQ** effect from the menu.
2. Set the parametric equalizer (**ParamEQ**) settings to match those in the following screenshot:

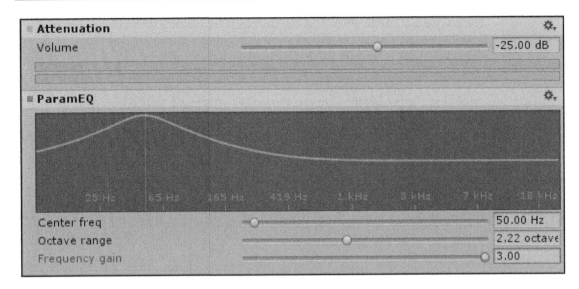

Setting the parametric equalizer effect

 You can use the sliders, text fields, or select and drag the curve with your mouse to make changes to the ParamEQ effect.

3. Press play to run the scene. Click on the **Edit in Playmode** button at the top of the **Inspector** window as shown in the following screenshot:

Clicking on Edit in Playmode from the Inspector window

4. After the scene starts running, click on the **S** button on the **Music** group to solo that channel. The first thing you may notice about the music now is how the lower tones, especially the drums, are emphasized now. This exactly matches the center frequency we are applying to gain with the **ParamEQ** effect.

The frequency range shown in the diagram represents the typical human hearing range. Of course, if you were designing a game for dogs or elephants, you would likely use a much different range.

5. Try adjusting the parameters on the **ParamEQ** effect and notice how you can emphasize specific or broad ranges of the audio expressed in octaves. The following is a diagram showing the **ParamEQ** frequency graph over the top of the audible human frequency range and instrument chart:

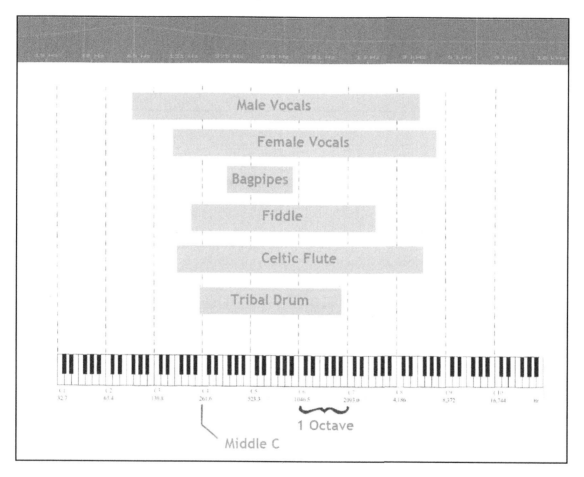

ParamEQ graph overlaid on top of the audible frequency range chart

The combination of the **ParamEQ** graph and audible frequency range chart should provide you with a good visualization of what ranges are affected by the equalization effect. For instance, if you wanted to highlight the high range of female vocals or other high pitched sounds such as the fiddle, you would shift the gain curve to the right, perhaps with a midpoint of 4,000 Hz and then a range of 1-2 octaves.

If you perform a search on Google images for **audible frequency range**, you will find plenty of more examples of good charts showing more instruments or other sound ranges. Having a good instrument frequency chart handy can be a good reference if you are trying to tune music, highlight instrumentals, or tune other audio.

6. Adjust the **ParamEQ** parameters to equalize the music to your personal preference. When you are done editing, press the play button to stop the scene. Then, be sure to save the scene and project.

If you do not have a musical background or audio editing experience, the preceding demonstration of visualizing the frequency range should be quite useful to you. Even if you do play a musical instrument, it may not be so obvious what frequency ranges another instrument or even a piece of music falls within.

As this section has demonstrated how a mixer group or channel can have effects layered to alter the frequency and corresponding sound, in the next section, we will look at how groups can by further mixed and routed to create even more complex audio effects.

The master mixer and controlling signal flow

The exercise in the last section demonstrated how to add and combine effects on a mixer group. You learned that the order of effects on a group is important to how the audio is processed. This also applies to how audio is routed through the mixers. At the top of every mixer is always a Master. In order to simplify our understanding of mixers, we named our primary mixer asset `Master`.

However, this doesn't have to be the case and we will conduct an exercise to demonstrate this further:

1. Click on the plus icon beside the **Mixers** element at the top of the **Audio Mixer** window. Rename this mixer **Music** and then select it; your view should be similar to the following screenshot:

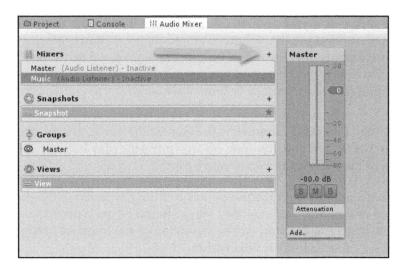

Creating a new mixer asset called Music

2. This will create another mixer asset called Music. Note how the first group is called **Master**. We can further confirm that this is a separate asset by going to the **Project** window and selecting the Mixers folder and expanding the mixer assets as shown in the following screenshot:

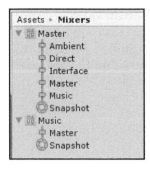

Mixer assets in the Project-Assets-Mixers folder

3. As you can see, both assets have a **Master** group. The `Master` group will always be the top routing path for any mixer or mixer group. You can in fact route mixer assets through other mixer assets. Go back to the **Audio Mixer** window. Select the **Music** mixer and drag it onto the **Master** mixer; this will make **Music** a child of **Master** as shown in the following screenshot:

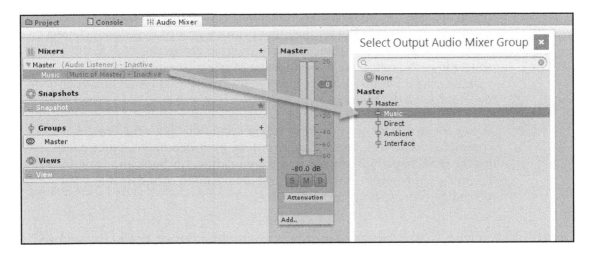

Routing the Music mixer into the Master mixer

4. A dialog titled **Select Output Audio Mixer Group** will then allow you to select the group you want to route the mixer asset through. Choose the **Music** group as shown in the preceding screenshot.

5. Now if you were to run the scene right now, nothing would change since the `viking_music` **Audio Source** is still routing directly to the `Master-Music` group. Let's fix that by selecting the **Music** mixer group and then clicking on the plus icon beside the **Groups** to create a new group. Rename that new group **viking_music** as shown in the following screenshot:

Adding the viking_music group to the Music mixer

6. Locate the `BackgroundMusic` object in the **Hierarchy** window. Select the object, and then in the **Inspector** window, change the `viking_music` **Audio Source** component's **Output** property to the new `viking_music` mixer group.

7. Press play now to run the scene. Click on the **Edit in Playmode** button at the top of the **Audio Mixer** window. Notice how you are now able to switch between the top level **Master** mixer and the **Music** mixer. Furthermore, you can control the music audio at multiple places as the signal is routed up to the top Master. Press the play button to the stop the scene when you are done exploring.

> If you are new to Unity, it is recommended you go though the process of creating new mixer assets for the other primary groups we defined: Direct, Ambient, and Interface. Then, create individual groups for each audio source in each group, like we did for the **Music** mixer and the `viking_music` audio source before. Finally, route all the new mixers as the children of the Master.
>
> If you are an experienced Unity developer and don't have the time, the completed scene with those changes will be provided in the source code for the next chapter. Of course, if you are reading this book and want to become a Unity audio master, you probably want to complete the preceding exercise on your own, anyway.

From the last exercise, we demonstrated mixing across multiple mixer assets. This allowed us to group and identify our various audio source assets in each mixer more clearly. While this did provide for some organizational benefits, it is not the only type of additional audio signal routing we can perform with the Audio Mixer. In the next section, we will explore other forms of signal routing.

Routing audio signals in the mixer to effects

You have most likely already have seen the **Send** and **Receive** effects listed on the effects context menu in one of the previous exercises. While they are considered effects, they really are a way of routing a group signal to another group for additional processing. This allows us to split and combine multiple signals through the same group or multiple groups for additional effects processing. The following is a diagram showing how this may work and a sample of the type of effects that use multiple signal processing:

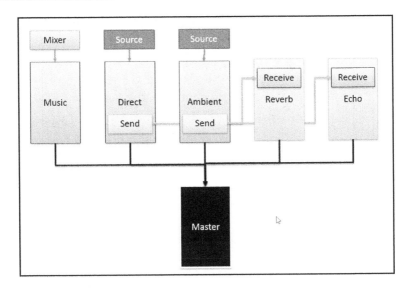

Mixer signal routing through return effects groups

The preceding diagram represents the routing we will connect in the next exercise. For simplicity, the **Interface** mixer group, which is just a placeholder for now, was removed. As the diagram shows, the `Direct` and `Ambient` groups will have their signal split to the `Master` and either a `Reverb` or `Echo` return effect. In turn, the `Reverb` and `Echo` effect after processing the signal will route to the `Master`. Finally, the `Master` will combine all the groups and send the signal to the audio listener in the scene.

 When a signal is split, the output from the original group is not cut or reduced. Instead, the portion of the signal that is split is added to the original by an amount set by the send level.

In the example, we are using the `Reverb` and `Echo` as return effects. We call them return effects to denote that they are processing a return or split signal. By doing this split and routing the signal back to another group or groups, it allows us to enhance or layer additional dynamics or physical characteristics about a sound we couldn't do otherwise. For instance, if we wanted to simulate a real-world sound we would want to create an echo or reverb to our audio mix. However, we wouldn't want all our audio processed through the same effect. This would make our audio sound over processed; instead we would want to simulate the actual and reflected sounds in multiple channels, just as we would experience them in the real world.

Check out the following diagram, which demonstrates how sound travels in the real world:

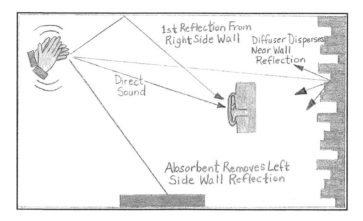

Direct, diffuse, absorbed, and reflected sounds

As you can see in the diagram, sound can appear from multiple sources and at slightly different times to the listener. If you have ever stood in a large empty room or cavern, you will hear this effect magnified. With the sound seeming to echo on and on as it is reflected off the walls or other surfaces. Both the SFX Reverb and Echo effects simulate those various physical effects, such as sound reflection and diffusion. This is why, for both effects, we will generally process them through a signal return, in order to add that additional echo or reverb effect on top of the original audio.

Let's put all this sound physics theory to practice by adding a Reverb and Echo effect to our mixer by following the exercise:

1. Open up the village scene in Unity and make sure the **Audio Mixer** window is visible. Be sure the `Master` mixer is selected and the **Master** group is selected in the **Groups** list.
2. Create a new group by clicking on the plus icon next to the **Groups** list. Rename the group `Reverb Return`. Click on the **Add** button at the bottom of the new group. Then, from the context menu select **Receive**, to add the `Receive` effect to the group. Click on the **Add** button again, and from the context menu, select **SFX Reverb**.

2. Select the `Master` group from the **Groups** list and then click on the plus icon to create a new child group. Rename this new group `Echo Return`. Click on the **Add** button at the bottom of the new group to open the context menu and then select the **Receive** effect. Then, click on the **Add** button again, and this time, select the **Echo** effect. Your **Audio Mixer** window should now match the following screenshot:

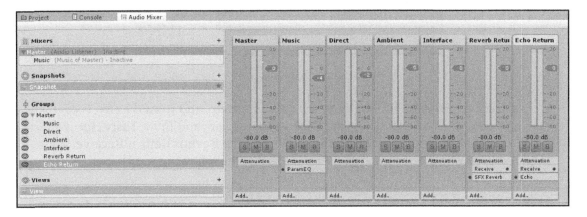

Audio Mixer window with new return groups added

4. Next, in order for us to visualize our Send/Receive signal connections, we are going to turn on a feature that is disabled by default. Click on the menu icon at the top right of the **Audio Mixer** window. Then, from the menu, select **Show group connections** and make sure the option is checked as shown in the following screenshot:

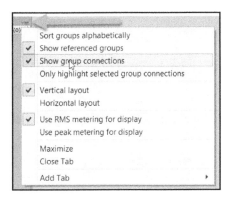

Setting the Show group connections on the Audio Mixer window

5. Click on the **Add** button under the `Ambient` group, and from the effects context menu, choose **Send**. Then, select the `Ambient` group and in the **Inspector** window under the **Send** effect **Receive** selector choose '**Echo Return\Receive**' from the list and as shown in the following screenshot:

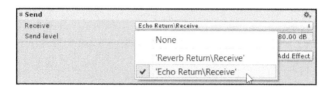

Selecting the output for the Send effect

6. Click on the **Add** button under the `Direct` group, and from the effects context menu, choose **Send**. Select the **Direct** group again, and in the **Inspector** window, set the **Receive** setting on the **Send** effect to the **Reverb Return\Receive**. Your **Audio Mixer** window should now look like the following screenshot:

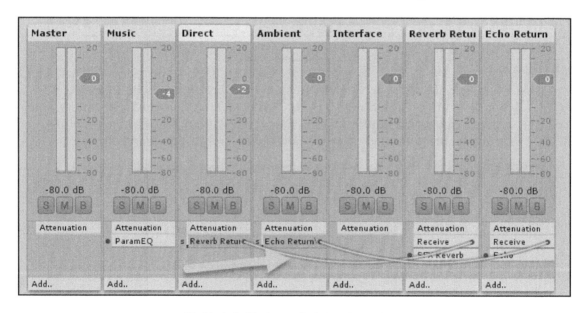

Visualizing the Send/Receive connections in the Audio Mixer window

 Notice how the order of effects is still important. If we put the Echo effect above the Receive effect, there would be nothing processed since the signal doesn't enter the group until Receive. Remember signal flow is from top to bottom through the mixer group.

7. Press play to start the scene running. Click on the **Edit in Playmode** button to turn on editing. Initially, you should notice no change in the audio and that is expected. The reason for this is that both our send effects are not sending any signal to the return effects.

8. Click on the **Ambient** group, and then in the **Inspector** window, adjust the Send Level slider on the Send effect all the way to the right. This will create an audible echo from the torches and possibly the lake waves depending on your position. If you move beside a torch, the effect will be amplified and obviously overwhelming. What we want is just a bit of echo to denote the ambient sounds reflection off the buildings and water. Adjust the **Send Level** slider to about halfway and notice how the ambient sound becomes even more natural with a slight echo.

> For those astute readers who may start thinking that while the Echo effect works well in some areas, where the buildings are close together, but what about the more open areas or inside buildings. These are questions we will start to answer in `Chapter 4`, *Advanced Audio Mixing*. In this chapter, we will introduce snapshots and environmental zones.

9. Click on the **Direct** group, and then in the **Inspector** window, adjust the **Send Level** slider on the **Send** effect all the way to the right. Then, select the **Return Reverb** group and in the **Inspector** window on the **SFX Reverb** effect, set the **Dry Level** to −10000, **Room** to 0, and the **Reflections** to 1000 as shown in the following screenshot:

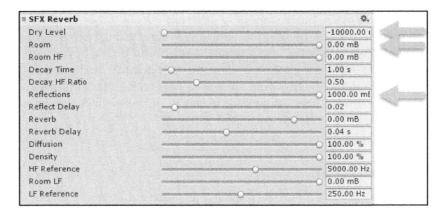

Setting the SFX Reverb settings

The **SFX Reverb** effect is a **CPU** intensive effect, which is the reason we only added the effect to the `Direct` group. If you want, you could route the `Ambient` group through the `Reverb Return` instead of the `Echo Return` group. However, be wary if the game frame rate drops or occasionally freezes. We will cover more about performance in `Chapter 11`, *Audio Performance and Troubleshooting*.

10. After you are done editing, click on the **Game** view to throw an axe and listen to the sound reverberate. Of course, this is far from the sound we want, so let's turn down some settings. Adjust the **Room** and **Reflection** sliders to about half, and then set the **Send** output from the `Direct` group to also about half. When you finish editing, throw another axe and see if the changes feel more natural. Feel free to adjust the reverb return effect to your auditory preference. When you are done testing, click on play to exit the play mode and then save your scene.

By now, you can see that as we progress through the book, our examples will become more complicated. Yet, if you have followed along with the exercises, most of what we just did should seem almost natural and intuitive by now. Of course, at this point, it should be obvious that we are only scratching the surface of what is possible with signal routing and effect mixing in the Audio Mixer. In the next section, we will breakdown the other audio effects for your reference.

Audio effects breakdown

If you have never mixed audio before, all these different effects can be overwhelming and abstract on how or where to use them. In this section, we are going to review each of the effects at a basic level, what they do, and a typical application for each. We won't go into extensive details on the effect parameters as they are well documented in other areas. For some of those effects that may have a direct benefit to our scene, we will provide an example. Of course, as always, take some time to test all of these effects on your own to get a better understanding of how they work.

Equalization effects

Equalization effects are used to alter the frequency response of an audio signal. As we have seen in the musical keyboard demonstration from `Chapter 2`, *Scripting Audio*, the higher the frequency equates to a higher octave, pitch, or tone. Conversely, the lower the frequency, the lower the octave, note, or tone.

Lowpass and Lowpass simple

We have already spent time looking at the Lowpass effect. Just remember that the Low in Lowpass means it allows frequencies lower than the cutoff. So if you wanted to emphasize low tones, such as a kick drum, you would use a Lowpass effect.

Highpass and Highpass simple

As we have seen, a Highpass effect allows for those upper frequencies above the cutoff to pass through and is effectively the opposite of the Lowpass effect.

ParamEQ

Since we have already spent a fair bit of time on this effect, we will just mention it here. This effect is used to isolate a frequency range and then either increase or decrease the signal strength. This is useful to isolate or highlight certain instruments or vocals in a mix.

Delay effects

A delay effect stores and then plays back or echoes the original signal back onto itself. The effect originated for the need to spatialize or create the sense of space in audio playback. We generally equate a sound with an added delay or echo as being in a large space. Since this is something we already covered when we looked at **SFX Reverb**, we don't need to elaborate much further. However, delay effects have had a broad use in other areas of mixing, especially in modern music, so don't think a delay effect can't be used for some other cool sound.

Echo

You can think of the Echo effect as the base delay effect. The effect creates an echo by playing the input signal delayed over a period of time. This is a good effect, if you want to create a sense of space to your audio without using one of the more CPU intensive delay effects. Since this effect is the base for the other delay effects, let's take a closer look at the parameters in the following screenshot:

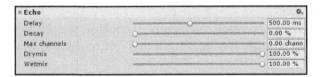

Echo effect default settings

- **Delay**: This sets the amount of time before playing the original (dry) signal and the modified signal (wet).
- **Decay**: This displays the amount of decay or loss of signal when the echo is played.
- **Max Channels**: Nothing about this is provided in the Unity documentation.
- **Drymix**: This is the amount of original audio to use with this effect. If you are using Echo as a return effect, like we did previously, then Drymix should always be 0.
- **Wetmix**: This shows the amount of modified signal to play.

 The terms wet and dry are used frequently in audio mixing. Dry always refers to the original unmodified signal, with wet denoting the modified or affected signal.

SFX reverb

We really only covered the surface of this effect earlier, so it is worth taking a closer look at. It is also worth mentioning that the Unity documentation on most of these effects is severely limited and inaccessible to newcomers. However, if you are an old mixing pro, most of the parameters will likely be quite familiar to you. For those without a mixing background, we will identify some of the important settings here:

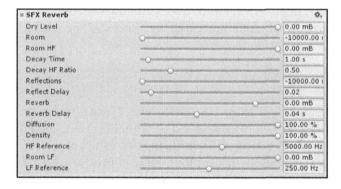

Default settings for SFX Reverb

- **Dry Level**: This is the same as Drymix. It controls the amount of the original signal to pass through. Again, if used in a return set, the **Dry Level** goes down to `-10000`.

- **Room**: This is the amount of gain applied to the original or source signal.
- **Reflections**: This is a reverb that will use multiple delays to denote the various sets of reflections. The Reflections setting denotes how strong the first delay or echo should be. It is called Reflections to denote how much sound the walls in the room immediately reflect back sound. This first set of reflections will also be called early reflections.
- **Reverb**: This is the amount of strength of secondary or late reflections. Essentially, the sound that is coming back to the listener after it has been reflected off at least a couple walls or objects.
- **Reverb Delay**: This is the late reflections. The sounds that have bounced a while before returning to the listener.
- **Room HF and HF Reference**: This controls the gain on the input high frequency and cutoff point. It is similar to a Highpass effect.
- **Room LF and LF Reference**: This controls gain on the input low frequency and cutoff point. Again, it is similar to a Lowpass effect.
- **Diffusion and Density**: These control the correlation among the delay lines in the internal reverb system.

The Audio Mixer in Unity is built on top of the FMOD plugins. As such, all the effects we look at here are also available in FMOD Studio with a better interface and documentation. In `Chapter 6`, *Introduction to FMOD*, we will download and install FMOD Studio and also cover more effects then.

Flange

this is another delay effect that produces a more synthetic synthesizer sound by remixing the dry and wet signals offset by usually less than 20 ms. This effect is used quite heavily in the music industry to produce interesting instrumental or vocal effects. Like the other delay effects, it is best used with a Send/Receive on a return group or bus. This would be a good effect to enhance machinery, lasers, spells, or other non-natural sounds.

Bus in mixing terminology denotes a single audio channel or group where multiple sources may be routed through. In the Unity Audio Mixer this is synonymous with group, and we may use the term bus to denote a mixed group. The Master group is a bus, for instance.

Chorus

A Chorus effect is a way of taking multiple audio sources of a similar timbre and pitch and then harmonizing them together to produce a single blended sound. This is another heavily used effect in modern music where instruments and vocals may be tuned to more closely harmonize without any noticeable differences. It is a good effect to use when you want to create distinct new tones from various audio sources.

 Timbre is often used to denote the tone quality or color of a sound. It is that tonal quality of a sound, instrument, or playing style that allows you to determine different instruments and/or singers even though they may be playing the same note or frequency.

Other effects

The last category is for those effects that don't fit into any of the preceding or more general categories. All of these effects are especially useful, and we will look at an example using each.

Pitch Shifter

Another one of those effects that has had a huge impact in the modern music industry. This effect allows you to pitch shift or tune a sound up or down in frequency without changing playtime. Typically, if you alter the pitch on an audio clip, you may reduce or increase the playtime. The Pitch Shifter, however, preserves the playback time while still adjusting the frequency. Since this is such a cool effect, let's take a look at the following example:

1. Open up Unity to our village project and focus your attention to the **Audio Mixer** window. Select the `Music` group, and then in the **Inspector** window, click on the **Add Effect** button. Select **Pitch Shifter** from the context menu.
2. Set the **Pitch** setting to `1.25` as shown in the following screenshot:

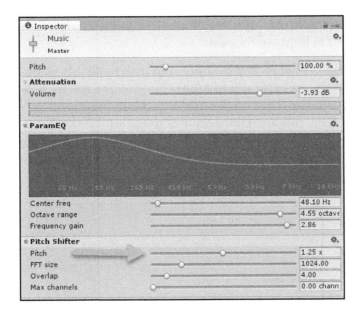

Setting the Pitch on the Pitch Shifter effect for the Music group

3. Press play to run the scene and listen to the change the effect has on the music. Feel free to alter the Pitch to your preference. When you are done testing, stop the scene and then save your changes.

Normalize

Normalization is the addition of constant gain to a signal in order to increase the average or peak loudness. It is commonly used with the compression effect, so we will demonstrate its use that way in the next section.

Compressor

Compression or dynamic range compression is a process to reduce loud sounds and amplify quieter sounds. This effect narrows or compresses the audio signal's dynamic range, unlike the Normalize effect, which does not alter the dynamic range of an audio signal. Typically, these two effects are used together to increase the overall loudness of a clip or source and to remove areas that are quiet.

The following is an example of adding the **Normalize** and Compressor effects to our Echo Return group in order to improve the echo:

1. Open up the village project in Unity, and direct your attention to the **Audio Mixer** window, yet again. Select the `Echo Return` group, and then in the **Inspector** window, click on the **Add Effect** button. Select the **Normalize** effect from the menu. Just keep the default settings for the effect.

2. Click on the **Add Effect** button, and this time select **Compressor** from the effect context menu. Adjust the effect settings to match what is shown in the following screenshot:

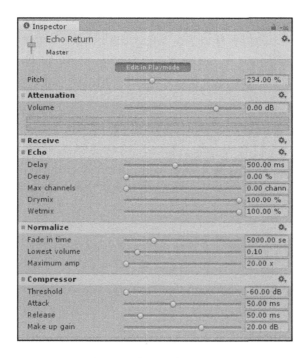

Echo Return effects and effects settings

3. Press play to run the scene and click on the **Edit in Playmode** button. Notice how the echo effect is much more pronounced now. Adjust the Ambient group's Send level up and the **Attenuation** down to set the amount of depth you want for Ambient sounds. Feel free to alter the various settings to your preferred auditory taste as well. Always keeping in mind that you are looking to create the most natural and immersive sound for the player.

4. When you are done editing, stop the scene and save your changes.

If you ever wondered how or why the sound in television commercials is so loud, the reason is normalization and compression. Television commercials will apply the Normalize and Compressor effects in order to maximize the volume of the audio.

The Compressor effect has a number of uses outside the example we have just shown. Another very common and useful use of compression is called side-chain compression or ducking. This is an effect where the output volume of one group is lowered or ducks the volume of another group. As this is such a heavily used effect, we will cover this effect in its very own section, next.

QUIZ TIME

What effect or effects would you use to accomplish each of the following tasks:

Eliminate high pitch sounds (over 5000 Hz) from an audio source?
a. Lowpass
b. Highpass
c. Send - Lowpass
d. both a and b

Emphasize or highlight a particular instrument from a music source?
a. Highpass
b. SFX Reverb
c. Param EQ
d. None of the above

Create the effect of a player yelling down a well?
a. Echo
b. Param EQ
c. Send - Receive - SFX Reverb
d. both a and c

Correct an out of tune singer's vocals to match an instrumental?
a. Compressor
b. Normalize
c. Pitch Shifter
d. Chorus

Think through these questions and the answers will be provided at the end of the chapter.

The duck volume effect

The duck volume effect, which may also be referred to as side chain compression, is an effect which controls the volume of one group using the volume of another. This is a powerful effect and has many applications in several areas where we want to highlight a specific group without it getting washed out from other competing audio. As this is a specialized effect, we will take a look at the following custom configuration to set this effect up:

1. Open up Unity to the village project and direct your attention to the **Audio Mixer** window. Select the `Music` group and click on the **Add Effect** button. Select the **Duck Volume** effect from the context menu.
2. Select the `Direct` group and click on the **Add Effect** button to open the effect context menu. Then, select the **Send** effect. Drag the new **Send** effect above the existing **Send** and then set the **Receive** to '**Music\Duck Volume**' and the **Send level** right up to 0 as shown in the following screenshot:

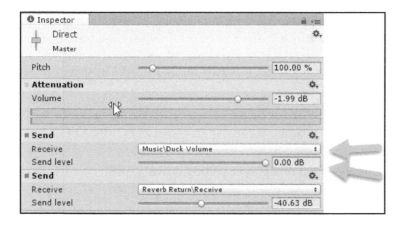

Setting up the Send to the Duck Volume effect

 The Send to a Duck Volume effect does not increase the output gain of the group as the signal is only used to trigger the effect. In our example, we moved the Send up a level in order to avoid any confusion. However, if you do notice the effect not being triggered, try moving the Send up or down in the chain. This may just be an issue in the way Unity updates in the play mode.

3. Select the `Music` group and then set the **Duck Volume** settings as shown in the following screenshot:

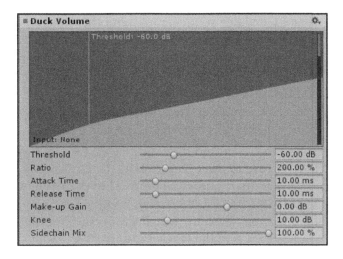

Setting the Duck Volume effect parameters

4. Let's take a closer look at what these settings mean and how they are used:

- **Threshold**: This is the required signal level (loudness) before this effect will be triggered. In our example, we set this to `-60 dB` in order to catch the fainter axe-landing sounds.

- **Ratio**: This determines the amount of reduction in gain or change in the volume. We use a value of `200%` in our example since it works well for our short-lived Direct audio.

- **Attack time**: This sets the amount of time between when the threshold is triggered and the reduction in gain starts. A value of `10 ms` is used here to allow for a quick attack, since the audio group we are ducking on has a short-lived audio.

- **Release tme**: This is the amount of time after the attack time has passed before the gain reduction is reset to the original. Again, we set this to a short release of `10 ms` because the grunt, throw, and landing sounds are short lived.

- **Make-up gain**: Use this parameter to alter the gain, positive or negative. We are keeping this value at `0 dB` in the example, since we don't want to alter the audio aside from the duck effect.

- **Knee**: This determines the behavior of when the effect is triggered. A low value will create a hard or linear transition, while a larger value will soften the transition. We will start by using the default value of 10 dB and then later in our sample alter this value to demonstrate the impact of this effect.
- **Sidechain mix**: This determines the amount of wet and dry audio mix. At 0%, only the original or dry signal is heard. While at 100%, only the modified or wet signal is heard. We use a value of 100% as the default, because we want the **Duck Volume** effect to completely control the volume of the Music group.

5. Press play to start the scene and then click on the **Edit in Playmode**. Listen to the scene and throw an axe or three. Notice how the **Direct** group of sounds now is not obscured by the **Music** group anymore. However, you may hear a pause or click when the **Music** group volume adjusts or is ducked.

6. In order to fix this issue, select the **Music** group and direct your attention to the **Inspector** window's view of the **Duck Volume** effect. Adjust the **Knee** setting on the effect to the maximum right as shown in the following screenshot:

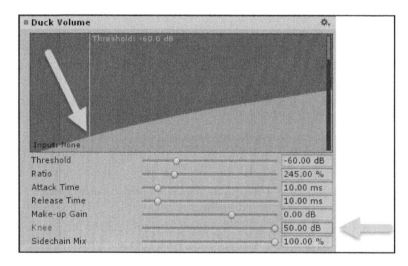

Adjusting the Knee on the Duck Volume effect

7. Notice how the graph smooths to a very gradual curve now. There is no longer a hard edge or change at the **Threshold** line on the graph. Go back to the **Game** view and throw a few more axes. Now, the volume change should almost be imperceptible.

You can also modify the various effect settings by clicking and dragging on the graph. Click on the **Threshold** line and drag it left or right to alter the setting in the graph.

8. When you are done making changes and testing, stop the scene and save your changes.

That completes our entire discussion about effects. If you have been following along, your **Audio Mixer** window should now resemble the following screenshot:

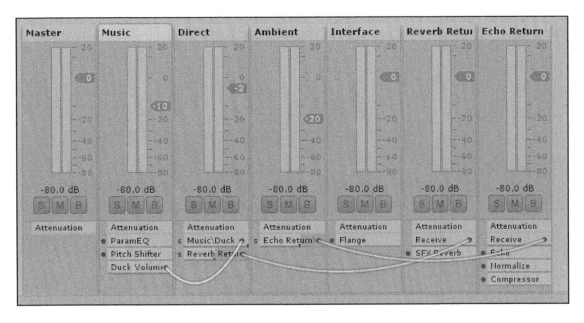

Audio Mixer window groups view from the end of the chapter

QUIZ ANSWERS

Here are the answers to each of the questions:

Eliminate high pitch sounds (over 5000 Hz) from an audio source?
a. **Lowpass** - *will remove sounds above a cutoff frequency*
b. Highpass
c. Send-Lowpass
d. Both a and b

Emphasize or highlight a particular instrument from a music source?
a. Highpass
b. SFX Reverb

c. **ParamEQ** - *parametric equalization allows you to highlight a frequency range or instrument range*
d. None of the above

Create the effect of a player yelling down a well?
a. Echo
b. ParamEQ
c. Send-Receive-SFX Reverb
d. **Both a and c** - *either answer will work*

Correct an out of tune singer's vocals to match an instrumental?
a. Compressor
b. Normalize
c. **Pitch Shifter-***can tune vocals or instruments to match a particular frequency*
d. Chorus

Summary

This chapter has dug deep into the world of audio mixology with the introduction of the Audio Mixer. We started with a basic introduction to the Audio Mixer, and how to set up mixers and groups. From there, we went on to introduce a few simple effects for equalizing frequencies and shaping our audio output. After that, we took a deeper look into mixers and groups and the Master group. This introduced us to other signal routing concepts with the Send and Receive effect, which introduced us to some more complex delay effects such as Reverb and Echo that worked best in a return group. We then spent more time reviewing all the effects the Audio Mixer supports and explored a couple examples with those effects. Finally, we focused our attention on the very useful Duck Volume effect.

In the next chapter, we will devote more time exploring further capabilities of the Audio Mixer. Here, you will learn about the use of: snapshots, parameters, and scripting the Audio Mixer, environmental effects and triggers, and interface controls.

4
Advanced Audio Mixing

In the previous chapter, we devoted most of our time to introduce the Audio Mixer and understand the capabilities of having a digital audio workstation in Unity. You learned the basic functionality of the mixer and how to use effects and route signals. While, we did look at a few recipes of using effects and the mixer, not much of what we did in the last chapter was applied to practical game development. Seeing how something works when it is applied to a real-world game development task or problem, reinforces a recipe or theory. Therefore, in this chapter, we will explore practical and advanced examples of how a mixer can be used.

For this chapter, we will spend time working through more practical and advanced examples that can be applied to a number of game development tasks. We will cover the following topics in this chapter:

- Recording audio changes with snapshots
- Audio Mixer scripting with parameters
- Dynamic audio wind effect
- Creating environmental audio zones
- Dynamic music mixing

Each of the main sections in this chapter will either be a practical example or provide an example of how to use the advanced capabilities of the Audio Mixer.

In order to complete the exercises in this chapter, you will need to have Unity installed on a computer, a downloaded copy of the book's source code, and the `Viking Village` Unity example project installed. All the instructions for downloading and installing these resources are provided in `Chapter 1`, *Introducing Game Audio with Unity*.

In this chapter, we'll continue from where we left off in the last chapter. As always, for those of you who have come here from another chapter, be sure that you have the Unity `Viking Village` project installed, and then import the **Chapter_4_Start.unitypackage** from the `Chapter_4_Assets` folder.

 If you are unsure on how to install the project or load an assets, go back to `Chapter 1`, *Introducing Game Audio with Unity*, and work through the introduction.

Recording audio changes with snapshots

An Audio Mixer snapshot is a way to record and save the complete state and settings of the mixer. A snapshot can then be restored later during editing or at runtime, and it is also possible to transition between multiple snapshots. You can use snapshot transitions for changes in a level, different rooms, or other effects. Let's take a look at how we can record and save a snapshot and then use it in play mode by following the example here:

1. Open up the Unity editor and load the `Viking Village` project. If you have been following along through the book, you can continue using the `GameAudio` project where we left it in the last chapter.

2. From the menu, select **Assets | Import Package | Custom Package;** this will open the **Import package** dialog. Use the dialog to find where you downloaded the book's source code to and open the `Chapter_4_Assets` folder. Inside that folder, select the **Chapter_4_Start.unitypackage** and click on **Open** to load the package. Follow the import dialog to load all the assets into Unity.

3. Open the **Project** window `Assets/GameAudio/Scenes` folder and double-click on the **The_Viking_Village_Chapter4_Start.scene** to open the scene in Unity.

4. From the **Project** window, select and double-click to open the **Master** mixer from the `Mixers` folder. This should open the **Audio Mixer** window if it is not already open at the bottom of the editor. Select the Master mixer from the Mixers list. Your window should match the following screenshot:

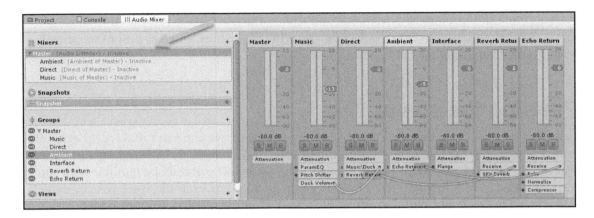

Audio Mixer loaded with sub mixers

If you cannot see the group connectors on in the mixer view, you can enable/disable them by opening the window menu and selecting the Show group connections option.

5. Click on the plus icon next to the **Snapshots** list to create a new **Snapshot**. Name the new snapshot, `Snapshot1`. Select the **Snapshot1** entry in the list and then set the Ambient group to `20 dB`. Click on the top Snapshot in the list and notice how the Ambient group volume drops immediately.

6. Press play to run the scene. Unlock the mouse by typing *Esc* and then click on the **Edit in Play Mode** button at the top of the `Audio Mixer` window. Click on the **Snapshot1** and notice the immediate change in the ambient sound volume.

7. At this point, you can make other changes to the mixer settings using the new snapshot as they will automatically be saved. Try switching back and forth between the original and new snapshot as you move around the scene.

The one thing you will immediately notice as you make changes is that you don't have to do anything besides selecting a snapshot and then making changes. These changes will be saved automatically. This ability to quickly make edits can, and likely will, get you into trouble. This makes it likely that you will overwrite changes you thought you were saving into different snapshots, for instance. The best way to overcome this is to be aware of which snapshot you have selected whenever you make edits. It also helps if you save your scene at points where you are happy with a particular mix.

8. When you are done making changes and recording them to `Snapshot1`, press the play button to stop the scene.

Well, as you can see, creating a snapshot and saving the mixer state is quite easy; in some ways, perhaps too easy. In the next section, we will look at how you can programmatically recall the state of a snapshot at runtime.

Pausing the scene

Now that we have seen how easy it is to create a snapshot, we can see a real-world example of how to recall a saved snapshot programmatically and at runtime, by building a pause feature. If you have played any single-player game, you will certainly be familiar with some form of pause button that pauses or freezes game play. In our example, the pause button will freeze the game, but will also adjust the audio to let the player know the game is paused. Let's see this in action by following the exercise here:

1. Open the **Audio Mixer** window and click on the on the Snapshot in the **Snapshots** list. Rename the snapshot, Unpaused. Click on the **Snapshot1** item from the **Snapshots** list and rename it Paused.

2. From the menu, select **GameObject | Create Empty**. This will create a new object in the **Hierarchy** window. Select this object, and then in the **Inspector** window, rename the object GameMenu and reset the **Transform** to 0, as shown in the following screenshot:

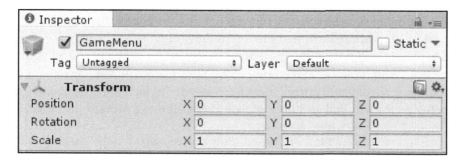

GameMenu with zero Transform

3. Click on the **Add Component** button at the bottom of the **Inspector** and type Game Menu in the search field. Select the **Game Menu** component from the list to add it to the object.

4. Then, click on the target icon beside the **Unpaused** slot of the **Game Menu** component, and then select the Unpaused Audio Mixer snapshot from the **Select AudioMixerSnapshot** dialog as shown in the screenshot here:

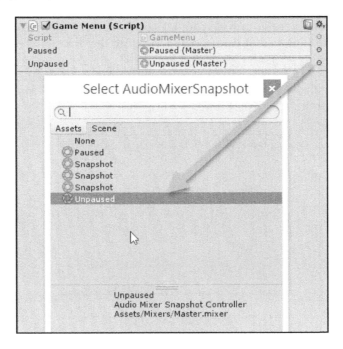

Setting the Unpaused snapshot slot

5. Repeat the procedure for the **Paused** slot on the **Gamemenu** component. Set the slot to use the **Paused** snapshot we renamed earlier.

6. Run the scene by pressing the play button. Pause the scene by pressing the *P* key. This will pause the game but the audio will still play, and you should notice a change in the ambient sounds becoming louder.

7. Obviously, having the ambient sound grow louder as we enter pause is not what we want. We probably want the audio overall to be more quiet. Click on the **Edit in Play Mode** button at the top of the **Audio Mixer** window.

8. Select the `Paused` snapshot from the **Snapshots** list. Reset the **Ambient** group attenuation (volume) to around -9 to -12 dB and set the **Master** volume to be around `-20`.

9. Now, press the *P* key to activate the pause mode and notice that the scene becomes much quieter. Feel free to adjust the **Paused** snapshot audio levels or other **Audio Mixer** settings to your preference. When you are done editing, stop running the scene and save your changes.

Now that we have seen the full example run, let's open up the **Game Menu (Script)** to see how the snapshots are switched at runtime by following the directions here:

1. Open the Game Menu script in your preferred code editor by selecting the gear icon beside the component and then selecting **Edit Script** from the context menu as shown in the screenshot here:

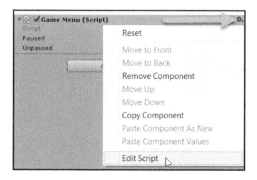

Opening the component context menu and selecting Edit Script

2. This will open your script in your preferred editor. The script is shown here for a quick review as well:

```
using UnityEngine;
using UnityEngine.Audio;  //addition of Audio namespace

public class GameMenu : MonoBehaviour {
    public AudioMixerSnapshot paused;
    public AudioMixerSnapshot unpaused;

    void Start()
    {
        if(paused == null || unpaused == null)
        {
            this.enabled = false;  //disable the component if missing
snapshots
        }
    }

    // Update is called once per frame
    void Update () {
        if (Input.GetKeyDown(KeyCode.P))
        {
            Pause();
        }
```

```
    }
    private void Pause()
    {
        Time.timeScale = Time.timeScale == 1 ? 0 : 1;
        if (Time.timeScale > 0) //if time is not paused
        {
            unpaused.TransitionTo(.01f);
        }
        else
        {
            paused.TransitionTo(.01f);
        }
    }
}
```

3. As we covered in `Chapter 2`, *Scripting Audio*, this script is consistent with the standard Unity script. How about we go through and discuss the main points of interest here:

- `using UnityEngine.Audio;`: This helps to add in or use the Audio library in order to work with snapshots.

- `this.enabled = false;`: This line of code will disable the component. We do this if either the paused or unpaused snapshots are missing, since the reset of our code will just break. Disabling a component means that the `Update` method will never run.

- `Pause();`: This calls the `Pause` method, which is listed after the `Update` method.

- `Time.timeScale = Time.timeScale == 1 ? 0 : 1;`: The `?` denotes a ternary operator, which you can think of as just a shortened form of an if statement. In the line, if the Boolean expression before the `?` is true, the value 1 is returned. Otherwise, if the expression is false, it returns the value after the `:` or in this case 1.

- `unpaused.TransitionTo(.01f);`: This calls the `TransitionTo` method on the `AudioMixerSnapshot`, which takes a `float` parameter to denote the transition time. In the example, `.01f` is used to mean the transition to the `unpaused` snapshot should take `.01` seconds.

- `paused.TransitionTo(.01f);`: This is exactly the same as the preceding point, except this time it is transitioning to the `paused` snapshot.

The *P* key was used for the pause function, but it is also typical to use the *Esc* key. Since this key is already bound to unlocking the mouse, it only made sense to use the *P* key for our pause action.

The `Game Menu` script is really just the start of a game menu script that would manage other things besides pause. Feel free to expand on this script and add other functionality such as displaying a menu interface, for instance. In the next section, we will continue to go into further scripting functionality with the Audio Mixer.

Audio Mixer scripting with parameters

In the last section and example, we looked at a partial way in which we can control the Audio Mixer through snapshots and transitions. While snapshots work well for setting multiple parameters quickly, they offer less control than being able to alter a parameter directly during every frame, for instance. That level of fine-grained control requires us to script directly against the mixer using exposed parameters. Let's take a quick look at how we expose parameters from the mixer in the exercise here:

1. Open up Unity and direct your attention to the **Audio Mixer** window. Select the **Ambient** group and then in the **Inspector** window, right-click on (*Ctrl* + click on Mac) on the **Volume** setting to display the parameter context menu. Select the **Expose 'Volume (of Ambient)' to script** option as shown in the screenshot here:

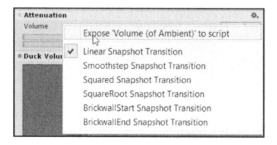

Exposing the Volume parameter to scripting

2. Next, select the **Exposed Parameters** selector at the top right of the **Audio Mixer** window to open the menu. Double-click on the **MyExposedParam** entry to rename it `ambisentVolume` as shown in the screenshot here:

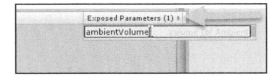

Setting the name of the exposed Volume parameter

3. Now, in a script, we could set the `ambientVolume` parameter by calling the `SetFloat` method of the `AudioMixer` class like so:

```
masterAudioMixer.SetFloat("ambientVolume", -15);
```

4. In the line of code, we are setting the `"ambientVolume"` parameter on a mixer called `masterAudioMixer` to the value of `-15` using `SetFloat`.

At this point, we could go back and modify the pause button example we did earlier to now use the exposed parameter method we just covered, but that example works just fine with snapshots. So instead, we will explore a more thorough example demonstrating the power of exposed parameters in the next section.

A dynamic audio wind effect

One of the sounds we avoided or missed up until now is the sound of the wind. The wind certainly has an affect in our scene. Run the game and walk up to a torch, and you will notice the smoke blows in a direction away from the water. Here is a screenshot showing the smoke blowing away from the torch by the rock in the scene:

Showing the direction of the wind in our village scene

The smoke may be faint to see if you are too close; so stand back a little from the torch.

If you run the game for a while, you will even notice that the smoke (particles) is blown around in what looks like gusts of wind. So ideally, if we want to add a natural wind sound, we want the audio controlled by the same element that is blowing the smoke particles, which is exactly what we are going to do in the next exercise:

1. Open up Unity and direct your attention to the **Hierarchy** window. Search for or see if you can spot the `Wind Zone` object near the top of the list. After you find the object, double-click on it to focus it in the **Scene** view as shown here:

Showing the Wind Zone focused in the Scene view

2. That big blue arrow is called a Wind Zone, which represents a special environmental effect in Unity. A Wind Zone can be used to blow particles, such as smoke, or even trees and grass. Notice how the direction of the arrow exactly matches the direction the torch smoke was blowing. With the Wind Zone still selected, look at the **Wind Zone** component parameters as shown in the **Inspector** window. We won't go into what each of those settings does; you can look at the Unity documentation for that, but just know that the current values represent just casual breeze. However, for our example, we want a wind with more force and gusto.

Set the **Wind Zone** component parameters to match those in the screenshot here:

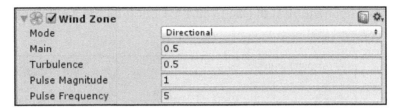

Editing the Wind Zone parameters for a more gusty wind

3. If you run the game again, you will now see puffs of smoke blown though the air in the direction of the wind. Yet, we are still missing the wind sound, so let's add one to the scene. First, open up the **Audio Mixer** window at the bottom of the editor and make sure the **Master** mixer is loaded and the **Master** group is selected in the **Groups** list. Click the **+** icon next to the **Groups** to create a new child group, and then name this group **Wind** as shown in the following screenshot:

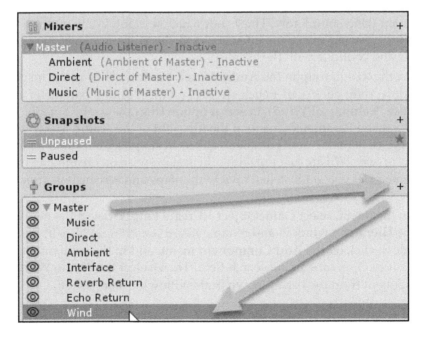

Adding a new Wind group to the Master mixer

4. Go back to the **Hierarchy** window and select the Wind Zone object again. Then in the **Inspector** window, click on the **Add Component** to open the component context menu. Enter `audiosource` into the search field and then select the **Audio Source** component from the list to add it. Configure the **Audio Source** to match the screenshot here:

4. Setting the Audio Source on the Wind Zone game object

5. Press play to run the scene. You should immediately notice the addition of a constant wind sound now. This is not what we want. We want the sound of the wind to gust and match the intensity of the blowing smoke particles. Stop the scene and continue with the exercise.

6. Select the `Wind` group in the **Audio Mixer** window. Then in the Inspector window, right-click (*Ctrl* + click on Mac) on the **Volume** parameter and select the **Expose 'Volume (of Wind)' to script** option from the context menu. Then, open the E**xposed Parameters** menu at the top right of the **Audio Mixer** window. Double-click on the new parameter called **MyExposedParam** to rename it `windVolume`. We are just repeating the last exercise on creating an exposed parameter. If you get lost, just review the steps and screenshots from the last exercise.

7. From the menu, select **GameObject | Create Empty**. Select the new **GameObject** in the **Hierarchy** window and rename it `AudioWeatherVane`. In the **Inspector** window, click on the **Add Component** menu, and in the component menu, enter `audioweathervane` in the search field. Then, select the **Audio Weather Vane** component from the list as shown in the following screenshot:

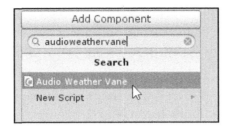

Adding the Audio Weather Vane component

8. This will add the **Audio Weather Vane** component to the new object. Click on the target icon next to the **Particle Tracker** setting. This will open the **Select ParticleSystem** dialog; just select one of the fx_smoke items in the list and close the dialog. Then, set the other parameters on the component to match the screenshot here:

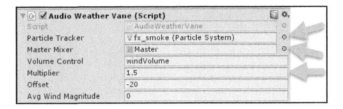

Setting the Audio Weather Vane parameters

The reason we need a particle effect in the Audio Weather Vane script is to to be able to track the force of the wind. Unfortunately, the Unity API can be a black box at times and this is especially true of the Wind Zone component. There isn't actually a direct way of querying the Wind Zone to determine the wind velocity during runtime. Instead, we use an indirect hack to track the velocity of particles being affected by the Wind Zone.

9. Press the play button to run the scene. Notice how the wind sound now is much more dynamic and matches the intensity of the wind as it blows the smoke particles around the scene. We will explore the details of the AudioWeatherVane script next, but try adjusting the multiplier and offset parameters to see the effect it has on the volume changes. You can also try adjusting the Wind Zone component parameters as well, if you would like to see what effect that has. When you are done testing, stop the scene and save your changes.

This dynamic wind effect we just created uses the exposed `windVolume` parameter to set the volume of the wind based on the current velocity of the wind. All of this magic occurs within the `AudioWeatherVane` script, so let's open that script up and take a closer look at the interesting points here:

1. Open up the `AudioWeatherVane` script in your favorite editor of choice. For review, the entire script is shown here:

```
using UnityEngine;
using UnityEngine.Audio;

public class AudioWeatherVane : MonoBehaviour
{
    public ParticleSystem particleTracker;  //ParticleSystem must have
External Forces set
    public AudioMixer masterMixer;
    public string volumeControl = "windVolume";
    public float multiplier = 1f;
    public float offset = -20f;
    public float avgWindMagnitude;
    private ParticleSystem.Particle[] particles;

    void Start()
    {
        particles = new ParticleSystem.Particle[10];
    }

    //FixedUpdate runs every physics update
    void FixedUpdate()
    {
        var magnitude = 0f;
        if (particleTracker.GetParticles(particles) > 0)
        {
            for (int i = 0; i < particles.Length; i++)
            {
                magnitude += particles[i].velocity.magnitude;
            }
            avgWindMagnitude = magnitude / particles.Length;
            masterMixer.SetFloat(volumeControl, avgWindMagnitude *
multiplier + offset);
        }
    }
}
```

2. Now, we will cover the highlights, changes, or differences of this script here:

- `public ParticleSystem particleTracker;`: This is the particle system we will use to track the strength of the wind. It is `public`, so it can be set in the editor.

 The **External Forces** setting is a particle system setting that allows wind to affect the particle when it is enabled. This setting needs to be enabled on the particle system in order for it to be used as a tracker.

- `public AudioMixer masterMixer;`: This is the mixer that has the exposed parameter we want to control. We called it the master, but just realize it could be any mixer with exposed parameters.
- `public string volumeControl = "windVolume";`: Instead of using a hardcoded setting for the exposed parameter, we are going to use a string, set to a default value. That way, in the future, we can change the parameter name to some other value we want to control.
- `public float avgWindMagnitude;`: Unlike the other two public float fields, we have this one made public for convenience. Making this field public allows us to monitor the value during runtime from the editor. If you were following the preceding exercise closely, you are already likely to notice this.
- `particles = new ParticleSystem.Particle[10];`: This is just an initialization of an array of `10` particles. Essentially, this is the rolling array of particles we track in order to determine velocity changes.
- `void FixedUpdate()`: We use `FixedUpdate` instead of `Update` in this script to run our code. `FixedUpdate` runs every physics calculation cycle of the game, whereas `Update` runs every graphics frame update. We won't get into why there needs to be two different update methods, but just understand that the physics timing is different than the graphics timing. Needless to say, we use the physics update cycle in this script, because we are tracking the physical properties of particles.

The bulk of the other code in the `FixedUpdate` is to track the effect of the wind on the particle system particles. We won't review the details of that code since it is a hack or workaround.

- `masterMixer.SetFloat(volumeControl, avgWindMagnitude * multiplier + offset);`: Finally, just as we have seen in the earlier example, we use the `SetFloat` method on the mixer to adjust the volume of the exposed parameter. This allows us to quickly adjust the parameter for every physics update and provides for that dynamic audio wind effect.

 For this example, we use `FixedUpdate` to execute `SetFloat`, but just realize that we could also do something similar in the regular Update method as well.

Feel free to reuse the `AudioWeatherVane` script wherever you want to track the wind and be able to adjust the mixer parameters for whatever effects suit you. Perhaps a creaky door sound or leaves rustling based on the strength of the wind, the possibilities are endless here. Before completing this example, we are just going to add one more tie-in effect to the `Ambient` audio group.

1. We are going to add a **Duck Volume** effect to the **Ambient** group in order for the ambient sounds to duck when the wind audio volume increases. Start by selecting the **Ambient** group in the **Audio Mixer** window and clicking on the **Add** button. Select the **Duck Volume** effect from the context menu in order to add it to the group.

2. In the **Inspector** window, select and drag the **Duck Volume** effect above the **Send** effect that is already in the **Ambient** group. Then, set the parameters on the **Duck Volume** to match those as shown in the screenshot here:

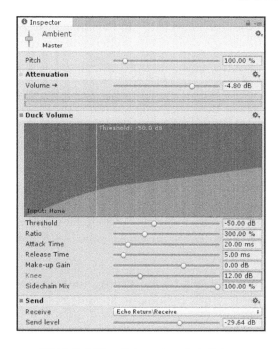

Setting the Duck Volume effect parameters on the Ambient group

You may notice that the suggested audio settings may not always sound the way you think they should. This could come from a number of differences in the way your audio is playing and the system you are using. In fact, this is something you should be especially mindful of. Be sure to try and listen to your game audio through multiple different system and mediums, such as headphones, speakers, and so on. Then, adjust your settings to match what you feel sounds best overall or what works best on each system. Perhaps, even using snapshots, if there are major differences.

3. Next, select the **Wind** group and add a **Send** effect to it by clicking on the **Add Effect** button in the **Inspector** window. Set the effect to point to the **AmbientDuck Volume** Receive level and adjust the **Send level** to max as shown in the screenshot here:

Setting the Wind group Send effect Receive and Send level

4. Press play to run the scene and listen to the changes in audio. As always, feel free to adjust the audio to suit your needs. When you are done editing, stop the scene and save your changes.

If you ever walked around on a windy day, you probably will have noticed how the sound of rushing air around you blocks out other noises. That is the effect we wanted to achieve by adding that additional Duck Volume effect. We didn't add a ducking effect to the **Direct** group of audio, but if you feel that would make the wind sound more natural, go ahead.

 If you talk to any experienced sound engineers or mixers, one thing they will generally point out is don't be afraid to do your own thing. Audio mixing and sound design are after all artistic endeavors, and as such there may come a time where breaking rules makes sense. In general, don't be afraid to break the rules and always do the best you can to see your vision through.

In the next section, we will continue by demonstrating another practical effect you could use in other game development efforts by looking at environmental audio zones.

Creating environmental audio zones

As it stands right now, our whole game level or scene uses a single global audio mix. We did create a couple of snapshots to allow us to switch audio during game pause, but overall everywhere we go, it all sounds the same. Sure, we have several audio sources providing 3D spatial sound, but nothing describing the changes to the physical space around us. Remember, when we talked about the SFX Reverb and Echo effects, how they are used to denote space by providing more realistic reflections. Unfortunately, all our audio uses the same Reverb and Echo effects everywhere, so again, it all sounds the same. Ideally, we want to be able to create zones of where the audio should sound differently and then make changes to our mix when a player enters those zones. Let's take a look at a high level view of the village scene and identify areas where sound should be different:

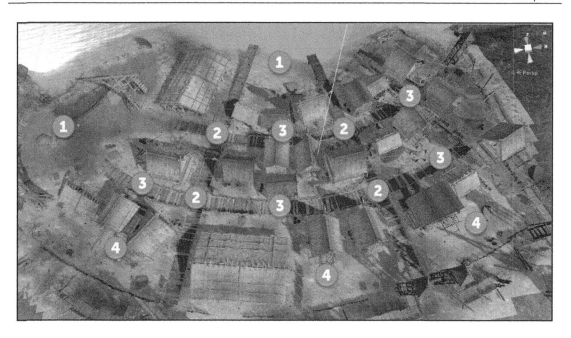

A map of the village scene with environmental zone-types labeled

The map shows the entire village scene labeled with environmental zone types. Each number represents a different type of environmental according to the description here:

- **Exposed**: These zones are very exposed to the elements and represent large open areas. In order to emphasize this with audio, we would increase the wind volume, reduce reverb or echo, and lower the volume on the direct audio.
- **Crossroads**: These may be especially windy or turbulent areas because of the funneling effect caused by surrounding buildings. In these areas, we will increase the wind volume but maintain the other global settings.
- **Sheltered**: These areas are all directly sheltered from the wind by the buildings, which should significantly reduce the wind volume in these areas. Because these areas are between buildings, we also want to increase the reverb and echo volumes. Increasing the direct audio will provide a sense of a smaller or confined space as well.
- **Fringe**: These areas are just on the outside of the village. Despite being away from the wind, they are not subjected to being a closed area. In this area, we would reduce the wind and direct audio.

You could of course add other environmental zones to what we described earlier. For instance, you may want indoor zones, underground zones, flying zones, and so on. The list is endless.

Now that we understand the concept behind environmental zones, it is time to put this to practice. Follow the exercise here to start defining and then laying out the environmental zones:

1. Open up Unity and direct your attention to the **Audio Mixer** window. Select the **Wind** group in the **Groups** list and then click on the **+** icon to create a new child group. Rename this new group `WindRaw`, as shown in the screenshot here:

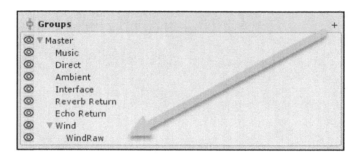

Creating a new WindRaw child of the Wind group

2. Select the **Wind Zone** game object in the **Hierarchy** window and then in the **Inspector** window redirect the **Audio Source** to the new `WindRaw` group. Since `WindRaw` is a child of `Wind`, the group will route all audio to the parent. We create this child group so that we can change the volume of the wind audio using a child group. If you recall, our **AudioWeatherVane** script dynamically changes the volume of the `Wind` group, which would override any snapshot settings.

3. Right-click (*Ctrl* + click on Mac) on the `Unpaused` snapshot. From the context menu, select **Set as start snapshot** and then **Duplicate** as shown in the following screenshot:

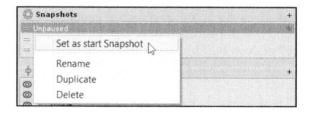

Setting the start or global snapshot

4. This will set the **Unpaused** snapshot as our starting point for our audio mixes. This also means that it will be our global mix settings. Rename the duplicate snapshot we created earlier to `Exposed`.

5. It is time for us to mix the audio settings for the `Exposed` snapshot. Be sure the `Exposed` snapshot is selected and make the following audio changes to your mix:
   - `WindRaw`: This increases the **Volume** to `10` dB.
   - `Direct`: This reduces the **Volume** to `-10` dB and decreases the **Send level** to `-60` dB on the **Reverb ReturnReceive**.
   - `Ambient`: This decreases the **Send level** on the **Echo ReturnReceive** to `-60` dB.

6. From the menu, select **GameObject | Create Empty**. Rename the new object **EnvironmentalZones** and reset the **Transform** to **0** (**Position: 0,0,0**).

7. Right-click (*Ctrl* + click on Mac) on the new object and select **Create Empty** from the context menu. This will create a child object attached to the `EnvironmentalZones` game object. Rename the new object `Zone_Exposed_1`. Click on the **Add Component** button in the **Inspector** window to open the component context menu. Enter `environmentalzone` in the search field and then select the Environmental Zone component. Set the parameters on the **Zone_Exposed_1** game object to match what is shown in the following screenshot:

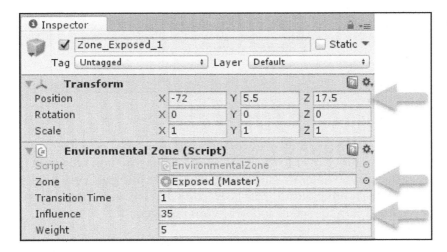

Setting the Zone_Exposed_1 Transform and Environmental Zone parameters

8. Double-click on the `Zone_Exposed_1` game object in the **Hierarchy** window after you set the parameters. This will highlight the object in the **Scene** view and allow you to see where this zone is placed. The zone is in the large wide open construction area with the boat, which is marked #1 in the preceding village map.

9. Select the `EnvironmentalZones` object in the `Hierarchy` window and then click on the **Add Component** button in the **Inspector** window. Enter `environmentalzonemanager` in the search field and then select the **Environmental Zone Manager** component from the list to add the component. Then, set the parameters for the component to match what is shown in the screenshot here:

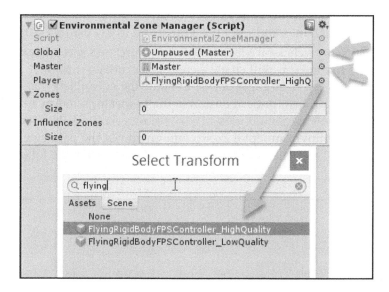

Setting the Environmental Zone Manager parameters

10. After you are done editing, press play to run the scene. Walk the player around the scene and move over to the large exposed construction area with the boat. Notice that as you enter this area now, the wind noise gets very loud, and it is difficult to hear other audio. This is exactly what we were after. When you are done testing, stop the scene and save your changes.

Okay, before we see the full effect, we should understand what is happening inside the `EnvironmentalZoneManager` script. Open up the script in your editor of choice and look for our old friends the `Start` and `Update` methods, shown for reference here:

```
void Start()
{
```

```
    zones = GetComponentsInChildren<EnvironmentalZone>();
    globalInfluenceZone = new InfluenceZone
    {
        Snapshot = global,
        Weight = 1
    };
}

void Update()
{
    influenceZones.Clear();
    influenceZones.Add(globalInfluenceZone);

    for (int i = 0; i < zones.Length; i++)
    {
        //zones only influence if they are within their influence
        var distance = Vector3.Distance(player.position,
zones[i].transform.position);
        if (distance < zones[i].influence)
        {
            influenceZones.Add(new InfluenceZone
            {
                Snapshot = zones[i].zone,
                Weight = (1 - distance / zones[i].influence) *
zones[i].weight
            });
        }
    }
    //blend the zones together
    master.TransitionToSnapshots(GetSnapshots(), GetWeights(), 1);
}
```

First off, if you are not a developer or have only a little knowledge of scripting, this script will likely be intimidating. There are a few sections of code that use more advanced features of C# for instance, but we won't try to understand those. Instead, we will just identify the highlights of the script here:

- `void Start()`: We will just summarize what is going on in this method. The first line uses `GetComponentsInChildren` to load all the child zones of the game object. Next, the code creates a new `InfluenceZone` object called `globalInfluenceZone` and initializes some fields. This global zone represents the base or global audio mix. The definition for `InfluenceZone` is at the bottom of the script but really all it does is holds the data that describes a zone of influence.

- `influenceZones.Add(globalInfluenceZone);`: This line is second from the top of the Update method. The first line in Update clears the list (just a special container of objects) called `influenceZones`. This line of code then uses the list's `Add` method to add the `globalInfluenceZone`.

- `for (int i = 0; i < zones.Length; i++)`: This is the start of a `for` loop, which will loop through all the child zones we initialized earlier, using `i` as an indexer.

- `var distance = Vector3.Distance(player.position, zones[i].transform.position);`: This line of code calculates the distance between our player object and the current zone in the `for` loop, identified by `i`.

- `if (distance < zones[i].influence)`: This `if` statement then checks if the distance between the player and the zone is less than the zone's `influence`. Influence represents the range at which a zone can be effective; we look into this in detail later in the chapter. If the zone is within range, then a new `InfluenceZone` is added to the list inside the statement.

- `Weight = (1 - distance / zones[i].influence) * zones[i].weight`: This code calculates the effectiveness of the zone, based on the distance. Just recall, for the global zone we assigned a `Weight` of 1. Again, we will explain this later in the text.

- `master.TransitionToSnapshots(GetSnapshots(), GetWeights(), 1);`: Finally, at the end of the `Update` method, we use the `TransitionToSnapshots` method of the mixer (master) to blend those zones together. `TransitionToSnapshots` takes an array of snapshots and an array of weights (type float) it uses to blend to determine the final mix. In order to simplify things, the `GetSnapshots()` and `GetWeights()` are just helper methods used to extract the array of snapshots and weights from the `influenceZones` list.

There are other ways to implement audio or environmental zones using event triggers or even physics ray casting. We are not going to look at how those are implemented, but the same concepts would apply. If you are interested, you can easily find an example using triggers to control zones on the internet.

Well that explains the more relevant pieces of code, but you may still be having a hard time visualizing how all of this is supposed to come together. Here is a diagram that should help to explain the concept of zones further:

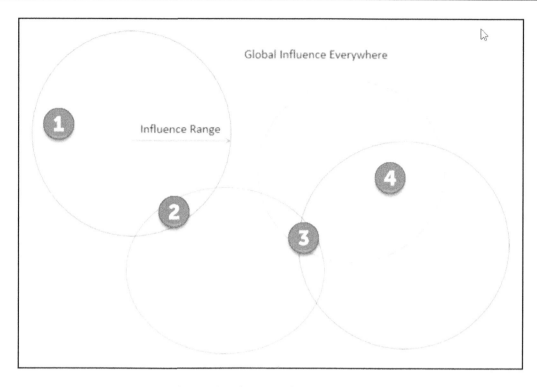

Diagram showing environmental or influence zones overlapping

In the diagram, there are four different environmental or influence zones represented. Each of these zones has a different influence range, denoted by their radius and strength. Imagine the player is at each of the numbered reference points in the diagram. How many influence zones affect each of the points in the diagram? Think about this question first, before looking for the answers:

- **2 zones**: The global influence zone and the single zone surrounding it
- **3 zones**: The global and the two overlapping zones
- **4 zones**: The global and the three overlapping zones
- **3 zones**: The global and the two overlapping zones

The influence range is not the only factor that affects what blend of snapshots is heard at any point however. We also provide a strength or weight factor to each zone. This allows us to control the amount of impact a zone has to the overall mix. The strength or weight of a zone will fall off as it moves from the center to the outside edge as shown in the diagram here:

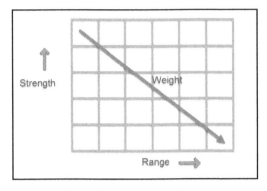

Linear calculation of weight based on zone strength and range to player

Depending on the strength you set for a zone, the more effective a zone will be overall. This allows us to control the transition between overlapping zones and the global zone. The stronger a zone, the more influence it will have. Although, you generally don't want a zone so strong that it creates an unnatural transition, unless that is what you want. For example, if you have a player entering a building or other closed space, you probably want only the zone to affect what the player hears. In that case, you would likely set a very high strength on the zone. With another option maybe to use a trigger zone effect like we mentioned earlier.

When we went through the exercise of exposing parameters for scripting; however you may have noticed a number of other options to control snapshot transition on parameters. Here is an example of what that context menu looked like:

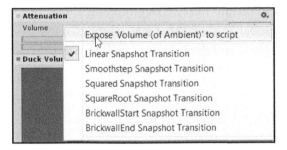

Parameter exposure and snapshot transition menu

Since our environmental zone method uses a linear transition, shown in the preceding graph, to blend snapshot weights, the additional transition settings won't have much affect. If you were mathematically inclined, you could implement other transition forms in the zone example we used.

 The variety of snapshot transitions made available by Unity are useful for simple transitions between snapshots using only a few parameters. Much like our first example, where we implemented the pause effect. For that reason, we won't be covering those transition types in any more detail here.

So, lets take a look at how all these zones come together in a complete example. Follow the directions to import the completed example:

 If you are disappointed that we didn't go through the exercise of setting up all the zones in the book. Don't worry; you will now have plenty of time to do that in your own game.

1. From the menu, select **Assets** | **Import Package** | **Custom Package**. This will open the **Import package** dialog. Use the dialog to go to the book's downloaded source code `Chapter_4_Assets` folder and select the **Chapter_4_Zones.unitypackage**. Then, click on the **Open** button to load the assets.

2. Select the defaults on the **Import** dialog and click on the **Import** button to import the assets.

3. After the assets import, go to the **Project** window and enter the text `zones` in the search field. This will filter the view to display a scene called **The_Viking_Village_Chapter4_Zones**. Double-click on the scene to open it.

4. Press play to run the scene. Move around the scene and notice how the sounds change as you move behind buildings or out in the open. When you are done testing, stop the scene. For the purposes of the samples in the book, we have generally over-emphasized various effects. This is to account for differences in a reader's hearing, equipment (headphones, speakers), and so on.

5. In the **Hierarchy** window, double-click on the `EnvironmentalZones` game object and then look at the **Scene** view. Zoom the camera out using the scroll wheel, or hold *Alt* + left-click, and drag until you see something like the following screenshot:

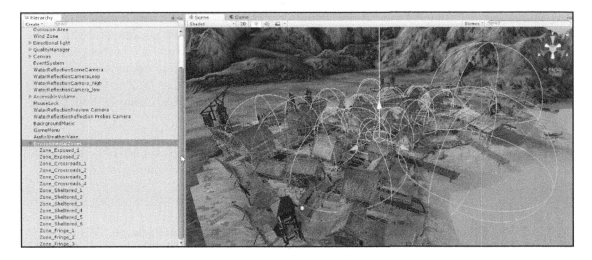

Viewing all the environmental audio zones in the scene

6. All the cyan spheres represent an environmental audio zone using based on one of those snapshot settings we discussed earlier. Feel free to go back to the running scene and listen for those zone transitions. If you are so inclined, you can certainly add additional zones or change the current zones and snapshot settings to match your taste.

QUIZ TIME
Time for another quiz.
Going back to the first chapter, which of the following audio sounds we have or will use in our scene are diegetic or non-diegetic? If you forgot what those definitions mean, jump back to `chapter 1`, *Introducing Game Audio with Unity*, and look it up.

Wind
Lake shore waves
Music

Answers will be provided before the end of the chapter.

In the last and final section of this chapter, we look at another way to dynamically mix content, which will be the basis for other exercises later in the book.

Dynamic music mixing

One of the truly powerful features of having your own DAW (digital audio workstation) right in Unity is the ability it provides for dynamic content mixing. Of course, we have already looked at some interesting ways to dynamically mix audio through environmental zones at runtime, but how about being able to create your own music mix within Unity? Being able to create your own music mix could certainly play into a number of interesting features, including adaptive music. We will forgo the discussion of adaptive audio until the next chapter; for now, let's dive in and create our music mix by following the instructions here:

1. Open up the Unity editor and, from the menu, select **File** | **New Scene**. Save your current scene if you are asked to do so.

As always, the exercises in the last section of each chapter will work very quickly and assume you have been following the exercises in the chapter. If you have trouble following the exercise, work hands-on through some of the earlier exercises.

2. From the menu, select **GameObject** | **Create Empty**. Rename the new object `Instruments` and reset the **Transform position** to 0.

3. Right-click (*Ctrl* + click on Mac) on the new game object in the **Hierarchy** window, and from the context menu, select **Create Empty**. Rename the new object `Fiddle`. Add an Audio Source component to the object and set its **AudioClip** to `fiddle` and check the **Play on Awake** and **Loop** settings as shown in the screenshot:

Fiddle Audio Source component settings

4. Select the `Fiddle` game object in the **Hierarchy** window and press **Ctrl+D** to duplicate the object. Rename the object `Tribe_Drum`. In the **Inspector** window, set the **AudioClip** for the new object to `tribe_drum`.

5. Repeat step 4 for two new objects called Celtic_Flute and Beat. Set the **Audio Source AudioClip** slots on each of those components to match their respective names: `celtic_flute` and `beat`.

6. Press play to run the scene. Obviously, the sound is far less than harmonious, and if anything, it verges on the horrendous. Stop the scene and save your changes.

Well obviously throwing a bunch of clips together certainly isn't going to create any music mastery. How about we see what the Audio Mixer can make of this? Follow the instructions here to create a new `MusicMix` mixer:

1. Open up the editor to the **Audio Mixer** window and click on the **+** icon beside the **Mixers** to create a new mixer. Rename this mixer `MusicMix`. Select the new `MusicMix` mixer.

2. Click on the **+** icon beside the **Groups** list to create a new mixing group. Rename this new group `fiddle`.

3. Repeat step 2 for the other instruments: **tribe_drum**, **celtic_flute,** and **beat**. Your mixer window should match the screenshot here:

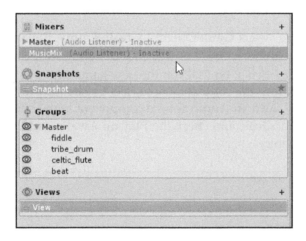

MusicMix groups

4. In the **Hierarchy** window, select the `Fiddle` object, and then in the **Inspector** window, set the **Output** slot of the **Audio Source** component to the **MusicMix | fiddle** mixer group as shown in the screenshot here:

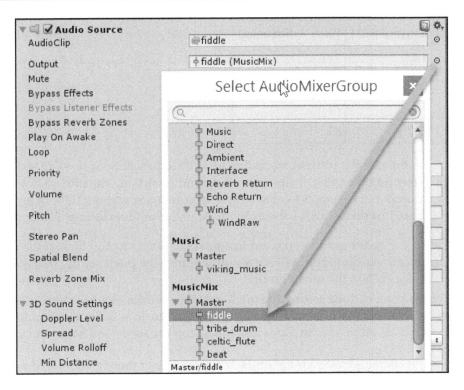

Setting the Output setting on the Fiddle Audio Source

5. Again, repeat the process for the other instrumentals: **tribe_drum**, **celtic_flute**, and **beat**. Match up the **Output** setting to their respective Audio Mixer group.

6. Next, one of the fundamental problems our various instrumental clips have is they are all playing at different beats per minute (or BPM). What we need to do, therefore, is align all our tracks to play at the same BPM. We can do that by simply adjusting the pitch of the audio in that mixer group. The following is a table of the pitch adjustments we need to make to each of our groups in order to bring all the audio to 100 BPM:

The BPM of each clip was determined by using BPM Counter from `http ://www.abyssmedia.com`, and then the pitch adjustment was calculated by using the following formula:

pitch% = desired BPM / actual BPM * 100

Example for fiddle adjusted to 100 PBM:
pitch% = 100 / 140 * 100 = .714 * 100 = 71%

Instrument	Current BPM	Pitch Adjustment
fiddle	140	71%
tribe_drum	120	83%
celtic_flute	137	73%
beat	120	83

Adjusting the pitch of an audio clip is the equivalent of slowing it down or lowering the pitch, to speeding it up and increasing the pitch. There are a number of free tools available to help you determine the BPM of an audio clip. Just do a search for `bpm counter` in your favorite search engine.

7. Select the mixer group you want to adjust the pitch on, and then at the top of the **Inspector** window, you will see a setting. Enter the pitch setting that matches the table for each of the mixer groups.

8. When you are done setting the pitch, run the scene again. This time notice how the instruments are harmonious now and the music is starting to sound like something. After you are done listening, stop the scene and save your changes.

Well those slight changes made a huge impact, but obviously there is more to do. At this point, most of the editing is really up to you on how to blend the instrumentals together into a sound you like. However, also keep in mind that now you could create any number of dynamic music blends controlled by snapshots or other exposed parameters.

Follow the suggestions here to add some useful effects and controls in order to balance your music mix better:

1. For each of the music groups, go ahead and add a **ParamEQ** effect. Do this by clicking on the **Add** button at the bottom of the group and then selecting **ParamEQ** from the context menu.

2. Press the play button to run the scene and then click on the **Edit in Play Mode** button. After the scene starts running, try adjusting the mix to match the settings shown in the combined screenshot here:

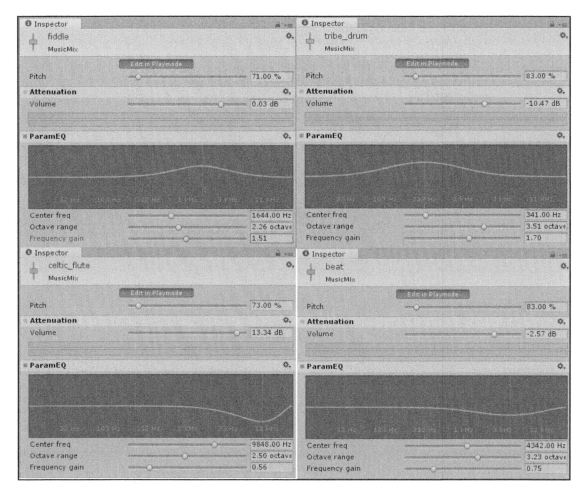

3. Again, that mix is just one way of combining those instruments. You could also add other effects to the various mixer groups. Try creating two-three different mixes you are happy with and save them as snapshots.

4. When you are done editing and mixing, stop the scene and save your scene and project.

Being able to mix your own music like this right within Unity provides for several possibilities. In the next chapter, we are going to put this concept into practice and even extend it further.

QUIZ TIME ANSWERS
Here are the answers for the short quiz we asked at the end of the last section. See how well you did.
Wind: If you can see it blowing objects, it is diegetic; otherwise, it is non-diegetic
Lake shore waves: If you can see the waves, it is diegetic; otherwise, it is non-diegetic
Music: If you can see musicians playing, it is diegetic; otherwise, it is non-diegetic.

All these sounds could be either diegetic or non-diegetic, so it was a bit of a trick question. Remember, if the sound matches some onscreen or in-game activity, it is classified as diegetic. Sounds made off-screen or to enhance mood, atmosphere, or theme are non-diegetic.

Summary

In this chapter, we looked at more advanced and practical examples of using the Audio Mixer. We started by looking at how to create, record, and transition snapshots, which we then applied to a practical example of a pause function for our scene. After that, we looked at constructing a dynamic wind effect that had several moving parts but could be used in other games. This led into another larger discussion of audio environmental zones. Audio environmental zones were areas where we wanted to simulate differences in our global audio due to things such as terrain, buildings, proximity to objects, and so on. We then implemented an environmental zone in one area of our village level, after which, we loaded the fully completed scene showing the addition of several zones representing areas of exposure, shelter, crossings, and partial cover. Finally, we diverged to create a new scene and worked on creating a dynamic music mix using four different audio clips.

In the next chapter, we will continue exploring the functionality of the Audio Mixer as it applies to an entire new era of mixing called adaptive audio. As this is the first chapter on adaptive audio, we will cover an introduction and discussion of definitions of dynamic and adaptive audio. After that, we will build a couple of examples using both sound effects and music.

5
Using the Audio Mixer for Adaptive Audio

Over the course of the last few chapters, we looked at several different ways to handle audio in a game. Starting from the basics of looped ambient audio clips to something a little more advanced using 3D spatial techniques. From there, we introduced processing and mixing techniques in order to refine the sound and music the game played. Then, we jumped into advanced mixing techniques in order to develop some dynamic audio effects with the wind and the environment. While all the techniques we have covered thus far could create excellent audio for your game, in this chapter, we start to bump things up to the next level by introducing adaptive audio.

For this chapter, we introduce new audio techniques in gaming called adaptive audio. Then, of course, as always, we will use these new concepts and apply them to useful and universal examples. Here are the main topics we will cover in this chapter:

- Introducing adaptive audio
- Building adaptive audio cues
- Creating mood with adaptive music
- Vertical remixing with the audio mixer
- Footsteps with adaptive sound

The examples in this chapter will continue from the work we completed in Chapter 4, *Advanced Audio Mixing*. For those of you that have jumped here from another part in the book, you can get going by installing the Viking Village Unity project and then importing the Chapter_5_Start.unitypackage found in the downloaded source code in the Chapter_5_Assets folder.

If you are unsure on how to install a project or import custom Unity assets, then in order to get the best experience from this book, go back and cover the exercises in `Chapter 1`, *Introducing Game Audio with Unity*, first.

Introducing adaptive audio

Mention adaptive audio to any group of game developers, and you will likely get quite a mixed bag of reactions from both positive to negative and everything in between. The reason for this has to do more with the definition of adaptive audio than what it means with respect to implementation. So, perhaps we should establish a proper definition of what is adaptive audio before we get too far into things. Here is a good broad definition of the term as it applies to modern game development:

> *"Adaptive audio" is a term used to describe audio and music that reacts appropriately to - and even anticipates - gameplay. Guy Whitmore (Gamasutra)*

While that definition does sound somewhat abstract, it really does a good job of defining what adaptive audio is. It is audio that anticipates, adapts to, and reacts with gameplay in order to enhance gameplay. The critical word in that definition is gameplay and that is what separates it from dynamic audio. We will define dynamic audio as audio that reacts to or is a consequence of environmental or level changes. The environmental zones and wind effect we developed in `Chapter 4`, *Advanced Audio Mixing*, would be classified as dynamic audio.

You may hear the terms dynamic, adaptive ,and interactive audio used interchangeably. We make the distinction between dynamic and adaptive audio in order to avoid confusion between terminology and definitions. As this aspect of audio development is still quite new, these definitions may still evolve and you may find a need to refer to adaptive audio as dynamic.

In case you are still a little confused on the definition of adaptive audio, we will look at some gameplay scenarios using it in games, as follows:

- As the player approaches a combat area, the music will quicken in pace, become louder, and feature more instruments.
- When a player is about to be surprised, the mood of the music becomes somber with undertones of apprehension and tension.
- If the player is quickly approaching the end of a level, the music quickens and becomes more celebratory. However, if the player fails, the music will become somber and express their defeat.

- The sound of the players, footsteps may quicken or become hushed, depending on the mood or state of the game.
- A player may make or hear encouraging or discouraging vocal cues based on the game state or other actions.

In the preceding list, there are three good examples of adaptive music, and if you have played any games recently, you will likely have come across them. The adaptive sound examples using footsteps and vocal cues are examples you are less likely to come across or notice but they are also out there.

In this book, we are going to spend plenty of time reviewing adaptive audio implementations using another tool. We will first start with Unity and demonstrate how the features you learned thus far can be used to implement adaptive audio. From there we will cover another professional mainstream tool for implementing adaptive audio as well as performing other audio tasks. By the end of those chapters, you should be more than comfortable enough to determine what audio tool will work best for your needs in the future.

The reason we will be covering two different implementations of adaptive audio isn't because it is the next big thing, which it is, but to demonstrate the crossover in skills and knowledge. Furthermore, while Unity has done a great job with the Audio Mixer, it still lacks functionality that is available in other tools and this will also be demonstrated.

Assuming we want to go ahead and implement adaptive audio, how should we go about it? How do we cue up or activate/deactivate it? The list here shows some strategies or options for controlling what triggers adaptive audio:

- **Event triggers**: These are used to detect when a player has entered an area, portal, or passageway. There will be typically several different triggers of various strength set around the level. This is similar to our environmental zones but it will typically be more structured.
- **Proximity triggers**: These are used to detect the distance to opponents or enemies. As the distance narrows, the adaptive level will increase. Each level will typically denote an additional increase in pace or tension in the audio.
- **Game state**: Elements, such as player health, enemy health, time to finish a task, and other similar game state elements can be used.

- **Others**: The list here could be endless based on the constant variations of gameplay game developers and designers will come up with. Use your imagination or try to think of some other examples of innovative triggers used to change audio. Think about this the next time you play an AAA game, and see if you can spot the triggers.

We use AAA games as the benchmark for users of adaptive audio, but it really is being used all over in various titles, whether developers want to admit it or not.

If you are still struggling with the definition of what is adaptive audio, do not worry, we will dig into some examples soon enough. In the next section, we cover how to build some triggers for cueing adaptive audio changes.

Building adaptive audio cues

As you learned from the last section, there are a number of ways of triggering adaptive audio changes. For our purposes, we are going to use two strategies that we mentioned earlier, the event and proximity triggers. Both of these triggers are good for general use and will transition well when we start to compare adaptive audio implementations for Unity in later chapters.

Thus far, we have omitted mentioning any elements of gameplay with our demo game. There really wasn't a need when all we were doing is talking about technical implementation. However, as part of our adaptive audio implementation, we need good definitions of gameplay elements so that we can create our triggers and audio to match. Therefore, in order to provide context for our gameplay, we will assume the following imaginary game design statement:

The player will assume the role of a not-so-fierce Viking warrior who has become abandoned in his village, with a ravaging dragon. All the other villagers have fled into the mountains to leave our lonely hero to defeat the dragon of his own accord. Playing the role of the hero, players must search the level for items that will help them defeat the dragon. As they move around, the level they may feel threatened and even potentially attacked by the dragon.

If you like the game design statement and want to develop this whole game concept further, by all means go ahead and do so.

Before we get into implementing the event triggers, let's take a look at what we want to accomplish. Here is an image of our level and how we propose to place our event triggers to control the adaptive audio:

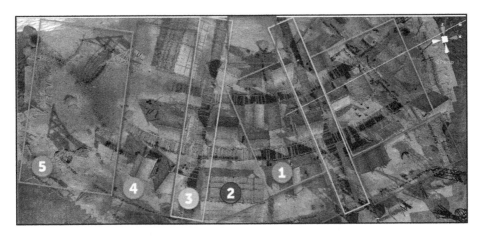

Event trigger area placement to control adaptive audio

The preceding map shows the placement of each type of trigger we plan to place. Notice how on the left side of the image there is a progression from areas numbered 1 to 5. That progression is relevant to our theme so let's review what each area color represents here:

- **Green** (1): This represents an area where the player is comfortable and not threatened. The player can move silently through these areas and not fear an attack by the dragon. All the audio in this area should give an uplifting tone and positive mood.
- **Black** (2): This is the global zone or all other areas not marked with an identified area trigger. The audio in this area should feel neutral. These are areas the player is not very likely to be attacked.
- **Yellow** (3): This area represents an area of exposure which will be identified with an audio tone of apprehension and caution. The player may be seen and attacked, but they are close to other areas they can move to cover quickly.
- **Purple** (4): The purple areas are even more exposed and further represent areas of tension and expectation of attack at any moment.
- **Red** (5): There most certainly will be an attack at any moment. The audio will be dramatic and full of anticipation. The player will need to run quickly through these areas in order to avoid attack.

Okay, now that we have our plans laid out, lets, get to it and create those audio triggers on the level by following the directions here:

1. Open up the Unity editor and load up the GameAudioBasics project. If you jumped here from another part of the book, create a new project and then import the Viking Village Unity project from the asset store.

   If you have made significant changes to your previous chapter's work and want to save those changes, then either start a fresh by creating a new project or duplicate your project folder to a new location.

2. Import the Chapter_5_Start.unitypackage from the downloaded source code in the Chapter_5_Assets folder by selecting **Assets | Import Package | Custom Package** from the menu. Then, use the **Import package** dialog to navigate to the Chapter_5_Assets folder and select the package. Click on the **Open** button to load and begin import of the package. Click on the **Import** button on the **Import** dialog to import all the package contents.

3. From the menu, select **GameObject | Create New**. Select and rename the new object to AdaptiveAudioManager in the **Hierarchy** menu. Reset the objects, **Transform position** to 0 in the **Inspector** window. Click on the **Add Component** button, and in the search field, type adaptiveaudiomanager. From the filtered list, select the **Adaptive Audio Manager** to add the component.

4. Right-click [*Ctrl* + click on Mac] on the AdativeAudioManager in the **Hierarchy** window and then select **Create Empty** from the context menu to create a new child object. Rename the new object AAT_1_1 (AAT = Adaptive Audio Trigger, level 1, #1) in the **Inspector** window.

5. From the menu, select **Component | Physics | Box Collider** to add a collider to the object. Click the **Add Component** button and then in the search field type adaptiveaudiotrigger to filter the component list. Select the **Adaptive Audio Trigger** component to add it to the object. While still in the **Inspector** window, carefully set the **Transform, Box Collider,** and **Adaptive Audio Trigger** component parameters to match the screenshot here:

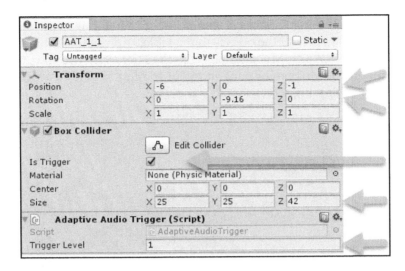

Setting the first triggers parameters

6. Select the AAT_1_1 object in the **Hierarchy** window and then press *Ctrl + D* to duplicate it. Rename the duplicate object AAT_1_2 and set its parameters to match those in the table here:

Name	Component	Parameter
AAT_1_2	Transform Box Collider Adaptive Audio Trigger	Position.X = 36.6, Position.Z = 5, Rotation.Y = -9.16 Size.X = 35, Size.Y = 25, Size.Z = 40 Trigger Level = 1
AAT_3_1	Transform Box Collider Adaptive Audio Trigger	Position.X = -31.5, Position.Z = 8, Rotation.Y = 19 Size.X = 11, Size.Y = 25, Size.Z = 75 Trigger Level = 3
AAT_3_2	Transform Box Collider Adaptive Audio Trigger	Position.X = -13.2, Position.Z = 5.3, Rotation.Y = -9.16 Size.X = 8, Size.Y = 25, Size.Z = 70 Trigger Level = 3
AAT_4_1	Transform Box Collider Adaptive Audio Trigger	Position.X = -7.4, Position.Z = 33.3, Rotation.Y = 8.5 Size.X = 12, Size.Y = 25, Size.Z = 12 Trigger Level = 4
AAT_4_2	Transform Box Collider Adaptive Audio Trigger	Position.X = -52.1, Position.Z = 7.4, Rotation.Y = 19 Size.X = 25, Size.Y = 25, Size.Z = 60 Trigger Level = 4
AAT_4_3	Transform Box Collider Adaptive Audio Trigger	Position.X = 41.2, Position.Z = -26, Rotation.Y = -9.16 Size.X = 37, Size.Y = 25, Size.Z = 20 Trigger Level = 4
AAT_4_4	Transform Box Collider Adaptive Audio Trigger	Position.X = -7.9, Position.Z = -33.9, Rotation.Y = -9.16 Size.X = 37, Size.Y = 25, Size.Z = 20 Trigger Level = 4
AAT_5_1	Transform Box Collider Adaptive Audio Trigger	Position.X = -81.9, Position.Z = 23.3, Rotation.Y = 19 Size.X = 36, Size.Y = 25, Size.Z = 60 Trigger Level = 5

7. Continue duplicating the objects using *Ctrl + D*, renaming them, and entering the parameters to match all the objects in the table. After you are done, double-click on the **AdaptiveAudioManager** object in the **Hierarchy** window, then adjust your camera view (zoom or pan) and your triggers should resemble something close to the following screenshot:

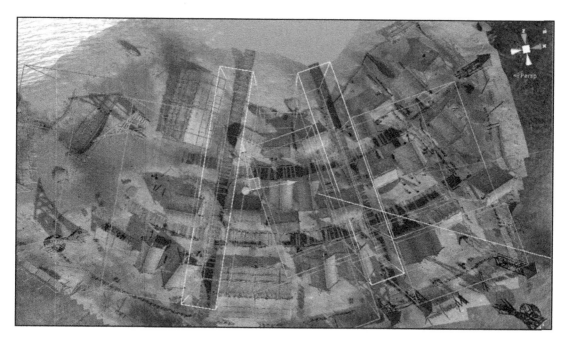

Village set up with various adaptive audio triggers added

8. Press play to run the scene. As you move through the scene, notice how the **Current Adaptive Level** setting on the **Adaptive Audio Manger** component changes as you move through the various triggers. Try to move outside an area where you know a trigger should be and see what the level gets set to.

9. When you are done testing the scene, press *Esc* to unlock your mouse and then press play again to stop the scene. From the menu, select **Save Scene** to save your changes.

Before we move on to adding the adaptive audio elements that will be cued off our trigger levels, lets, take a closer look at the Adaptive Audio Trigger script by following the exercise here:

1. Locate the **Adaptive Audio Trigger** component in the **Inspector** window as it is attached to one of the AAT objects. Click on the slot showing the AdaptiveAudioTrigger script. The script will become highlighted in yellow in the **Project** window as shown in the screenshot here:

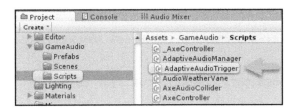

Highlighting the AdaptiveAudioTrigger script in the Project window

2. Double-click on the script to open it in your preferred code editor. The code for the AdaptiveAudioTrigger script is shown here for reference:

```
using UnityEngine;

[RequireComponent(typeof(BoxCollider))]
public class AdaptiveAudioTrigger : MonoBehaviour
{
    public int triggerLevel;

    void OnDrawGizmosSelected()
    {
        Gizmos.color = GetGizmoColor();
        Gizmos.matrix = transform.localToWorldMatrix;
        Gizmos.DrawWireCube(Vector3.zero,
GetComponent<BoxCollider>().size);
    }

    private Color GetGizmoColor()
    {
        switch (triggerLevel)
        {
            case 0:
            case 2:
                return Color.black; //default is black
            case 1:
                return Color.green;
```

```
                case 3:
                    return Color.yellow;
                case 4:
                    return new Color(.4f, .1f, .6f); //purple
                case 5:
                    return Color.red;
            }
            return Color.black;
        }

    void OnTriggerEnter(Collider collider)
    {
    AdaptiveAudioManager.Instance.AdjustAudioLevel(triggerLevel);
    }

    void OnTriggerExit(Collider collider)
    {
        AdaptiveAudioManager.Instance.AdjustAudioLevel(2);
    }
}
```

3. The script is fairly simple, but as you may have noticed it doesn't follow our typical format. Let's take a closer look at the highlighted lines of code in more detail as follows:

   - `[RequireComponent(typeof(BoxCollider))]` : This line defines a special attribute, which makes it mandatory that this script be only used on an object that already has a `BoxCollider` attached. If you tried to add the `AdaptiveAudioTrigger` to an object, without a `BoxCollider`, the editor would throw an error and block you from doing so.

   - `void OnDrawGizmosSelected()` : This method is called by the Unity editor to draw the component when it is selected. It is this section of code that allows us to color our areas based on our trigger level. If you look at the `GetGizmoColor` method, which is just a `switch` statement; this is the bit of code that determines what color is used for what trigger level.

   - `void OnTriggerEnter(Collider collider)`: This is a special method that is triggered, when the boundaries of a collider are entered by another game object also with a collider (our player object). The collider, in our case a `BoxCollider`, needs to have the `Is Trigger` option set on its component properties as shown in the screenshot here:

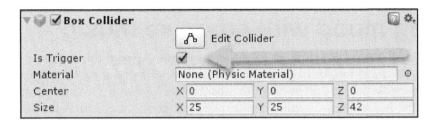

Setting the Is Trigger setting on a Box Collider

 If a colliders Is Trigger, the property is not set and the object will function as any other collider, meaning it will prevent any other object from passing through it that has a collider attached to it. The majority of objects in the scene will not be triggers.

4. `AdaptiveAudioManager.Instance.AdjustAudioLevel(triggerLevel);:` This line of code is activated inside the `OnTriggerEnter` method. It sets the current trigger level on the `AdaptiveAudioManager` using the `AdjustAudioLevel` method. Don't worry about the strange way we are calling the method just yet, we will cover that later when we cover the manager script.

5. `void OnTriggerExit(Collider collider)` : This method is called when a collider exits from the boundaries of the trigger collider.

6. `AdaptiveAudioManager.Instance.AdjustAudioLevel(2);` : This method is called inside the `OnTriggerExit` method as a way of setting the trigger level back to our global level of **2**. Ideally, you would want to script this value but for simplicity we hardcoded it. Thus, when a player exits a trigger area, then the level will be set to **2**, our global level.

We are using triggers to cue up our adaptive audio changes but just understand that we could have just as easily used the environmental zone method we used from Chapter 4, *Advanced Audio Mixing*. Alternatively, we could have just as easily used triggers to create the environmental zones. However, that would have given us less control for how our environmental sounds transitioned. For our needs, the hard boundary trigger zones will work well with the way we are going to implement the scenes, adaptive music. In the next section, we will discuss other options for controlling adaptive music and then use one of those methods to add music to our scene.

Creating mood with adaptive music

Music has been used to set the tone or mood in movies and games now for decades. It is almost always the most influential non-diegetic audio element a director, editor, producer, or game developer will focus on in order to add depth and quality to their production. Music, therefore, has become an important production element in games for decades. In the early days of game development, developers found themselves using static or linear music tracks throughout their game to great success. However, as games became more sophisticated, linear music tracks just didn't cut it anymore. After all, unlike movies, games are not linear and ideally need gameplay to drive the tone of the music. It was with that realization of having gameplay drive the music and not the other way around, is what became adaptive music.

Okay, so now we decided that we want adaptive music for our game, and we have five levels or areas that need different music. Why don't we just go ahead and add those five different music tracks to our game and change them when a player enters a trigger. Unfortunately, it isn't that easy. After all, if we had five very different music tracks, it would sound painfully harsh to switch between them whenever a player moved to a new area of the level. Our audio needs to smoothly transition between tracks so as not to jar the players, experience. What sounded like a simple process of adaptively changing music, really is not that easy after all. In fact, it can be downright tricky from an audio or sound designers, perspective. Here is a list of the top current ways adaptive music has been implemented in games, with a general list of advantages and disadvantages of each method:

1. **Horizontal re-sequencing** : This is a way of blending those multiple tracks together using techniques such as cross-fading, phrase branching, musical demarcation branching, and/or bridge transitions.
   - **Advantages:**
     - Easier to compose and implement than other methods
     - Allows for full changes to tempo, harmony, instrumentation, or melody
   - **Disadvantages**:
     - Often still very disruptive and still jarring to the player when a change occurs
     - Changes are often non-immediate except for cross-fading
     - Audio changes feel more scripted than adaptive

2. **Stinger-based sequencing:** This is a another type of horizontal re-sequencing that works by being triggered off events and then uses stingers (short audio clips) to cover transition points or changes in music.

- **Advantages:**
  - Ability to transition quickly between full changes to tempo, harmony, instrumentation, or melody
  - Highlights the music change by the game event
  - Easier to implement and mix than other horizontal re-sequencing methods

- **Disadvantages**:
  - Changes are limited to one event at a time
  - Changes may appear to be disjointed

3. **Vertical remixing (layering)**: The music is typically mixed on the fly into layers by adjusting tempo, harmony, instrumentation, or melody but while sharing common points of transition. Each transition may require multiple control inputs in order to adapt the music mix.

- **Advantages:**
  - Allows for very quick and seamless transitions
  - Music changes are very natural
  - Supports the ability to adapt after composition

- **Disadvantages:**
  - Difficult to compose for if not given the right tools
  - Can be difficult to drastically change tempo and harmony on some compositions
  - The transition may be too quick and possibly missed

The following diagram demonstrates the difference between horizontal re-sequencing and vertical remixing visually. With the arrows representing possible audio changes or track transition points. Horizontal is appropriately named because changes may only occur horizontally on the audio timeline. While vertical allows for changes to occur anywhere on the timeline, since the tracks overlap by sharing common reference elements.

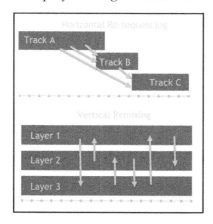

Diagram showing the difference between horizontal re-sequencing and vertical remixing techniques

The methods we will look at in this book will be number 2 and 3 from the preceding list. In the next section, we will get into implementing number 3, the vertical remixing (layering) system to use for our adaptive music with the Audio Mixer.

Vertical remixing with the Audio Mixer

Fortunately, the Unity Audio Mixer provides us with an excellent toolset in order to perform vertical remixing of the adaptive music we want in our scene. In fact, the current Unity mixer (at the time of writing) would really provide little use if we wanted to do some form of horizontal re-sequencing. This is what we will look at in Chapter 7, *FMOD for Dyanmic and Adaptive Audio*, when we will learn to use horizontal re-sequencing techniques for our scenes, adaptive music.

 Just for clarification, it's not that the Unity Audio Mixer could not implement any of the horizontal re-sequencing techniques, it just isn't well suited to do so.

The capabilities of the mixer allow us to easily breakup our music into distinct layers using snapshots. Just as we did at the end of Chapter 4, *Advanced Audio Mixing*, when we created the dynamic music mix. After we have the snapshots of the different music changes, as we have already seen in previous chapters, it is a simple matter to do transitions. As we will see, the tricky part in vertical remixing is just choosing your reference and control points. Let's take a look at how we can compose some vertical remixed layers with the Audio Mixer here:

1. Open up the editor and search for the MusicMix scene in the **Project** window. After you find the scene, double click on the scene to open it up. If you are prompted to save your current scene, then do so.

You can search for any asset, game object, or component in the various windows by just using the search box at the top of the window. Just start typing your search term and the window will automatically filter its contents.

2. From the menu, select **Window** | **Audio Mixer** to open or focus on the mixer window. Select the **MusicMix** mixer from the list of mixers and then the **level1** snapshot from the list of snapshots. Your window should match the screenshot here:

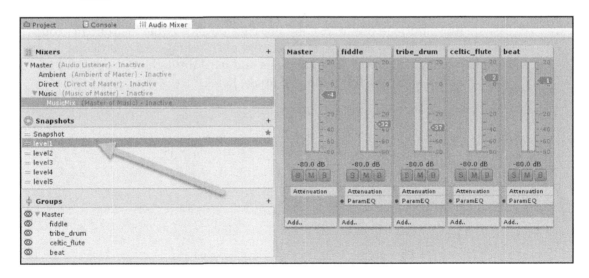

Viewing the MusicMix mixer and level1 Snapshot in the Audio Mixer window

3. Notice how the `MusicMix` mixer already has the level or snapshot layers we need to define. If you click through the various snapshots, you will see the settings change as well.

As much as some readers may have wanted hands-on experience mixing the various layers, explaining the numerous amounts of group changes could have filled almost an entire section on its own.

4. Click on the play button to start the scene. Then, press *Esc* to unlock the mouse while the scene is running and then click on the **Edit in Play Mode** button at the top of the **Audio Mixer** window. Switch between the various snapshots to hear the change in music. Notice how the snapshots have multiple variations, including tempo (BPM) and changes in instrument focus.

In order to change tempo, we used the same pitch adjustment trick from `Chapter 4`, *Advanced Audio Mixing*. Recall, the trick is to adjust the pitch by a ratio of the desired BPM over the actual recorded BPM. The formula is shown again for reference:

pitch% = Desired BPM / Actual BPM * 100

5. As you move through the snapshots, also click on each of the instrument groups and pay attention to the effects, volume, and pitch settings. Pay particular attention to the way the `beat` group is set and used throughout the various layers (snapshots) as shown in the combined image here:

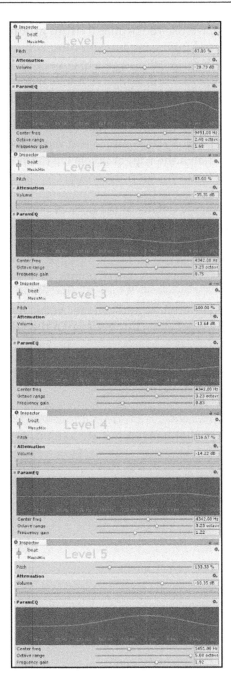

Vertical remixing of the beat group through the various layers or levels

For the example, we use the beat and drum groups to provide our reference or control points for transitioning between layers. The beating of the drums in both mixes also works to cover harsh changes as we will see later. We will dig more into adaptive music composition and techniques for vertical remixing in Chapter 10, *Composing Music.*

6. Be careful and avoid making any changes to the settings, since they will be saved to the mixer. Instead, listen to the music and remember how each of the snapshots needs to match the trigger levels we defined earlier in the chapter. When you are done listening, stop the scene.

We won't get into any more specific details of the how of vertical remixing at this time. Our intention in this chapter is just to identify the use and implementation of adaptive audio and music. Describing how to vertically remix audio using just the Audio Mixer would be difficult, if not painful. The Audio Mixer lacks the visual display of audio that we would need to talk about with these reference or control points. Instead, we will cover a section on vertical remixing in Chapter 10, *Composing Music.* In that chapter, we will work with a tool that can provide us with visual references and cues for vertical mixing. Having said all that, you are still encouraged after we get everything set up in the village scene to try and vertically remix on your own.

So now that we have seen how the vertical remix is composed, let's take a look at setting up the village scene by following the directions here:

1. Find the scene The_Viking_Village_Chapter_5_Start and drag it onto the **Hierarchy** window so that both scenes are loaded, as shown in the screenshot here:

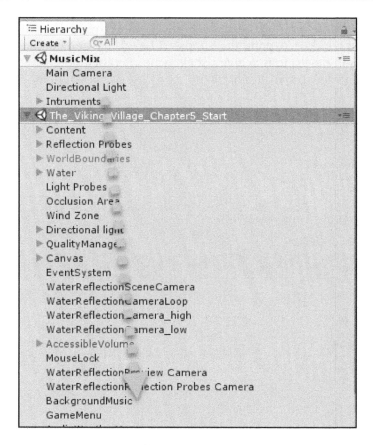

Working with two scenes in the Hierarchy window

2. Drag the `Instruments` object from the **MusicMix** scene and drop it onto the `BackgroundMusic` object in the village scene (as shown in the screenshot).

3. Right-click [*Ctrl* + click on Mac] on the **MusicMix** scene, and from the context menu, select **Remove Scene**. You will be prompted to save your changes, but don't save your changes. You may want to come back and work with the mix scene later.

4. Select the `AdaptiveAudioManager` object in the **Hierarchy** window. Then in the **Inspector** window, expand the **Snapshot Levels** list and enter a size of 5. This will expand the list to five items or elements. Set each of the levels to the appropriate level snapshot of the `MusicMixer` as shown in the screenshot here:

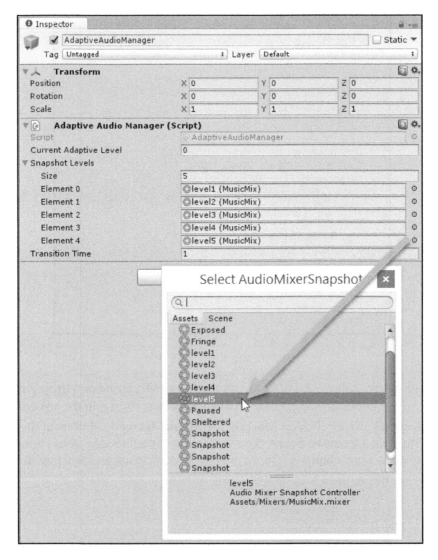

Setting up the Snapshot levels on the Adaptive Audio Manager

5. Open up the **Audio Mixer** window and select the **MusicMix** mixer. Then, right-click [*Ctrl* + click on Mac] on the `level2` snapshot. Then from the context menu, select **Set as start Snapshot** as shown in the screenshot here:

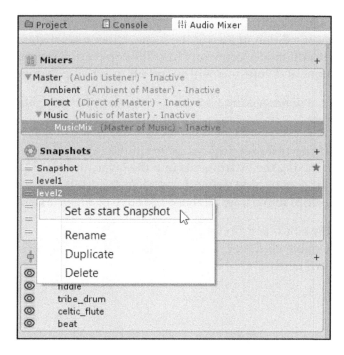

Setting the MusicMix mixer starting snapshot to level2

6. Press play to start the scene. Move around the scene while paying special attention to how the music changes as you move from trigger level area to area. Try and get to all of the five different areas. As you do, pay special attention to how the music transitions from one layer/level to the next.

7. At this point, if you want to change the mix in a particular area, press *Esc* to unlock the mouse and then click on the **Edit in Play Mode** button to turn on editing. Make the changes you feel are appropriate to the area and when you are done, click on the **Edit in Play Mode** button again to turn off editing. Then, you can move around the scene more.

When you click on the Edit in Play Mode button and engage editing, mixer transitions become disabled. Therefore, when making edits to dynamic or adaptive mixes, such as the music and wind, be sure to keep the audio listener (the player) in the scene stationary while making edits. Turn off editing, and move the listener (player) when you want to edit the settings of a different area of the scene. Otherwise, if you move around while in edit mode, you won't hear the correct dynamic/adaptive transitions and your mix will sound off in actual play mode.

8. After you are done making your own edits, stop the scene and of course save your changes.

As you can see, setting up that exercise was quite simple. After all, most of the work had already been done in mixing the instruments into the layers or levels. You would think that there certainly must be a lot of code doing the work in the AdaptiveAudioanager script. We will open up the script to see how all those adaptive changes take place:

1. Open up the editor and find the AdaptiveAudioManager script in the **Project** window. Double-click on the script to open it in your preferred code editor and it is also shown here for review:

```
using UnityEngine;
using UnityEngine.Audio;

public class AdaptiveAudioManager : Singleton<AdaptiveAudioManager>
{
    public int currentAdaptiveLevel;
    public AudioMixerSnapshot[] snapshotLevels;
    public float transitionTime = 1;

    public void AdjustAudioLevel(int level)
    {
        currentAdaptiveLevel = level;

snapshotLevels[currentAdaptiveLevel-1].TransitionTo(transitionTime);
    }
}
```

2. Here is a breakdown of the highlighted sections of code that are the most important:

- `public class AdaptiveAudioManager : Singleton<AdaptiveAudioManager>` : Notice how we are extending the `AdaptiveAudioManager` not from `MonoBehaviour` but rather a class called `Singleton`. `Singleton` is a programming pattern that essentially says we only ever want to have one type of object and that object should be globally accessible from all our code. By extending `AdaptiveAudioManager` from `Singleton`, we are only allowing one object of its type to be created and it will be accessible from everywhere in other parts of our code using a special `Instance` property. Remember when we passed the level from the trigger to the audio manager with this line of code: `AdaptiveAudioManager.Instance.AdjustAudioLevel(triggerLevel)`.

- `public AudioMixerSnapshot[] snapshotLevels;` : This line of code is just a definition for the array or list of snapshot levels we want the audio manager script to control.

- `snapshotLevels[currentAdaptiveLevel-1].TransitionTo(transitionTime);` : This line of code is what indexes into the list of snapshot levels and calls the `TransitionTo` method of the `Snaphot`. The reason we subtract 1 from the `currentAdaptiveLevel` is because we always start counting at zero in programming. So, the first element in the snapshot levels array is actually at index 0. Aside from that, we have already covered the `TransitionTo` method in the last chapter.

 Be aware that most of the samples in this book are used to demonstrate concepts and are not a how to on writing robust production code. In some cases, some robust error checking has been done but only for the safety of the demo. If you will be scripting code for your game, do yourself a favor and read a book or blog on coding best practices.

Hopefully, as you looked at the simplicity of the preceding code, and the code we needed for setting up the triggers, you can realize how well Unity is suited for quick development. It also goes to show how well suited the Unity Audio Mixer is for supporting adaptive music with vertical remixing. For the next section, we are going to look at how well the Audio Mixer can support adaptive sound.

> **QUIZ TIME**
>
> Which adaptive music technique would best match each of these situations:
> a) **Horizontal re-sequencing**
> b) **Horizontal re-sequencing with Stingers**
> c) **Vertical remixing**
>
>
>
> 1) Your team is fairly new to game development so it is decided to outsource the music for your game. Which means the music will come in completely composed and each piece will change dramatically. Which option works best: a, b, or c?
>
> 2) Your team has experience working with the Audio Mixer and have found a number of instrumental sounds they like. Which option works best: a, b, or c?
>
> 3) The game you are developing needs event-driven full changes to the music (tempo, harmony, and instrumentation). Which option works best: a, b, or c?
> The answers to the quiz will be provided at the end of the chapter.

Footsteps with adaptive sound

While adaptive audio is often synonymous with adaptive music, it doesn't have to be as we will see in this section. In order to demonstrate adaptive sound, we will implement footsteps audio that is controlled by the current adaptive level. Until now, we have avoided working with footstep sounds so as not to clutter up the other audio we were mixing. Follow the instructions here to add footsteps to our scene:

1. Open up the **Audio Mixer** window in the editor, select the **Master** mixer from the **Mixers** list. Then, right-click [*Ctrl* + click on Mac] on the **Direct** group and from the context menu select **Add child group**. This will add a new child group to `Direct`. Rename this new group `Footsteps` as shown in the following screenshot:

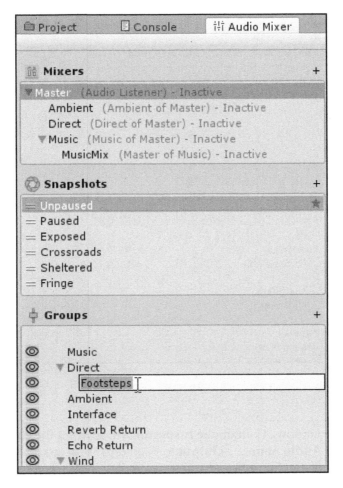

Adding new Footsteps group to the Master mixer

2. Type the text `fps` in the search field of the **Hierarchy** search window. Then, type the text `footstepsaudio` in the search field of the **Project** window. Drag the `FootstepsAudio` script from the **Project** window and drop it onto the `FlyingRigidBodyFPSController_HighQuality` object to add the component to it as shown in the screenshot here:

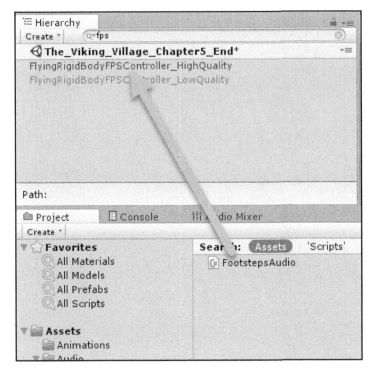

Drag and dropping the FootstepsAudio script onto the controller

3. Select the `FlyingRigidBodyFPSController_HighQuality` object in the **Hierarchy** window. Then, in the **Inspector** window, set the component properties: **Audio Source | Output** to **Footsteps (Master)** and the **Footsteps Audio | Footstep Sounds** to the array as shown in the screenshot here:

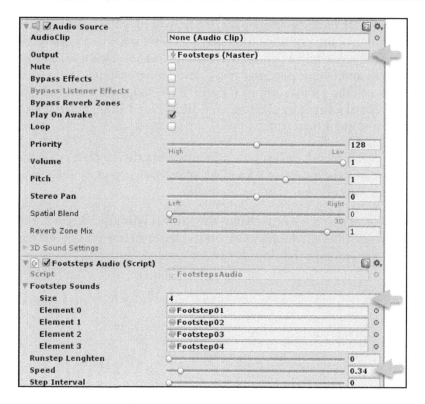

Setting the Audio Source and Footsteps Audio sources and parameters

4. Back to the **Audio Mixer** window, select the `Direct` group and then in the
Inspector window reduce the **Send level** to `-80 dB` for the **Music\Duck Volume**
as shown in the screenshot here:

Turning down the send to the Duck Volume effect

5. Press **Play** to run the scene. Notice how the character now has footstep sounds
that change as you move around the scene. The footsteps, pace and occurrence
depend on the trigger level you are moving through.

6. Since we have added a new mixer group, you may also want to adjust the environmental area settings for the Footsteps or Direct group as well. Move around the scene and as you move through one of the zones: exposes, crossroads, sheltered, and fringe, pay attention to how the footsteps, audio sounds. If you want to edit the group settings for any of the snapshot sounds, be sure to stop moving, start editing by clicking on **Edit in Play Mode**, make your adjustments, and then stop editing.

With the script in place, our character now generates adaptive footstep sounds. This is great, but has come at the expense of a lot of scripting. Let's open up the FootstepsAudio script here to take a look at what is going on inside:

1. Search for footstepsaudio from the **Project** window. When the contents of the window are filtered, double-click on the script to open it in your editor of choice. Here is the entire horrendous script for review:

```
using UnityEngine;
using UnityStandardAssets.Characters.FirstPerson;

[RequireComponent(typeof(AudioSource))]
[RequireComponent(typeof(RigidbodyFirstPersonController))]
public class FootstepsAudio : MonoBehaviour
{
    public AudioClip[] footstepSounds;
    public float runstepLenghten;
    public float speed;
    public float stepInterval;
    private RigidbodyFirstPersonController characterController;
    private AudioSource audioSource;
    private float stepCycle;
    private float nextStep;

    void Start()
    {
        characterController =
GetComponent<RigidbodyFirstPersonController>();
        audioSource = GetComponent<AudioSource>();
    }

    void FixedUpdate()
    {
        switch
(AdaptiveAudioManager.Instance.currentAdaptiveLevel)
        {
            case 0:
            case 2:
```

```
            speed = 1; stepInterval = 3;
            Time.timeScale = 1f;
            break;
        case 1:
            speed = .5f; stepInterval = 2.5f;
            Time.timeScale = .5f;
            break;
        case 3:
            speed = 1.5f; stepInterval = 2.5f;
            Time.timeScale = 1.5f;
            break;
        case 4:
            speed = 2.5f; stepInterval = 3.5f;
            Time.timeScale = 2f;
            break;
        case 5:
            speed = 3.5f; stepInterval = 5f;
            Time.timeScale = 2.5f;
            break;
    }
    ProgressStepCycle(speed);
}
private void ProgressStepCycle(float speed)
{
    if (characterController.Velocity.sqrMagnitude > 0 )
    {
        stepCycle += (characterController.Velocity.magnitude
+ (speed
                    * (characterController.Running ?
runstepLenghten : 1f)))
                    * Time.fixedDeltaTime;
    }

    if (!(stepCycle > nextStep))
    {
        return;
    }

    nextStep = stepCycle + stepInterval;

    PlayFootStepAudio();
}

private void PlayFootStepAudio()
{
    if (characterController.Grounded == false)
    {
        return;
```

```
        }
        // pick & play a random footstep sound from the array,
        // excluding sound at index 0
        int n = Random.Range(1, footstepSounds.Length);
        audioSource.clip = footstepSounds[n];
        audioSource.PlayOneShot(audioSource.clip);
        // move picked sound to index 0 so it's not picked next
time
        footstepSounds[n] = footstepSounds[0];
        footstepSounds[0] = audioSource.clip;
    }
}
```

2. This script is similar in some ways to our other scripts that have interacted with physics objects. This is exactly what we are doing in this script. For the most part, aside from the maths perhaps, you should be able to understand most of what is going on in this script. The highlighted lines either represent important methods or actual code. Here is a detailed description for each of the highlighted lines:

   - `FixedUpdate()`: Since we are interacting with the physics system, the character controller, we process our code in the `FixedUpdate` rather than the `Update`.

   - `switch (AdaptiveAudioManager.Instance.currentAdaptiveLevel)`: This **switch** statement is called at every fixed update and it switches base on the `AdaptiveAudioManager` singleton objects `currentAdaptiveLevel` property. Remember that since our `AdaptiveAudioManager` is a singleton, it can be called from any script running in the scene. This means that when a trigger updates the `currentAdaptiveLevel` on the `AdaptiveAudioManager` by calling `AdjustLevel`, this will in turn indirectly send an update to this script. Inside the switch statement, each of the levels is split into case statements that set the particular parameters for how the character will move and how frequently the footstep sounds will occur.

   - `Time.timeScale = 1.5f;`: This line sets the scale of time for the scene. So in this instance, we are not only controlling audio characteristics with our adaptive triggers but also the time scale characteristics as well. In essence, we are putting our character in various time warps for a more dramatic effect on gameplay. These types of time warping effects are used all the time in modern gaming for everything from slow motion shots of dying to warp movement effects not unlike what we are doing here.

You could also accomplish the same sense of speed increase by just speeding up the character controller. However, it is generally not recommended to alter the physical characteristics of an object because this could dramatically effect other physical systems in the game. For instance, a character moving at a greater speed will generate a higher force to impacts, which could allow previously immovable objects to move, just by having a character run into them. Whereas, this would not be an issue with time warping, since the character is still moving at the same speed but just perceives time faster or slower.

- `private void ProgressStepCycle(float speed)`: The code in this method was extracted from the Unity first person character controller and it is what controls the step length based on speed. We won't get into the details of this method too much but just realize there are two important variables that determine the number and frequency of footsteps. They are the stride length or `stepInterval` and `speed`. In the `FixedUpdate` method, these variables are set based on what trigger area the player is in. If you can understand the math in this method, then also feel free to adjust those parameters a little for each of the trigger areas.

It is important to notice that we are hardcoding a number of values in this script, which is bad programming practice. We will look to rectify this issue in later chapters when we look at more advanced tools that can provide alternatives to hardcoding.

- `private void PlayFootStepAudio()` : Finally, we get into the last method where the footstep sounds are actually played. Notice how the various footstep sounds are used randomly. This is the same practice we followed with our audio randomization we did for various sources in Chapter 2, *Scripting Audio*. The sounds we are using for the footsteps are actually part of the original Unity project. In further chapters, we will look to add dynamic footsteps that change as the player moves across different surface materials.
  - `if (characterController.Grounded == false)` : This line of code checks if the character is grounded. Obviously if the character is not grounded, we don't want to play footsteps.

Well, that was quite a lengthy script to do what we needed compared to the other scripts in this chapter. Unfortunately, most of it was necessary to get just the basic footsteps working. This is because the controller we are currently using for the scene is not set up to use footstep sounds. The standard FPS Controller script is equipped to use footstep audio and actually was the source for a couple of the methods in this script. While this script works for our demonstration, it is less than perfect for our development needs since all of the settings need to be defined in code. The `FootstepsAudio` script is a good starting point for demonstrating the basic concepts. Ideally, we want to be able to dynamically make changes to the adaptive audio changes the same way we did for the music. In `Chapter 7`, *FMOD for Dyanmic and Adaptive Audio*, we will look to improve on this script in a few interesting ways.

QUIZ TIME ANSWERS

Here are the answers to the previous chapters quiz:

1) Your team is fairly new to game development, so it is decided to outsource the music for your game. This means the music will come in completely composed and each piece will change dramatically. Option a (horizontal re-sequencing) works best here. Since the team is new and the music is outsourced, it is best managed using more traditional horizontal re-sequencing techniques.

2) Your team has experience working with the Audio Mixer and have found a number of instrumental sounds they like. Option c (vertical remixing) is the best choice. The team alone, given their knowledge of the Audio Mixer, could use vertical remixing to create the needed adaptive music.

3) The game you are developing needs event-driven full changes to music (tempo, harmony, and instrumentation). Option b (horizontal re-sequencing with stingers) works best for this case. Event-driven music that needs full changes is best done with horizontal re-sequencing with stingers.

Summary

In this chapter, we looked into new techniques that are used to enhance gameplay in most modern games these days and especially in AAA titles. We started with an introduction to adaptive audio, which is a way to adapt to, react with, and enhance gameplay. After that we looked at a technique for triggering adaptive audio and then implemented that into our village scene. From there, we took a closer look at adaptive music and the various techniques used to implement seamless music transitions. We then used one of those techniques best suited for the Unity Audio Mixer called vertical remixing to implement adaptive music within our demo scene. As we implemented this remixing technique, we began to understand the need for learning some basic music composition skills. Finally, in the last section of this chapter, we looked at adaptive sound using footstep audio. We introduced and examined a starting script that demonstrated how adaptive footstep sounds could be accomplished with a heavy amount of scripting.

For the next chapter, we will continue with the theme of implementing adaptive sound. However, in the next and following chapters, we will look at FMOD, which is powerful commercial tool that is able to do the job just as well as the Audio Mixer, if not better.

6
Introduction to FMOD

FMOD is the oldest commercial audio engine, first published in March 1995, and originally just worked with MOD files, hence the name. It is without exception the standard in audio development tools for game development and has been used for hundreds of AAA titles. The Unity audio engine is FMOD, although that shared heritage may not become evident until you start working with the Audio Mixer. Of course, no book on audio development with Unity or any other game engine would be complete without at least one chapter on working with FMOD. Therefore, we are going to spend a couple of chapters working with FMOD and this entire chapter will be an introduction. We will cover the basics of setting up and using FMOD for Unity and how it can work to develop adaptive audio. However, as we will see, FMOD is a choice not all teams may want to take or decide they need, especially if they have become comfortable working with the Audio Mixer.

We are going to devote this entire chapter to introducing FMOD Studio and how it integrates into Unity for your projects (games) audio development. FMOD Studio is the DAW software, that is powered by FMOD, and is used for audio game development that was previously known as FMOD Designer. While a whole book could likely be devoted to working with FMOD Studio, we are going to keep it simple by just adapting some of the demonstrations we have worked on thus far. Not only will this allow you to compare tools, it will also show you the similarities between the Audio Mixer and FMOD Studio. Here is the list of topics we will cover in this chapter:

- Getting started with FMOD Studio
- Back to the basics
- Effects and mixing
- Mixing in a reverb effect
- Parameters, snapshots, and triggers

When we speak of FMOD, we are referring to the entire audio system, which in our case, also encompasses FMOD Studio. Assume from now on that any reference to FMOD is a reference to FMOD Studio unless mentioned otherwise.

While our goal will be to demonstrate the capabilities of FMOD Studio in the development of adaptive audio and music, we certainly will need to cover some of the basics first. FMOD is a complicated piece of software, and we will need to understand some setup before diving into the deep end and developing an adaptive audio example. Therefore, in the next section, we will indeed start with the basics by covering FMOD installation and the basic setup.

Getting started with FMOD Studio

FMOD Studio is a commercial product and standalone tool that provides free licensing to independent developers, which is inline with the Unity license. Since it is a standalone tool, it actually does not need to be used with Unity and in fact is compatible with many other commercial game engines. This is even a more powerful feature if you develop audio assets across game engine platforms. However, the compatibility within Unity with existing tools is another matter.

> *And now for something completely different. - John Cleese (Monty Python)*

Unfortunately, as the preceding quote suggests, working with FMOD in Unity uses an entirely different set of components which are incompatible with any of the work we have already covered. Perhaps, in the future, there may be an integration path between FMOD and the Audio Mixer but as of now the audio systems are completely different. As such, we will need to relearn some basic tasks, but if you have covered most of the exercises in the book thus far, that transition should be relatively straightforward.

Installing FMOD Studio

As we discussed, FMOD Studio is a standalone commercial software package that will require a separate installation to that of Unity. Follow the directions here to install the software onto your computer:

1. Proceed to the following site: `http://www.fmod.org/download/` by clicking on the link or entering it in your browser.

2. In order to download any software from the site, you will need to register for an account, just as you did with Unity. Click on the **Register** link found at the top of page and shown in the screenshot here:

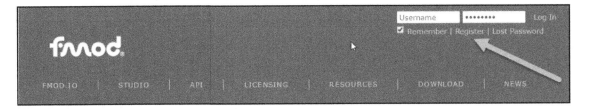

Registering for an account of the FMOD site

3. Complete the account registration just as you did for Unity. After you have verified your email, log into the site and proceed to the download page again. Select the download that matches your computers, OS and platform from the **FMOD Studio Authoring Tool** section as shown in the screenshot here:

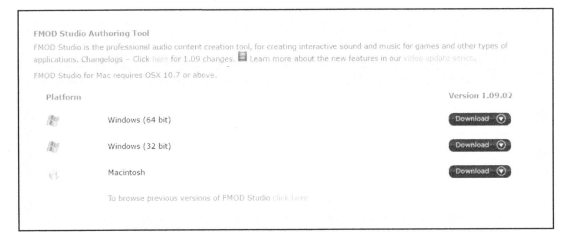

Selecting the download that matches your system

4. After the download completes, run the installer and follow the default instructions to install the software.

5. Scroll down on the FMOD download page to the **FMOD Studio Unity Integration** section as shown here:

Downloading the Unity integration package

6. Click on the **Download** button to download the
   `fmodstudio{version}.unitypackage` file to a well-known location. You will need to import this package later into Unity.

7. Open up the Unity editor and create a new empty 3D project called `GameAudio_FMOD`. After the project opens, select **Assets | Import Package | Custom Package** from the menu. This will open the **Import** package dialog. Use the dialog to locate and import the file you just downloaded, `fmodstudio{version}.unitypackage`. Follow the **Import** dialog as you have done before to import the package.

8. When the package finishes importing, there will be a new menu entry called **FMOD**. You will also notice the following error in the **Status** bar/**Console** window: **FMOD Studio: FMOD Studio Project path not set**. In order to fix the error, we need to launch FMOD Studio, create a new project, and attach to Unity. Launch FMOD Studio as you would with any other software.

9. When FMOD Studio has finished loading from the menu, select the **File** | **Save As...** . Use the **Save As** dialog to locate the folder where you created the Unity project. Enter a name of `GameAudio_FMOD` and then click on **Save**.

10. From the menu, select **File** | **Build** to build the empty project.

11. Open back up the Unity editor, and from the menu, select **FMOD** | **Edit Settings**. Click on the **Browse** button beside the **Studio Project Path** in the **Inspector** window as shown in the screenshot here:

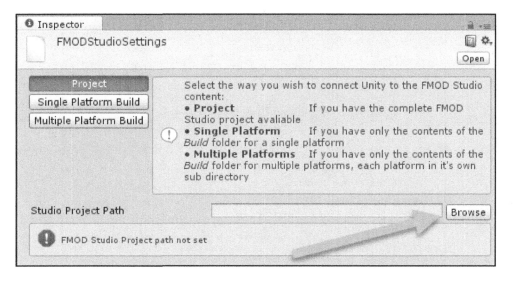

Setting up the FMOD Studio Project Path

12. This will open the **Locate Studio Project** dialog. Use the dialog to open the FMOD Studio project folder and select the project file you just saved. Click the **Open** button to set the project path. When the path is set, the **Inspector** window will now show the following:

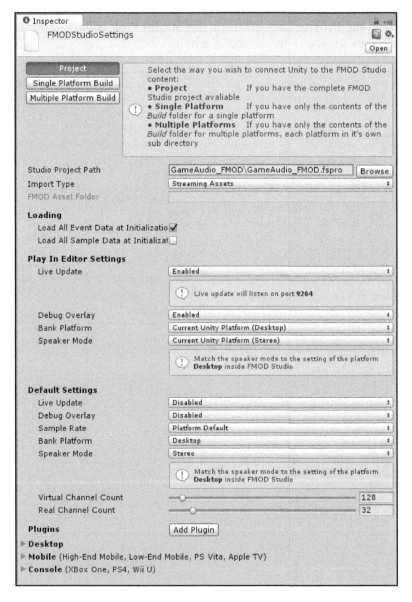

Inspector window showing properly configured FMOD Studio Project settings

Good job, that finishes the installation of FMOD. In the next section, we will cover the basics of using FMOD for audio in our scene.

Back to the basics

As we already discussed, FMOD provides its own audio implementation within Unity. This means that we need to relearn the FMOD way of putting sound into our scene. While this may sound like we are starting over, that is far from the case. Although FMOD uses different components and terminologies, as we will see, the concepts are all the same.

Open up the Unity editor to the new project we created in the last section and let's get started working with importing the Viking Village asset into the new project by following the instructions here:

1. From the menu, select **Windows** | **Asset Store**. After the store page loads, type `unity viking village` in the search box and enter to start searching for the example project. Select the first item from the list of results (as you did previously) and then from asset page, click on the **Import** button as shown in the screenshot here:

Importing the Unity Viking Village example project, again

If you have jumped ahead to this chapter from earlier in the book or not completed any of the previous exercises, you may instead see a **Download** button. That is fine, just click on the **Download** button to download and import the asset.

2. We won't go over step by step on importing the project as we already covered this in Chapter 1, *Introducing Game Audio with Unity*. Just follow the steps as you did previously to import the asset into the new project. Remember, this can take a while so stay hydrated and don't be afraid to grab some of your favorite beverage.

3. When the asset has completed loading, locate and then open the **The_Viking_Village** scene as shown in the screenshot here:

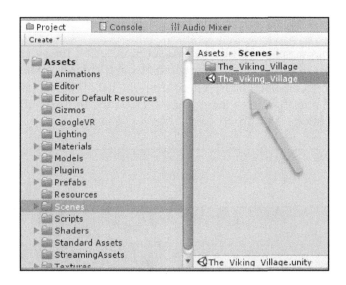

Opening the The_Viking_Village scene

4. From the menu, select **File | Save Scene as** and then save the scene with the name Chapter_6_Start in the Scenes folder. It is best to always make a copy of a scene you are modifying.

Remember you can easily locate anything in the various editor windows quickly by using the search field. Just start typing the name of your asset, scene, or script and the window will filter the contents to match your search.

Now, we have a completely fresh install of our Viking Village asset in our project we can get back to the FMOD integration pieces. First, we will open up FMOD Studio and take a bit of a tour on how to import audio and set up events by following the directions here:

1. Open up FMOD Studio and be sure that the **GameAudio_FMOD** project is loaded by taking note of the software's title bar.

2. From the menu, select **File | Import Audio Files**. Use the **Open** dialog to locate and open the `Chapter_1_Audio` folder from the book's downloaded source code. Inside the folder, select the `torch.wav` and `lake-shore-waves2.wav` files to import them into the project. After the files are selected, click on **Open** to import them.

3. The files will quickly import and the **Audio Bin** window will open showing both files. Select the `torch.wav` file as shown in the screenshot here:

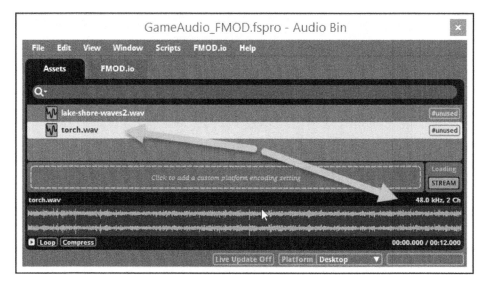

Audio assets imported into the FMOD projects Audio Bin

4. Notice that the information is similar to what we seen in Unity after importing the same files. Close the **Audio Bin** window as we no longer need it. Back in Studio, select the **Assets** tab and then right-click [*Ctrl* + click on Mac] on the `torch.wav` asset. From the context menu, select **Create Event** as shown in the screenshot here:

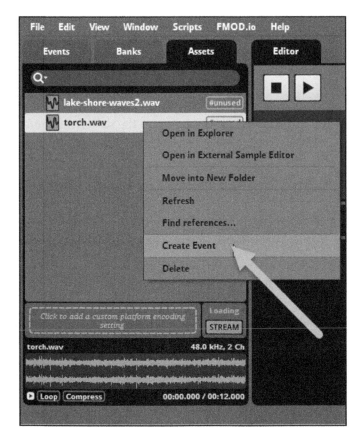

Creating an Event from the torch asset

 FMOD uses the term Event to refer to what we would call in Unity an audio source and mixer group combined. It may seem strange after working with sources and groups, but as we will see, it actually simplifies things.

5. You will then be prompted with the **Create Event** dialog asking you to choose between **2D** or **3D**. Select **3D** and then click on the **Create** button as shown in the following screenshot:

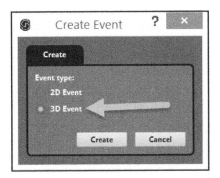

Creating an event

6. After the **Create Event** dialog closes, not much will appear to change. Select the **Events** tab and then select the new **torch** event in the list and the interface will now completely come alive as shown in the following screenshot:

7. First off, try not to panic or get overwhelmed. Sure, there is a lot of new stuff going on here, but as we will see, most of it will be similar to using the Unity Audio Mixer. As you can see, the major points of the interface have been labeled on the diagram and and a brief explanation for each is given here:

- **Events tab**: This shows a list of the events that are defined for the project.
- **Playback control**: This allows you to play the event and monitor timing/beats and so forth.
- **Event editor area**: This allows you to horizontally edit the tracks or modules. The control area provides what separates FMOD Studio from the Unity Audio Mixer. We will spend a lot of time working in this window.

As a clarification, you will notice that the entire window in the preceding screenshot is showing is called the event editor. FMOD Studio uses a series of actual windows or sub-applications to control various phases of the audio editing process.

- **Overview window**: As this sound is 3D, the interface provides a spatial overview window that allows you to move the listener.
- **Deck region**: This is named after the old mixing recorder used in the early days of audio editing. It is essentially like the Unity Inspector window view of a mixer group. This is where effects are added on the event or tracks.
- **Master control**: Just like the Unity mixer, this Event or group is controlled by a Master control.

8. Next, right click [**Ctrl+Click** on Mac] on the `torch` track in the **Event** window and from the context menu select **New Loop Region** as shown in the following screenshot:

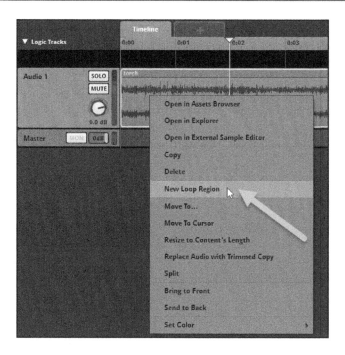

Making the torch track loop

9. Click on the play button to play the **Event** and make sure the audio is looping. As the sound is looping, use your mouse to drag the pointer (listener) in the **3D Preview** around the area, notice how the sound changes to reflect the change in position. Next, change the **Distance Attenuation** in the **3D Panner** effect in the mixing window to the graph shown in the combined screenshot here:

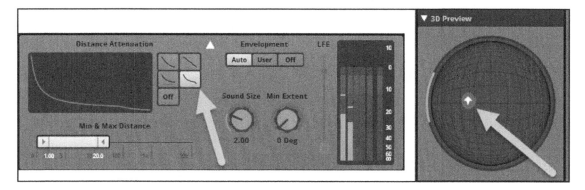

Setting the Distance Attenuation graph on the 3D Panner effect and 3D previewing

If you are unable to see any effects, select the **Master** track (always the bottom track) in the Track region. The **3D Panner** effect is always applied to the **Master** track.

10. Feel free to play around with the controls until you get a distance attenuation you like. As you can see, this interface is much more visual and powerful than Unity's 3D settings controls. When you are done exploring, press the Stop button.

11. Right-click [*Ctrl* + click on Mac] on the torch event in the Events tab, and from the context menu, select **Assign to Bank | Master Bank**. You will notice that the **#unassigned** tag has been removed from the event. Then, from the menu, select **File | Build**. This will build the project and we will be ready to integrate the audio into Unity.

We now have created our first audio Event in FMOD Studio, and it is time to integrate that event in Unity to see how it sounds. Open up the Unity editor and return to the Viking Village scene and follow the instructions to wire up the audio:

1. We are going to assign the `torch` event to all our torches just as we did previously. Enter `prop_torch` in the **Hierarchy** window search field, to filter down to just all the torches in the scene. Select all the torches in the scene using any method you prefer (*Shift* or *Ctrl* select).

2. In the **Inspector** window, click on the **Add Component** button. Type `fmod` in the search field and from the filtered list select **FMOD Studio Event Emitter** to add the component. On the new component, set the **Play Event** to be **Object Start** and then click on the search button to open the **Event** finder. Select the **torch** event and the component will expand to display other properties as shown in the screenshot here:

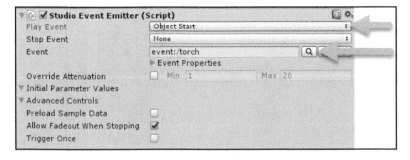

FMOD Studio Event Emitter configured

3. Back in the **Hierarchy** window, enter `camera_high` in the search field to locate the **Camera_high** object. Select the object and add the **FMOD Studio Listener** component to it from the **Inspector** window.

 If you forget to add the **Studio Listener** component, you won't experience any spatial/3D characteristics, that you will still be able to hear the audio though.

4. Press play to run the scene. Move around the scene and pay attention to the sound of the torches. Do the torches sound better or worse? We will leave that up to you to decide. When you are done testing, stop the scene and save your changes.

As mentioned, this certainly is a diversion from where we started in Unity. Hopefully though, as you progress through this chapter, you can appreciate the power of working with a full featured DAW such as FMOD Studio. In the next section, we will continue introducing the basics by covering effects and mixing.

Effects and mixing

The capabilities for applying effects and mixing with FMOD Studio go well beyond what is possible with the Audio Mixer, and it can be intimidating to grasp for novices. Fortunately for us, while the interface may be quite different, the theory and practice we already covered in previous chapters will apply well here. In order to demonstrate effects and mixing, we will add the lake shore waves ambient sound we used previously, as a new event in Unity, by following the directions here:

1. Open up the FMOD event editor window to the `GameAudio_FMOD` project. The one we have been working with.

2. Locate the `lake-shore-waves2.wav` audio clip in the `Chapter_1_Audio` folder of the book's downloaded source code. Drag this file from the folder and drop it into the event editor **Events** tab as shown in the screenshot here:

Importing the lake-shore-waves2.wav file into the FMOD event editor

3. You will then be prompted by the **Create Event** dialog to select the type of event, choose **3D** as we did earlier, and then click on **Create**. Right-click [*Ctrl* + click on Mac] on the and then from the context menu, select **Assign To | Master Bank**.

 In order to avoid confusion, we will call the work areas within FMOD Studio region or area as opposed to windows like we do in Unity. This is because FMOD actually creates and uses actual windows for various functionality such as mixing, event editing, and so on.

4. Right-click [*Ctrl* + Click on Mac] on the audio clip in the **Tracks** region, and from the context menu, select **New Loop Region**, just as we did for the `torch` event earlier.

5. Select the **Master** track in order to view the event's **3D Panner** effect and adjust the settings to match those shown in the screenshot here:

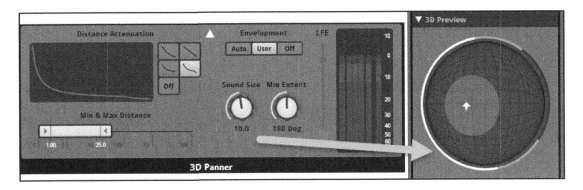

Adjusting the 3D Panner effect on the lake-shore-waves2 event

Notice that as you change the **Sound Size** and **Min Extent** (angle) on the **Panner** the way the 3D preview plot updates. This not only allows us to control how the sound drops off but how wide and deep the sound is. Creating that depth is essential for us on our lake waves sound. Otherwise, we would need to place multiple sounds in our scene to generate the same effect.

We don't have the time to break down all the FMOD effects like we did for the Audio Mixer, but it will be invaluable to you to spend time playing with each effect at some point.

6. From the menu, select **File** | **Build** to build the project. This will also update the connect project in Unity as well. Next, open up the Unity editor and locate the `Capsule 5` object in the **Hierarchy** window. Rename the object to `Ambient_lake-shore-waves` and set its **Z** position to `60`, just like we did in the first chapter.

7. Click on **Add Component** and then locate and add an **FMOD Studio Event Emitter** component to the object. Set the **Play Event** to **Object Start** and the **Event** to **event/lake-shore-waves2** as shown in the following screenshot:

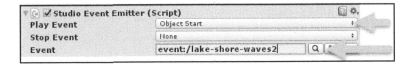

Setting the Studio Event Emitter properties

8. Press play to run the scene. Move around and listen to the sounds of the torch and the waves. Obviously, one of the more powerful features of the Audio Mixer is to be able to edit while the scene is running. Fortunately, you can also do this in FMOD. While the scene continues to run, go back to FMOD, and from the menu, select **File** | **Connect to Game**. The **Connect to Game** dialog will open, prompting you to select the host, just use the defaults as shown in the following screenshot:

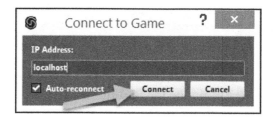

FMOD Studio connecting to Unity

9. After FMOD connects to Unity, you can now edit your events in real time and notice the changes automatically just like the mixer. Unlike Unity, however, you have full control over all the audio effects, including control of the **3D Panner** in one interface. This is a very powerful feature, but you may find it distracting moving between interfaces unless you have two+ monitors.

FMOD Studio is designed to be used with multiple monitors. Everything is still completely functional, if you only have a single monitor. When it comes down to it, you will be more productive with multiple monitors if you are doing a lot of fine edits.

10. Go ahead and continue exploring and making edits. When you are done, stop the scene and save your changes in Unity and FMOD.

Now that we have our couple of starter ambient sounds, we can look to add some effects to give them a little more quality and realism, just as we did previously. Of course, we won't cover all the techniques and effects we used earlier, but instead will go through a couple effects workflows in the next section.

Mixing in a reverb effect

Right now, our ambient audio is missing those physical characteristics of natural sound that we understand as early and late reflections off the environment. As we did before, we want to add a reverb or echo effect in order to provide that natural sound quality.

However, before we get into the exercise of doing that, it will be helpful for us to understand how the signal routing in FMOD works. If you recall, we already went over this for the mixer, so let's break down how this looks using the FMOD interface here:

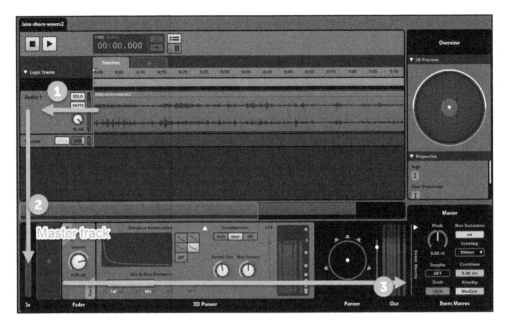

Signal flow through the FMOD interface

The interface screen shows how the signal is routed through the event editor. This is just the first half of the routing and we will cover how signals are routed through the mixer later. For now, let's break down what each step is:

- **Sound file or Module -> Audio track**: The sound is first routed from the audio file or files called a module to the track. A track essentially represents a grouping of audio, and in the name group, is used to represent the same level.
- **Audio track -> Master track**: The audio track is routed to the master. Again, just like the way groups are routed to the master in Unity.
- **Master track -> Input Bus**: We will get to the bus routing later when we talk about the mixer. For now though, just realize that all tracks, including the master, route through an effects processor. In the screenshot, the effects shown are the **Fader** and **3D Panner**. Just like in Unity, effects can be added to any track (group) and routed to other tracks as well using a **Send** effect.

Now that we understand the first phase of routing, we will see how this can be applied by adding a reverb effect to our `torch` event by following the directions here:

1. Right-click [*Ctrl* + click on Mac] on the track and from the context menu, select **Add Return Track**. This will add a new track to the area. Double-click on the **A** label to rename the track `Reverb` as shown here:

Adding a Return track to the event

2. With the `Reverb` track selected, go to the deck area and click on the **+** button after the **Fader** effect. Then, select **Add Effect I FMOD Reverb** from the context menu. This will add a reverb effect to the track. Right-click [*Ctrl* + click on Mac] inside the new effect and select **Presets I Mountains**. This will add the effect as shown in the following screenshot:

Setting a preset on the Reverb effect

 Notice that all the settings on the `Reverb` effect are very similar to the same effect in Unity. This is no accident since they ultimately use the same code base for both. However, look at all the preset options you have available to choose from. Ultimately, if you decide not to use FMOD, you can still borrow those preset settings and apply them to the SFX Reverb.

3. Select the `Audio 1` track again and return to the deck region. Click on the **+** button again, and this time, select **Add Send | Reverb** to add a Send effect. Set the send level to `0 dB` as shown in the following screenshot:

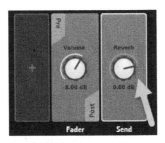

Adding a Send effect and setting the send level to the Reverb track

This is the exact same workflow we used with the Audio Mixer in Unity to add the reverb and echo effects, so we won't explain the reason why we do this here. If you missed that section, head back to `Chapter 2`, *Scripting Audio*, to review.

4. From the menu, select **File | Build** to update the project and jump over to Unity. Press the play button in Unity to run and test how the reverb effect sounds. Walk up to a torch and listen to the reverb. If there is too much reverb, go back to FMOD while the scene is running, and turn down the signal level.

5. When you are done testing and tweaking the audio, stop the scene and save your changes in FMOD.

Hopefully, at this stage of our journey, you feel comfortable enough to add other regular or return effects to the audio tracks. You should be able to replicate the same steps and add a reverb return effect to the lake-shore -waves event as well. However, having to set the same reverb effect for each track could become tedious. So, let's look at a better way of doing this with the mixer by following the instructions here:

1. First, remove the existing reverb return effect by right-clicking [*Ctrl* + click on Mac] on the `Reverb` track and selecting **Delete** from the context menu. Then, select the `Audio 1` track and in the deck region, right-click [*Ctrl* + click on Mac] on the **Send** effect and from the context menu, select **Delete**.

2. From the menu, select **Window | Mixer**. This will open up the **Mixer** window, and you will see both of the events in the routing list, plus a default reverb. Upon first opening this window, you will notice it is quite similar to the Audio Mixer, again not by accident.

The **Mixer** window allows you to define the Input buses that will be mixed like groups in Unity and will all get routed to the Master bus. This may be slightly confusing at first, but this is just like how we created child groups that routed to groups in Unity.

3. Right-click [*Ctrl* + click on Mac] on the `torch` event, and from the context menu, select **Reroute to New Group**. Rename the new group `Ambient` and then drag the `lake-shore-waves2` event into the same group as shown in the following screenshot:

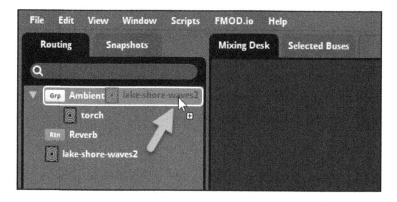

Transferring the lake-shore-waves2 event to route through the Ambient group

4. Select the `Ambient` group, and then in the deck area, click on the **+** button and from the menu, select **Add Send | Reverb**. Then, adjust the send level to `0 dB`, just as you did in the last exercise.
5. Select the `Reverb` group, and then in the deck area, right-click on an empty space on the **Reverb** effect to open the context menu. From the menu, select **Presets | Mountains**. Here is a screenshot showing the completed window:

Mixer window showing the Ambient group and signal route

6. From the menu, select **File** | **Build** and then go to Unity. Press play in Unity to run the scene. Again, feel free to return to FMOD and adjust the mix as you would have done in Unity. When you are done editing and testing, stop the scene and save your changes.

As discussed before, if you notice a dramatic decrease in performance on your system you may need to weigh the benefits of using the Reverb effect, perhaps instead choosing to use a cheaper delay effect such as echo.

Well, that completes our very basic introduction to effects and mixing with FMOD. As you have seen, the concepts and certain interface elements are quite similar to the Audio Mixer in Unity. In the next section, we will get up to speed further on working with parameters and triggers.

QUIZ TIME

Which of the following are classified as delay effects?
a) Reverb
b) Echo
c) Flange
d) Equalization
e) 3D Panner

Which of the following effects is it standard to use through a return or sidechain?
a) Reverb
b) Duck Volume
c) Equaliztion
d) 3D Panner
e) Equalization

Which of the following is a valid signal routing path in FMOD?
a) Sound file -> Audio Track -> Master Track
b) Master Track -> Audio Track -> Sound file
c) Input bus -> Sound file -> Master Track
d) Audio Track -> Input bus -> Master Track

The answers will be provided at the end of the chapter.

Parameters, snapshots, and triggers

Like Unity, FMOD provides the ability to control audio with parameters, snapshots, and triggers. However, unlike Unity, you actually get more control with FMOD out of the box, and it is possible to develop advanced audio handling without any scripting. In order to demonstrate this capability, we are going to replicate some of the functionality of one of our more advanced examples without writing a single line of script.

We are going to partially replicate the wind zone effect in order to demonstrate how we can automate or control audio playback within Unity. There isn't enough time to cover the entire example and really we just want to demonstrate the concepts here. Follow the directions here to start building this new version of a dynamic wind effect:

1. Open up the FMOD event editor, and from the menu, select **File | Import Audio Files**. Use the dialog to locate the `Chapter_6_Audio` folder in the book's downloaded source code. Select the `wind.wav` file and click on **Open** to import the file. When prompted by the **Create Event** dialog, this time choose 2D, not 3D, and then click on **Create**.

2. Right-click [*Ctrl* + click on Mac] on the new `wind` event in the **Events** tab and select **Assign to Bank | Master Bank** from the menu. Then, right click [*Ctrl* + click on Mac] on the audio clip in the **Audio 1** track and select **New Loop Region** from the menu. Right-click [*Ctrl* + click on Mac] the **Audio 1** track and select **Add Audio Track** from the menu. You will now have **Audio 1** and **Audio 2** tracks.

3. From the menu, select **Window | Mixer** to open the **Mixer** window. Right-click [*Ctrl* + click on Mac] on the **wind** event in the **Routing** tab and select **Reroute to New Group** from the menu. Rename the new group `WIND` and then turn the resting volume up to max at `10 dB`.

4. Select the **Snapshots** tab. This should be empty since we have not created any snapshots. Right-click [*Ctrl* + click on Mac] on the empty area, and from the menu, select **New Blending Snapshot**. Rename the snapshot `wind_snapshot`. Then, click within the green dotted region that represents the `WIND` groups, volume and turn it down to `-50 dB` as shown in the following screenshot:

Adjusting the volume setting of the Wind group in the wind_snapshot

What we just did was create a blending snapshot. This is a little different than in Unity since FMOD actually allows us to control the blending within FMOD, instead of having to write code to do it. However, the procedure to control a snapshot is a little counter-intuitive, especially after all our discussions about routing.

5. As soon as you click on the volume knob, it will turn into the standard looking control, which will allow you to adjust the volume. Next, select and then drag the `wind_snapshot` from the **Mixer** into the event editor and drop it on the `Audio 2` track as shown in the following screenshot:

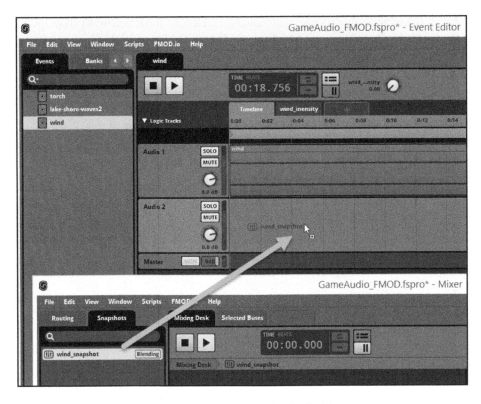

Dragging the wind_snapshot into the Audio 2 track on the wind event

6. Move to the event editor window now and use your mouse to select and adjust the snapshot so that it fills the track in the same area as the `wind` clip does. This is shown in the following screenshot:

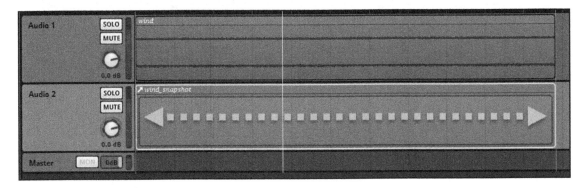

Setting the wind_snapshot to fill the audio track

7. Next, select the `wind_snapshot` in the track and look below to the **Deck** region. Right-click [*Ctrl* + click on Mac] on the **Intensity** knob and select **Add Automation** from the menu. After you do this, you will notice a new track gets added to the **Tracks** region called **Intensity**.

8. Click on the **+** button beside the **Timeline** tab at the top of the **Tracks** region. Select **Add Builtin Parameter** | **Distance** from the menu that opens. This will prompt you with a **Parameter** dialog; enter in a range of [0,20]. With this new parameter tab open, use your mouse to select the gray line in the **Intensity** track and adjust it so that it matches the screenshot here:

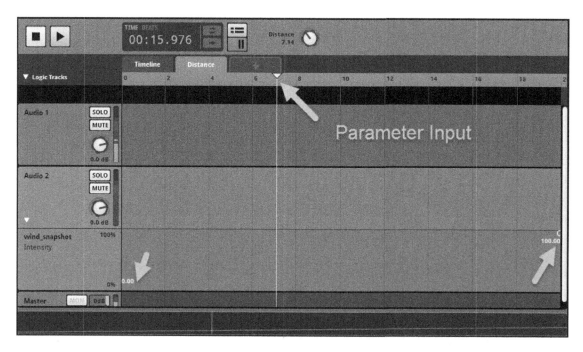

Adjusting the wind_snapshot intensity in the parameter

9. Press play, to play the event and then use your mouse to drag the input parameter control left to right in the track. Notice how the wind audio becomes louder when the distance is small and softer when the distance increases. This may seem a bit backwards but remember we set our snapshot base to **-50 dB** on the `Wind` group. So as the **Intensity** of the snapshot increases, it actually turns the volume down. After you are done testing, stop the event and then save and build the project.

We just created a new parameter called distance that controls the intensity of the `wind_snapshot`, depending on how close the listener is to the event target. Take your time and think about that. It isn't the most intuitive way you may think of doing this, but let's see how it works in Unity.

Open up Unity and follow the directions here to connect to the new event:

1. Open up Unity and make sure the Viking Village scene is loaded from before. From the menu, select **GameObject | Create Empty** to create a new object in the scene. Rename the object `AudioZones` and reset its **Transform Position** to 0.

2. Right-click [*Ctrl* + click on Mac] on the new `AudioZones` object and from the menu, select **3D Object | Cube**. Rename the object, add or remove components, and set the parameters to match the screenshot here:

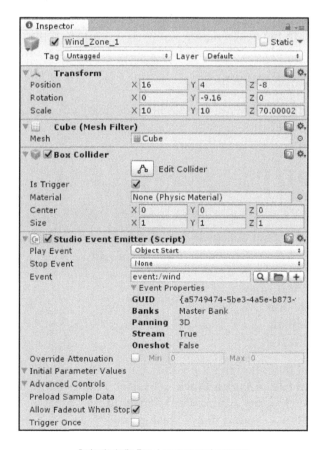

Setting the Audio_Zone_1 components and parameters

You will need to remove one of the components to complete the task. If you need help, just review earlier sections in this chapter or others.

3. After you are done editing, press play to start the scene. Move around the scene and notice that as you get farther away or closer the way the wind audio decreases and increases, respectively. When you are finished testing, stop the scene and save your changes in Unity and FMOD.

Essentially what we have just demonstrated is being able to replicate the environmental audio zones controlled by a snapshot from the dynamic wind zone example. Keep in mind that although we only adjusted the wind volume, we also could have controlled numerous other settings in the mixer. Furthermore, while we only demonstrated controlling one snapshot, we could have controlled multiple snapshots all on the same or different tracks within the same event. In the next chapter, we will continue to replicate the functionality of the previous dynamic wind effect by upgrading some scripts to work with FMOD.

QUIZ TIME ANSWERS

Which of the following are classified as delay effects? *Correct answers are marked in bold*
a) **Reverb**
b) **Echo**
c) **Flange**
d) Equalization
e) 3D Panner

Which of the following effects is it standard to use through a return or sidechain? *Correct answers are marked in bold*
a) **Reverb**
b) **Duck Volume**
c) Modulation
d) 3D Panner
e) Equalization

Which of the following is a valid signal routing path in FMOD?
a) **Sound file -> Audio Track -> Master Track - is the only correct answer**
b) Master Track -> Audio Track -> Sound file
c) Input bus -> Sound file -> Master Track
d) Audio Track -> Input bus -> Master Track

Summary

In this chapter, we undertook a new journey by beginning to look at the leading third-party audio development tool called FMOD Studio. First, you learned about the origins of FMOD and how relevant it is to the industry as an audio development tool. From there, we downloaded and installed FMOD Studio. After that, we returned to doing some basic exercises of setting up audio in our village scene the FMOD way. You then spent some time learning how effects and mixing worked in FMOD, how it differed from Unity in some ways but also shared many similarities in others. Finally, we looked to replicate some of the functionality in one of our previous examples using FMOD. What we found is that we were able to do most of the same things with only a little code using the functionality provided by parameters, snapshots, and triggers within FMOD.

In the next chapter, we will continue our work with FMOD Studio and get into more advanced development exercises, including scripting and, of course, enhancing our adaptive audio examples we worked with in the previous chapter.

7
FMOD for Dyanmic and Adaptive Audio

As we saw in the last chapter, FMOD Studio is a powerful audio workstation that integrates seamlessly with Unity. It gives the sound designer or developer the ability to create professional quality audio that can be used across platforms and even game engines. Getting experienced with such a tool will take some time and certainly not all the capabilities can be explored in a single chapter. While in the last chapter, we only started covering the basics of using FMOD with Unity by completing some simple and familiar tasks. For this chapter, we will go far deeper into FMOD and explore the complex tasks of creating dynamic and adaptive audio, which took us a couple of chapters using the Unity Audio Mixer. We plan to only cover the same material in a single chapter, not because FMOD is so powerful, but because all the background material was previously covered in earlier chapters. Of course there will still be plenty of sample exercises and tasks for you to get up to speed with using FMOD quickly.

In this chapter, we are going to cover the tasks of creating dynamic and adaptive audio with FMOD. Since we have covered all the background material already in previous chapters, this chapter will be almost entirely hands on and in the software. There will also be plenty of repetitive tasks using FMOD that should make you more familiar and comfortable with the tool. Here is a summary of what we will cover in this chapter:

- Dynamic wind and environmental zones
- Unity scripting with FMOD
- Revisiting the footsteps example
- Adaptive music with FMOD
- Transition timelines and stingers

As already mentioned, this chapter will cover several complex examples and it is strongly suggested, as always, that you work through the exercises. Ultimately, you will be rewarded for your work. For those FMOD masters or readers that just don't have the tools or time, unfortunately no single completed project can be provided. However, the individual completed FMOD and Unity projects will be available for you to combine into the final example on your own.

Dynamic wind and environmental zones

In the previous chapter, we quickly touched on how to implement a simple audio zone with FMOD and no scripting. For completeness and practicality, we are going to revise the Environmental Zones example we created in Chapter 4, *Advanced Audio Mixing*, using FMOD, but this time without any scripting. This example will demonstrate the full capabilities of snapshots within FMOD.

In this chapter, we will start fresh with just the basic Viking Village and add the other project assets as needed. If you have not already done so, be sure to download the required assets from the Unity Asset Store and the book's source code from here. Be sure to refer back to Chapter 6, *Introduction to FMOD*, for instructions on how to install the village project and FMOD if you need to.

Open up Unity and follow the instructions, to get started:

1. If you are continuing from the previous chapter, open up the **GameAudio** project we created. For those of you just getting here, create a new Unity project called GameAudio and then import the Unity Viking Village project from the Asset Store.

2. From the menu, select **Assets | Import Package | Custom Package** and use the Import package dialog to locate and open the Chapter_7_Assets folder located in the book's downloaded source code. Import the **Chapter_7_Start.unitypackage** by selecting the file and clicking on the **Open** button. Follow the instructions to import the asset as you normally would.

3. Locate the Chapter_7_Start.scene file in the Assets/GameAudio/Scenes folder of the **Project** window and double-click to open it.

4. For the next step, you will need to manually copy the FMOD project folder from the book's downloaded source code into the Unity project folder. Before proceeding, make sure that FMOD Studio is closed. Use your computer's file explorer to locate and open the Chapter_7_FMOD folder found in the book's source code folder. Copy the FMOD project folder called GameAudio_FMOD by any means you prefer.

5. Again, use your computer's file explorer to locate and open the GameAudio Unity project folder. Paste the GameAudio_FMOD folder into the GameAudio folder so it looks similar to the following screenshot:

Copying the GameAudio_FMOD project folder to the Unity project folder

 You may be prompted to confirm overwriting existing files. Be sure to accept and overwrite the files from last chapter. If you are blocked from copying over FMOD files, be sure that all instances of FMOD Studio are closed.

6. Open the Unity editor and from the menu, select **FMOD** | **Edit Settings**. Go to the **Inspector** window and confirm that the **Studio Project Path** is still set correctly from the last chapter or set it using the **Browse** button as shown in the screenshot here:

Confirming the Studio Project Path is set correctly

 If you don't see the FMOD menu option, you will need to return to Chapter 6, *Introduction to FMOD*, to download and install the FMOD Unity integration package.

7. Launch FMOD Studio and from the menu select **File** | **Open Recent** | **GameAudio_FMOD.fspro** | **GameAudio** to open the project. If you have never launched Studio before or have it installed, return to the previous chapter and follow the instructions to download, install, and setup FMOD Studio.

8. From the menu, select **File** | **Build**. This will make sure the streaming assets folder is updated within the Unity project.

9. Return to the Unity editor and press play to run the scene. Move around the scene and you should hear the torches flickering and the sound of the lake waves. After you confirm things are working correctly, stop the scene.

10. Locate the **EnvironmentalZones** prefab in the **Project** window and drag and drop it into the scene. This will add the **EnvironmentalZones** locations we used previously but the scripts have been removed. Expand the object and just review the zones as shown in the screenshot here:

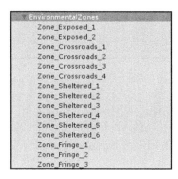

EnvironmentalZones object expanded showing the various zones around the scene

 If you recall from the previous example, each of the zones was classified by type as summarized here:

Exposed: The areas that are exposed to the wind and out in the open, minimal reflections, and additional wind.

Crossroads: The junctions of the pathways; these areas are not as windy and provide almost no reflections.

Sheltered: The areas covered from the wind and close to buildings, maximum reflections and minimal wind.

Fringe: Just on the wall side of the village, partially covered, still some wind and audio reflections.

Now that we have a fresh scene in Unity and the base FMOD project open, we can continue by creating blending snapshots that our environmental zones will use to mix audio across the scene.

Remember, this is the exact same concept we worked with previously using snapshots and mixer transitions with the Unity Audio Mixer. With FMOD though, we will be able to generate the same effect but without scripting. Open up the FMOD Studio and follow the instructions:

1. From the menu, select **Window** | **Mixer** to open the **Mixer** window. Click on the **Snapshots** tab in the window to open the tab.

2. Right-click [*Ctrl* + click on Mac] on the **Snapshots** tab, and from the menu, select **New Blending Snapshot**. Rename the new snapshot crossroads and then select it. Since the crossroads represents an area of high wind but low reverb, adjust the mix to what is shown in the screenshot here:

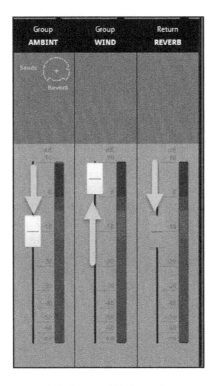

Setting the crossroads blending snapshot

 The settings don't have to be exact, after all you are ultimately in control and can decide what works best for you.

3. Repeat step 2 for the sheltered, fringe, and exposed snapshots. The mixer settings are shown in the screenshots here:

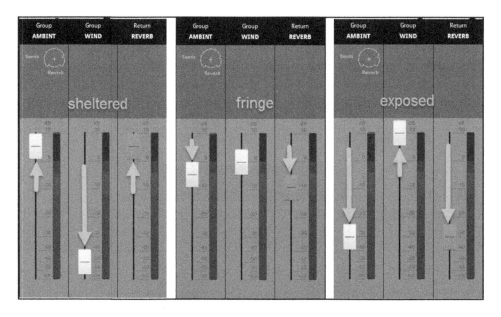

Adjusting the mixer settings for each of the snapshot zones

 After you have the four blending snapshots created, we then need to configure how the snapshots will be blended. If you recall from our previous example, we controlled the blending using a simple linear distance function written in a script. We are going to do something similar with FMOD, but without the need for scripting.

4. Select the **crossroads** snapshot and then click on the tracks button at the top of editing window to expose the tracks, as shown in the screenshot here:

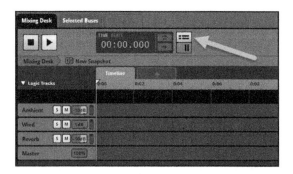

5. Click on the **+** button beside the **Timeline** at the tracks view, and from the menu, select **Add Built-In Parameter | Distance**. When prompted by the Parameter dialog, enter a range of 0 to 20.

6. Select the **Master** track and then go to the bottom right corner of the mixer window in the deck area. Right-click [*Ctrl* + click on Mac] on the **Intensity** dial, and from the menu, select **Add Automation**, as shown in the screenshot:

Adding Intensity automation to the snapshot

7. This will add an `Intensity` track to the **Tracks** view. Use your mouse to adjust the line so that it starts at 100 at 0 distance and goes to 0 at 20 distance. This is shown in the screenshot here:

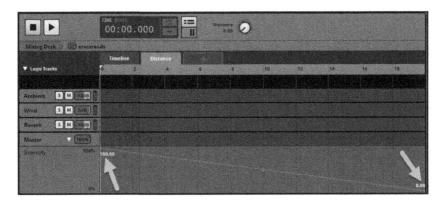

Adjusting the Intensity over distance

Adjusting the Intensity in this manner allows you to set how snapshot will be blended. For this example, we are using a simple linear slope, but you could adjust the line into a curve, based on your needs. Just click anywhere along to add new control points to the line and move those as desired. We have chosen a maximum range of **20** for this example but that could also be changed as well.

8. Repeat steps 4-7 for the remaining 3 snapshots (sheltered, fringe, and exposed). Be sure to keep the same distance range and linear control curves, at least for now. When you are done, build and save the project.

Now that we have all the mixer snapshots configured and the blending parameters set, its time to integrate this into Unity. Open up the Unity editor to the scene as we last left it and follow the directions here:

1. Select the **EnvironmentalZones** object in the **Hierarchy** window, and then in the **Inspector** window, click on the **Add Component** button. Locate the **FMOD Studio Event Emitter** component and add it to the object. Set the component properties to match those in the following screenshot:

Adding the wind event to the EnvironmentalZones object

2. Next, select (*shift* or *Ctrl* select) all the object zones beneath the **EnvironmentalZones** object in the **Hierarchy** window. With all the objects selected, add an **FMOD Studio Event Emitter** component just as you did in step 1.

3. Group select just the **Zone_Exposed** objects (2 objects) and set the **Studio Event Emitter** component parameters to match the screenshot here:

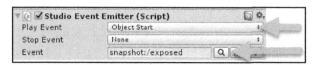

Setting the Zone_Exposed object to use the exposed snapshot

Notice that we are setting the Event to a snapshot called exposed. Make sure that you open the snapshot group and not the event group when locating the event using the search tool.

4. Repeat step 3 for each of the other zone groups (sheltered, crossroads, and fringe). Making sure to set the zone groups Event to the respective snapshot that we previously configured in the Mixer.

5. After you are done setting the snapshots for each of the respective zones, press play to start the scene. Move around the scene, as you have done plenty of times previously. Notice how well the zones blend together as you move through the areas. When you are done testing, stop the scene and save your Unity and FMOD projects.

As we have seen, we are able to duplicate the same effect as one of our more complex examples without writing a single line of script. What's more impressive is the number of additional options we have available now to change the way the blending occurs. Even being able to go so far as to change the way the distance or other parameters control the blending intensity. Now, having said all that, there still will be times when you still need to control a parameter directly through scripting, and that is what we will cover in the next section.

Scripting with FMOD

So far, we have managed to get away from doing any scripting and generated some fairly impressive results. Yet, as you can imagine, there always will be tasks you won't be able to complete with existing components. In fact, the `AudioWeatherVane` script we developed earlier is a very good example of that. If you recall, the script measured the force of the wind and then adjusted an Audio Mixer parameter to control the wind volume. This will be an excellent script we can upgrade to work with FMOD in order to demonstrate scripting.

First, we will start by laying the ground work by building a new parameter in FMOD. Open up FMOD Studio Event Editor and follow the instructions here:

1. Select the `wind` event in the **Events** tab and then click on the **Master** track. Then look to the deck region and right-click [*Ctrl* + click on Mac] on the **Volume** knob and from the menu select **Add Automation**.

2. Click the **+** button at the top of the **Timeline,** and from the menu, select **Add Parameter**. When you are prompted with the **Add Parameter** dialog, name the new parameter `Wind_Intensity` and keep the default range [0,1].

It is usually better to work with a normalized range of 0 to 1 for a parameter. This way if the game mechanics or other parts of a level change later, you won't need to go back and alter the parameter range. We will see how this range is calculated in the script later.

3. With the **Wind_Intensity** tab opened, adjust the **Volume** automation control line to what is shown in the screenshot here:

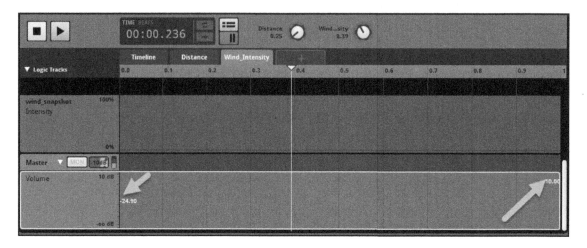

Adjusting the Volume automation line for the Wind_Intensity parameter

4. Select the Timeline tab to return to the timeline view and select the wind audio clip (blue wave forms). Then, look to the deck area again and right-click [*Ctrl* + click on Mac] on the **Volume** knob, and from the menu, select **Add Modulation | Random**. This will add a **Random** modulation effect. Right-click [*Ctrl* + click on Mac] on the **Volume** knob within the **Random** modulator and select **Add Automation** from the menu. This is shown in the screenshot here:

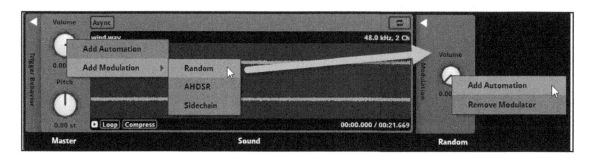

Adding a Random modulation on Volume and automating it

Remember in our earlier chapters, we added some randomization to audio in order to provide variation to the listener. FMOD provides different ways in which you can create an audio randomization. In this section, we will use the most frequently used one.

5. Right click [*Ctrl* + click on Mac] on the **Pitch** knob and then follow the same procedure as you did in step 4 to create an automated random pitch modulation.

6. After you complete steps 4 and 5, there will be two new **Random Modulator** tracks added. Select the **Wind_Intensity** tab and then adjust the automation lines to match what is shown in the following screenshot:

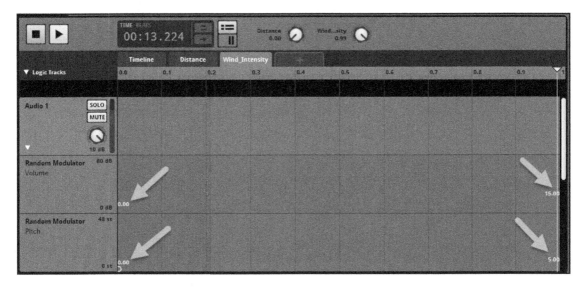

Setting the Random Modulator automation lines for Volume and Pitch

7. When you are done setting the automation curves, build and save the project.

Return to Unity and let's test this new **Wind_Intensity** parameter a little before we script it, by following the directions given here:

1. Select the **EnvironmentalZones** object in the **Hierarchy** window and then look at the **Studio Event Emitter** component in the **Inspector** window. Notice that a new parameter has been added to the component called **Wind_Intensity**. Ideally, we will want to script this parameter later, but for now, click on the checkbox to activate the parameter and then set the value to a maximum of 1, as shown in the screenshot here:

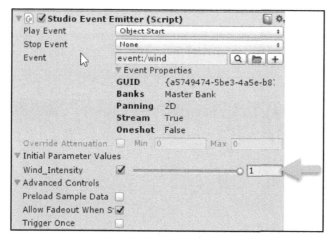

Setting the Wind_Intensity parameter on the wind event emitter

2. Press play to run the scene and move around to test. Move to an area where the wind sound is audible and wait.

Do you hear it? Yes, at some point, you will hear a break or stop in the wind audio. This is a result of our random pitch modulation. Sometimes, an audio file is played quicker and as a result it ends before the loop point. Fortunately, this is an easy fix but could be quite frustrating if you were not sure what was happening.

3. Stop the scene and open up the FMOD **Event Editor**. Select the **wind** event and make sure the **Timeline** tab is also open. What we want to do is shorten the loop region so that if the wind clip plays faster, the sound doesn't break but keeps playing. Select the far right end of the loop region above the wind clip and drag it over so that it stops around the 18 second mark, as shown in the following screenshot:

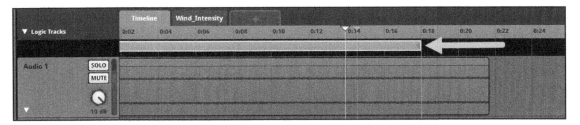

Adjusting the loop region to account for the random pitch modulation

4. After the adjustment, press play to play the audio and listen to how it loops. Be sure that you also turn the **Wind_Intensity** parameter up by selecting the tab and sliding the white parameter control. Adjust the loop end point if the looping is not natural.

5. When you are done setting the loop to your liking, go back to Unity and select the **EnvironmentalZones** object in the **Hierarchy** window. Then, disable the **Wind_Intensity** parameter on the **Studio Event Emitter** by unchecking the parameter checkbox in the **Inspector** window.

6. When you are done, save everything.

Now that we have the **Wind_Intensity** parameter working the way we think it should be, we can add the already updated `AudioWeatherVane` script to the scene, by following the instructions here:

1. Locate the **Wind Zone** object in the **Hierarchy** window. Select the object and then use the **Add Component** button in the **Inspector** window to open, locate, and then add the `AudioWeatherVane` script. Then, set the parameters in the component to match the following screenshot:

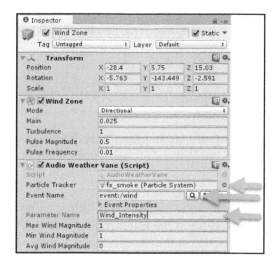

Setting the Audio Weather Vane component parameters on the Wind Zone

Remember to use the target icon to open a dialog a Select Particle System dialog to easily find an fx_smoke particle effect in the scene. Any effect will work as long as it has the External Forces option turned on. Which means the particle effect will respond to the force of the wind.

2. After you have added the script and set the parameters, press play to start the scene. Yes, it was that easy to set up the script, which says a lot about your ability to find your way around Unity now.

3. Keep an eye on the **Inspector** window and the **Audio Weather Vane** component as you wander around the scene. Notice how the **Max, Min,** and **Avg** wind magnitude values change and how the wind audio adjusts as well. When you are done testing, stop the scene and save the scene and project files.

4. Locate the `AudioWeatherVane` script in the **Project** or **Inspector** window and then open the script in your editor of choice. We will take a more detailed look at that script next.

Having seen the AudioWeatherVane script in action yet again, let's take a look at how this works with FMOD. Here is the entire script for review; you should also have the script open in your editor as well:

```
public class AudioWeatherVane : MonoBehaviour
{
    public ParticleSystem particleTracker; //ParticleSystem must have
ExternalForces set
    [FMODUnity.EventRef]
    public string eventName;
    public string parameterName;
    public float maxWindMagnitude = 1;
    public float minWindMagnitude = 1;
    public float avgWindMagnitude;

    FMOD.Studio.EventInstance windEvent; //the event
    private ParticleSystem.Particle[] particles;

    void Start()
    {
        particles = new ParticleSystem.Particle[10];
        windEvent = FMODUnity.RuntimeManager.CreateInstance(eventName);
    }

    //FixedUpdate runs every physics update
    void FixedUpdate()
    {
        var magnitude = 0f;
        if (particleTracker.GetParticles(particles) > 0)
        {
            for (int i = 0; i < particles.Length; i++)
        {
        magnitude += particles[i].velocity.magnitude;
        }
        avgWindMagnitude = magnitude / particles.Length;
        minWindMagnitude = Mathf.Min(avgWindMagnitude, minWindMagnitude);
        maxWindMagnitude = Mathf.Max(avgWindMagnitude, maxWindMagnitude);
        windEvent.setParameterValue(parameterName,
                    (avgWindMagnitude - minWindMagnitude) /
maxWindMagnitude);
        }
    }
}
```

Since we have already covered the Unity Audio Mixer version of this script, we really only need to review the changes we made to support FMOD. The following is a detailed explanation for each of the highlighted changes in the script:

```
[FMODUnity.EventRef]
public string eventName;
```

Adding the attribute FMODUnity.EventRef to the eventName allows for the cool event selector GUI to be added in the Inspector.

```
FMOD.Studio.EventInstance windEvent; //the event
```

These are the declarations for the event and parameter instances we will retrieve and set later. Don't be confused by the use of the explicit namespace (FMOD.Studio), it really is the same as declaring any other variable.

```
windEvent = FMODUnity.RuntimeManager.CreateInstance(eventName);
```

Inside the start method is where we see the instances of the event and parameter being set. Notice that the call to FMODUnity.RuntimeManager is similar to the way we have called our singleton class, [AdaptiveudioManager]. In fact, RuntimeManager is also a singleton. Essentially what we are doing is asking the FMOD RuntimeManager to create an event and then use the event to get the parameter.

If you are a developer, you will likely be familiar with the Factory method pattern, which we used. For those of you new to scripting, it is important to understand that this is just a more controlled way to create objects.

```
windEvent.setParameterValue(parameterName, (avgWindMagnitude -
minWindMagnitude) /         (maxWindMagnitude - minWindMagnitude);
```

Lastly, we set the parameter using the normalized [0-1] value of the wind magnitude. Recall that our preference is always to use a normalized value for parameters when we can since this will require less changes if game mechanics change later. The preceding highlighted line of code keeps the min and max values updated depending on how much the wind gusts.

The formula we use to normalize a value is fairly standard and is of the form:
normalized = (value - min) / (max - min)
This will always return a number from 0-1, as long as the value is within that range of course.

That about covers our discussion on FMOD scripting. As we have seen, while scripting is done a little differently with FMOD, the concepts should all be quite familiar by now. In the next section, we will cover more scripting and start developing adaptive audio with FMOD.

Revisiting the footsteps example

In order to give us more experience of the capabilities with FMOD and introduce some very simple adaptive audio techniques, we will revisit another earlier example, the footsteps example. If you recall, in that example we added footstep sounds to the game character. Those sounds also responded to a set of adaptive or transition areas we made for our scene. We used those adaptive areas to control the adaptive level, which in turn set the mood for our characters, movements, footsteps audio, and music. If you need to revisit how those areas work, consult `Chapter 5`, *Using the Audio Mixer for Adaptive Audio*. In that chapter, we discuss the why, what, and how for setting up those areas in much more detail.

By now you should be very familiar with Unity and FMOD, so this should be a quick example. Follow the instructions here to start updating the footsteps example:

1. Open up FMOD and right-click [*Ctrl* + click on Mac] on the **Events** tab; from the menu, select **New 2D Event**. Rename the event `footsteps`. Right-click [*Ctrl* + click on Mac] on the event, and from the menu, select **Assign to Bank | Master Bank** and the event.

2. Go back to the Unity project and search for `footstep` in the **Project** window. Select the group of four audio footstep sounds, as shown in the screenshot here, and drag them as a group to the FMOD **Event Editor** window:

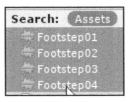

Selecting and dragging the four audio footstep sounds from Unity to FMOD

3. Drop the group of audio clips into the **footsteps** event **Audio 1** track. This will create a **Multi Sound** source clip, as shown in the screenshot here:

Creating a Multi Sound audio event

4. Confirm that the **Randomize Playlist** button is enabled by selecting the **Multi Sound** clip and looking in the **Playlist** area, and as shown in the preceding screenshot. Click on the **loop playback** button, also shown earlier, and then play the event by pressing play. As the event plays and loops, you should see and hear the various footstep sounds play.

 If you recall, we had to write code in our footsteps script to randomize the playback of the various clips. With FMOD that can all be handled with just a couple clicks.

5. Click on the **Master** track and then look to the bottom right of the window. Right-click [*Ctrl* + click on Mac] on the **Pitch** control and select **Add Automation** from the menu. This will add an automation track just below the **Master**.

6. Click the **+** button beside the **Timeline** tab, and from the menu, select **Add Parameter**. When prompted with the **Add Parameter** dialog, name the parameter `Adaptive_Level` and set the range from [1-5]. Yes, this does break our rule about normalizing, but in this case it simplifies our understanding. Since we already set the parameter to work with a range of 1-5, select the `Adaptive_Level` parameter and then adjust the **Pitch** curve to around [-2.25 - +5], or something similar to what is shown in the following screenshot:

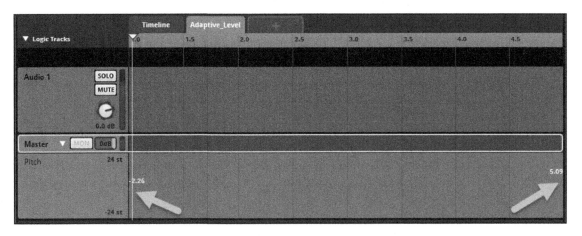

Adjusting the Pitch automation control for the Adaptive_Level parameter

7. After you have finished making your changes, build the project and then save.

That completes our updates to FMOD for our footsteps example. As you have seen, FMOD again offers us a couple of shortcuts and more control over parameters. You should note that in our previous example, we also didn't add any fine tuned parameter control. This was done more to simplify the example when we developed it for Unity. Speaking of Unity, let's jump back into the editor and get this example completed by following the exercise here:

1. Open up the editor and search for the `AdaptiveAudioManager.prefab` in the **Project** window. Remember a prefab is denoted by a blue box icon so try not to confuse for the script of the same name. Drag the prefab into the bottom of the **Hierarchy** window to add it to the scene. Double-click on the **AdaptiveAudioManager** in the scene. This zoom out/in is to display the colored zones in the **Scene** view.

2. Locate the **FlyingRigidBodyFPSController_HighQuality** object in the **Hierarchy** window and select it. Then, add the `FootstepsAudio` script to the component using the **Add Component** button in the **Inspector** menu. After the component is added, set the parameters to match what is shown in the screenshot here:

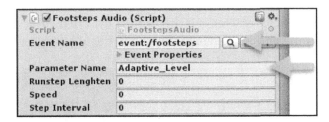

Setting the parameters for the Footsteps Audio script component

3. When you are done editing, save the scene and then press play. Move around the scene and listen to how the footstep audio changes. Remember that as the player moves through the various adaptive audio areas, they will experience various forms of time compression based on the danger level of the area. Now, with our updated script, the footstep audio playback speed (**pitch**) is more inline with that time compression.

If you recall from Chapter 5, *Using the Audio Mixer for Adaptive Audio*, where we discussed the premise of our pretend game, we described our character as the forced and very apprehensive hero. As such, we wanted to express those emotions through basic game mechanics in the form of time compression or distortion. Now that we have the footsteps sounding, the effect is working better. However, we can still add more cues or perhaps even vocal cues to enhance this effect. We will get into more detail about vocal cues in Chapter 9, *Character Lip Syncing and Vocals*.

Before we complete this example, we want to cover the scripting changes we need to perform in order to get this example to work. Open up the `FootstepsAudio` script in your favorite editor. Since we have already covered this script and the majority of other changes, we are only going to focus our attention on one method that has been updated, see here:

```
private void PlayFootStepAudio()
{
    if (characterController.Grounded == false)
    {
        return;
    }
    footstepsEvent.setParameterValue(parameterName,
                    AdaptiveAudioManager.Instance.currentAdaptiveLevel
);
```

```
footstepsEvent.start();
}
```

The two highlighted lines of code show the major differences. The first one we already covered in the previous section and is just an example called setParameterValue. The second line of code shows the use of the **start()** method to play an event.

 An excellent source for learning the FMOD API and how to use the library is the code itself. The complete FMOD Unity integration source code is written in C# and available. You only need to spend time to look through it and learn. Of course if you are not a developer, this may not concern you and you likely have more mixing to do anyway.

We really have only touched the surface of what is possible in scripting the FMOD audio system from within Unity. In the next section, we will dive back into adaptive music development with FMOD.

Adaptive music with FMOD

As the last part of this journey to replicate the Unity Audio Mixer examples, we will look at how FMOD can be used to develop adaptive music. If you recall, in our adaptive music example, we altered the tune depending on what area the player was in or moving through. With Unity, we did this using a system of area triggers that matched the footstep system and an adaptive music technique called vertical remixing. In Chapter 5, *Using the Audio Mixer for Adaptive Audio*, we used vertical remixing because the technique paired well with the capabilities of the Audio Mixer. As we discussed, the Unity mixer was not well suited for the other horizontal re-sequencing techniques that we also discussed in Chapter 5, *Using the Audio Mixer for Adaptive Audio*. Fortunately, FMOD is particularly well suited for using horizontal re-sequencing techniques and this is something we will spend a lot of time working with in the last sections of this chapter.

 If you only glanced over Chapter 5, *Using the Audio Mixer for Adaptive Audio*, then it is strongly recommended at this point that you review that chapter thoroughly before continuing. Of course, it still may not be a bad idea for readers that did work through that chapter to quickly review it, as well.

Before we start pulling in assets and laying audio tracks, let's look to some of the sources and techniques we used to derive the music pieces for the adaptive music. First off, the music we are using for our game will be a couple of tracks from `freemusicarchive.org`, which represent the taste and theme proposed by the designer. Second, we don't want to use the entire tracks and actually just want to use elements from each track to represent the five different levels of audio we need. Fortunately, FMOD gives us the capability for us to spliting out those elements, and example of how this is done is shown here:

1. Open FMOD **Event Editor** and right-click [*Ctrl* + click on Mac] on the **Events** tab, and from the menu, select **New 2D Event and** rename the new event `music`.

2. Locate and open the `Chapter_7_Music` folder from the book's downloaded source code using your file explorer. Select the `Artofescapism_-_Watching_from_Red_Hill.mp3` file and drag it into the **Event Editor** and drop it onto the new events `Audio 1` track. Make sure to align the clip so that it starts at `0`.

3. Right-click [*Ctrl* + click on Mac] in the black region above the track, and from the menu, select **Add Tempo Marker**. This will add a marker with a BPM number and time signature. Double-click on the number **120** and change it to `99`. Right-click [*Ctrl* + click on Mac] again in the black region to create a new loop region. Move the **Tempo** marker and **Loop Region** marker to the start of the audio, as shown in the following screenshot:

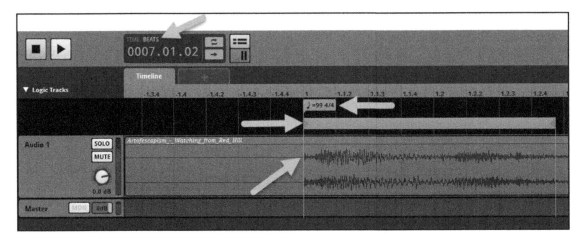

Moving the Tempo and Loop markers to the start of the audio

You may find it helpful to zoom into the tracks view by using the menu **View** | **Zoom In**, *Ctrl +]* (*command +]* on Mac) or the mouse to shrink the overview window in order to position the markers at the start of the sound, as shown in the preceding screenshot.

4. Select the **BEATS** timing on the timing control, as shown in the preceding screenshot. This will switch the timing from seconds to beats, which is especially useful when looping and sub-mixing music. If you previously zoomed in, be sure to zoom out to the entire clip now (**View** | **Zoom To Fit**). Move the end of the loop region marker using your mouse to the five or fifth measure and then play the event.

There are plenty of free tools out there that will allow you to quickly find the BPM or tempo of a song. As previously mentioned, BPM Counter for Windows works well. There are also plenty of free bpm counters available for Mac, Android, and iOS. Just use your favorite search engine or app store to find one.

5. The end result should be a very good loop of the first part of the clip. If the timing sounds off, make sure you set the tempo marker to the start of the audio. Right-click [*Ctrl* + click on Mac] on the loop marker line on the clip and from the menu select **Split**. Do this again for the end of the clip as well. This is shown in the screenshot here:

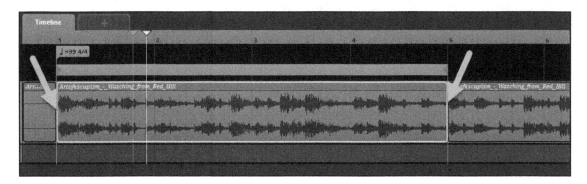

Extracting a trimmed looping clip from the original clip

6. Right-click [*Ctrl* + click on Mac] on the new clip, and from the menu, select **Replace Audio with Trimmed Copy**. This will create a new trimmed down version of the extracted loop.

7. When you are done, delete the `music` event and then recreate. This will quickly clean up the work area, so we can prepare for the real music setup. Be sure to also assign the `music` event to the **Master Bank**.

The example exercise is the same process that was used to extract all the looping clips we will use to build our adaptive audio example. Unfortunately, we won't have time to create all those examples within the book, but the preceding exercise should show you a useful technique if you have to work with music tracks in the future.

Now that we understand how the various looping clips were isolated and extracted from the two music tracks our designer selected, we can proceed to add them to our `music` event here:

1. Return to the `Chapter_7_Music` folder and this time drag in the `Music_Level_1.wav` file and drop it onto the `music` events `Audio 1 track`. Adjust the clip so that it starts at the beginning of the track.
2. Continue step 1 for each of the other `Music_Level` clips in the folder by their respective order as defined by the ending number. Then, after you drag all the files in your track, your view should resemble the following screenshot:

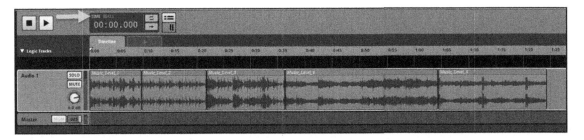

Aligning the Music_Level clips on the Audio 1 track

3. Play the event and listen to how the music plays through the various levels. Don't worry about the messy transition point between level 3 and 4, we will take care of that later. What we want to do next is create a control parameter that will set which music level clip plays at each adaptive level we have created in our game.
4. Click the **+** button beside the **Timeline** and from the menu select **Add Parameter**. When prompted by the **Add Parameter** dialog, name the parameter `Adaptive_Level` and set the range from **[1-5]** just as you did in the footsteps example.

5. Select the **Timeline** tab again to return to the view of the clips. Right-click [*Ctrl* + click on Mac] on each of the clips, and from the menu, select **New Loop Region**. Do this for all five clips. Then, drag each of the loop regions down in the marker region so that the loops are staggered vertically. This is shown in the following screenshot:

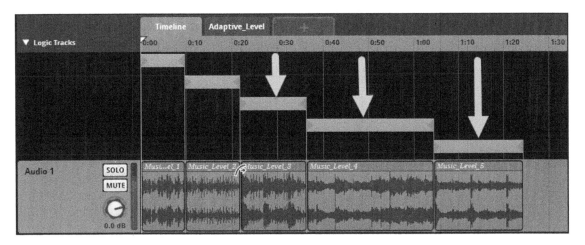

Adding and adjusting the loop regions

6. Select the first loop region above the Music_Level_1 clip and then look to the **Conditions** panel of the deck region. Click on the **Add Condition** button, and from the menu, select **Add Parameter Condition | Adaptive_Level**. Set the **Adaptive_Level** conditions bar to the range of 1 - 1.5, as shown in the following screenshot:

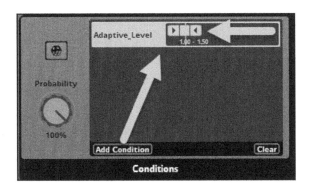

Adding a looping parameter condition to the loop region

7. Of course you will need to do this for each of the other looping regions except be sure to the condition range to encompass the level. For instance, the looping region for level 2 would have a conditional range from 1.5 - 2.5. Level 3 would be 2.5 - 3.5 and so on. After you are done setting the looping condition for each region, build and save the project.

8. Go to the Unity editor now and locate the `AdaptiveAudioManager` object in the **Hierarchy** window. Add an **FMOD Studio Event Emitter** component to the object and set its parameters to match those in the following screenshot:

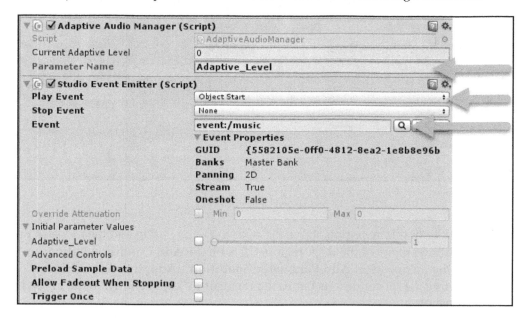

Setting up the Event Emitter and Adaptive Audio Manager components

9. After you are done setting the parameters, run the scene by pressing play. Wander around the scene as you normally would and pay particular attention to the music changes. After you are done testing, stop the scene and then save all your changes.

Did you notice how the music continues looping depending on the different area of the level you are wandering? This is what we want; however, you may have also noticed that the music never goes back down in levels and it easily gets out of sequence. We will fix those issues in the next section.

QUIZ TIME

Which of the following adaptive music techniques can FMOD support:
a) Vertical remixing
b) Cross fading
c) Phrase branching
d) Musical demarcation branching
e) Bridge transitions
f) Singer-based sequencing

Answers as always we be provided before the end of the chapter. Hint, you may want to refer back to Chapter 5, *Using the Audio Mixer for Adaptive Audio.*

Transition timelines and stingers

Thus far, our adaptive music works well for a simple horizontal re-sequenced linear progression of music. Of course, we would never expect our players to progress through a level like that unless our game mechanics required that, which they don't. Fortunately, FMOD is able to support several adaptive music techniques from horizontal re-sequencing to vertical remixing and will even allow the combination of techniques as well. As we progress through this section, we will try to identify each of the techniques in use and some alternative options as well.

Right now our music is an example of the **horizontal re-sequencing** technique called **phrase branching,** but unfortunately the transitions are only one way. Let's fix that by adding reverse transitions to our music event by following the directions given here:

1. Open the **Event Editor** and make sure the music event is up and ready. Right-click [*Ctrl* + click on Mac] on the region marker area and from the menu select **Add Marker**. Rename the marker `Level 1` and then drag it onto the start of the first loop region. Do this for all the other music level loop regions, as shown in the screenshot:

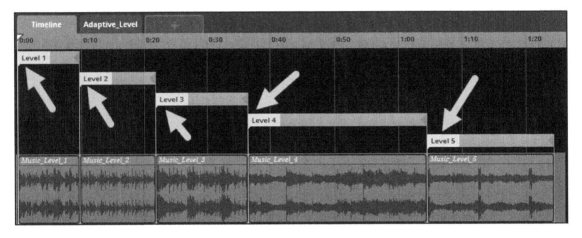

Adding and positioning the level markers

2. Right-click [*Ctrl* + click on Mac] beside the level looping region, and from the menu, select **Add Transition To | Level 1**. This will add a bright green transition marker with an arrow. Move the marker to the end of the `Level 2` looping area but at the same level as the `Level 1` looping region, as shown in the following screenshot:

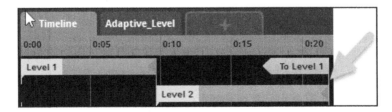

Setting the Transition marker to the end of Level 2 loop region

3. Select the marker and click on the **Add Condition** button in the **Conditions** area at the bottom of the window. From the menu, select **Add Parameter Condition |** **Adaptive Level**. Then, set the range to be from 1 - 1.5, just as you did for the looping condition.

4. Right-click [*Ctrl* + click on Mac] on the transition, and from the menu, select **Copy**. Right-click [*Ctrl* + Click on Mac] above the Level 3 loop and select **Paste**. This will add another transition marker at the end of the loop. Paste two more times so that there are transitions above the Level 4 and Level 5 loops as well.

5. Repeat steps 2-5 for each of the other music levels making sure to set the transition condition to the correct range. At the end of all of this work, your screen should resemble the following screenshot:

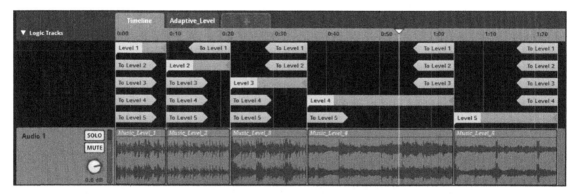

The completed view of the transition markers set for each music level

 Just use copy/paste to speed up the task. The critical part is to just be sure that the conditions for each of the markers is appropriate to its level.

6. After you are done, save and build the project. Return to Unity and run the scene by pressing play. Move around the scene and you will notice the music transition back and forth better now. Of course it is not perfect and that is what we will work on next. Stop the scene when you are done testing.

Moving through the level now should give you some appreciation of the amount of time it takes to move between areas. This was one of the defining characteristics in determining how long to make the looped sections, at least when using the **phrase branching** technique. A better technique for us would be to use what's called **musical demarcation branching**. This type of adaptive music technique allows us to transition at the next bar or measure and is really powerful. Let's see how this works by converting our current setup to use musical demarcation branching by following the exercise given here:

1. Open the **Event Editor** and select the **wind** event. Select the first transition marker we put down in the last exercise and delete it; do this for all the other music level transition markers as well. Right-click [*Ctrl* + click on Mac] on the marker region, and from the menu, select **Add Transition Region To | Level 1**. Then, select the new region and refer to the **Conditions** area at the bottom of the window. Add a new Adaptive_Level condition and set the **Quantization** settings to match those shown in the following screenshot:

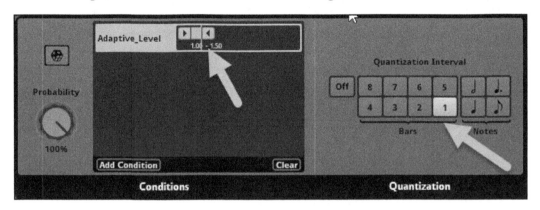

Setting the condition and quantization settings for the new transition region

In this case we are using a musical bar to denote the transition timing, which is fine for our needs. If you are unsure about musical notation of notes and measures not to worry, we will cover some of that theory in Chapter 10, *Composing Music*.

2. After you are done setting the conditions, drag the region so it covers the entire top area except for the looping section. Continue the procedure for the remaining levels. The following screenshot will show you how the finished view will look:

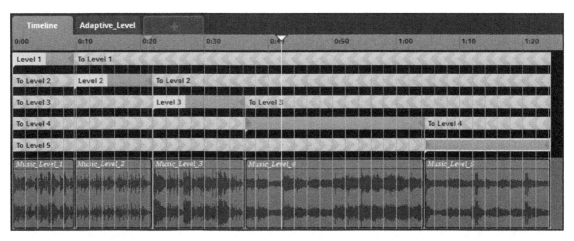

Transition markers converted to transition regions

3. Again, this may seem like a bit of work but using copy/paste you can probably complete this step quicker than the last. After you are done setting up all the transition regions with the correct conditions and quantization, save and build the project.

4. Open up Unity and run the scene by pressing play. Notice how the transition is far quicker now between clips this is the clear advantage of the **music demarcation branching** technique. When you are done testing, stop the scene.

 If you feel the changes are too quick or rushed, you can quickly adjust the quantization value you are using for the transition. You could even set different quantizations for different transition regions, the possibilities are endless here.

For the most part, everything sounds good, but there are a couple of problem spots we want to improve on. The transition between levels 1-3 to level 4 and 5 is abrupt because they were extracted from a different source. They also have a different tempo and instrument variation. To account for that we are going to introduce transition timelines, which will allow us to ease those differences with other horizontal re-sequencing techniques such as **cross fading and stingers**.

First, let's take a look at how we can perform cross fading in a transition timeline from the 1-3 levels to level 4 transition region by following the directions given here:

1. Go to the **Event Editor** and select the **music** event. Double-click on the **Level 4** transition region above levels 1-3. This will open up the timeline window and add a small circle icon to the end of the transition region marker. Adjust the timeline window by hovering the mouse over the time bar and when it turns to an arrow, drag the window so that only covers around 2 seconds.

2. Next, use the mouse to drag the **Level 4** drag halfway left into the timeline. Do the same thing on the other side so that they meet in the middle. Then, use the mouse to hover over the corner of each track until it turns to a fader cursor. After the cursor changes, drag it across the track to create a fade level over the portion of the track. This is shown in the following screenshot:

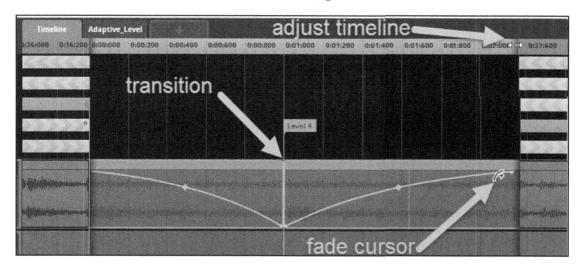

Setting up the transition timeline

You can also fade between different clips by just dragging the end of one clip over the top off another. You will see a cross fade region generated for you automatically.

3. Save and build the project and then jump to the Unity editor. Press play to run the scene and see if you can pick out how smooth the transition is now between areas 1-3 to 4.

   That corrects our problem for music level 4 transitions now we will cover a more advanced technique in order to resolve the level 5 transition. Follow the instructions given here to build on the previous example:

4. Start by building another transition timeline, this time using the `Level 5` transition region. Set the timeline range to around 4 seconds and cross fade just as you did before. After you are done with that, you should be at the point shown in the following screenshot:

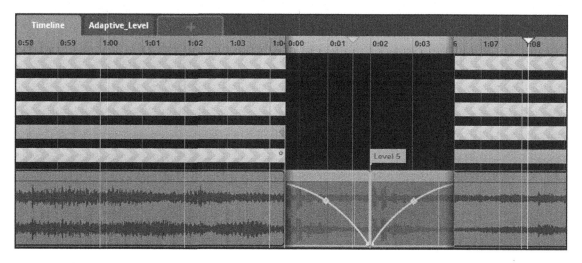

5. Now, we want to punch up the transition between the other levels and Level 5 by adding a short violin stinger into another track. Right-click [*Ctrl* + click on Mac] on the **Audio 1** track and select Add Audio Track from the menu. Drag the stinger-violin.wav file from the Chapter_7_Music folder and drop it onto the **Audio 2** track just after the Level 5 transition timeline. This is shown in the following screenshot:

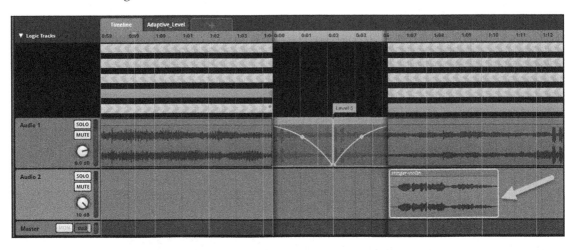

Level 5 transition timeline and stinger added on separate audio track

6. After you are done making the changes save and build the project. Return to Unity and run the scene. Test the scene and observe the changes. Of course feel free to make any other additional changes you want at this point.

The addition of the stinger in this example was derived and just as an example. In fact, our entire example is actually a use of stinger-based sequencing, because we are using a collection of clips as our music base. Keep in mind though that you could use any length of music clip and use the advanced techniques we worked through here.

A sting is a short musical phrase, primarily used in broadcasting and films as a form of punctuation. For example, a sting might be used to introduce a regular section of a show, indicate the end of a scene, or indicate that a dramatic climax is imminent. - Wikipedia

QUIZ TIME ANSWERS

Which of the following adaptive music techniques can FMOD support:
a) **Vertical remixing**
b) **Cross fading**
c) **Phrase branching**
d) **Musical demarcation branching**
e) **Bridge transitions**
f) **Singer-based sequencing**

FMOD could support any of the techniques listed precedingly.

Summary

This chapter was a mix of review and new content with FMOD. We covered a lot of advanced content using FMOD in this chapter, and hopefully you are fairly comfortable now using the tool for your game development needs. We covered a lot of material in this chapter quite quickly by starting on replicating the environmental zones we developed for Audio Mixer earlier. Then, we advanced to the next phase of the zones example by adding dynamic wind and this allowed us to review the internals of FMOD scripting in Unity. After that, we jumped back to adaptive audio and the footsteps example that we upgraded to run with FMOD, while also adding other enhancements along the way. From there, we moved onto working with adaptive music again using FMOD, where we spent an extensive amount of time reviewing various techniques for extracting and re-sequencing the various musical phrases our game level would use. Finally, we looked into more advanced transition techniques that allowed us to blend our more awkward transitions seamlessly.

In the next chapter, we will go back to Unity and this time look at how we can visualize audio. Being able to visualize the beats of music or frequency changes can provide your game with new and interesting effects.

8
Visualizing Audio in Games

Thus far, we have been primarily focused on using audio to enhance or as a response to game visuals or mechanics. Essentially, all the audio we have used has been the result of some action, activity, or visual, from the sound of the wind, background music, axe throwing, and other sound effects. We have layered audio on top of the game's activity, in order to enhance the player's experience, which is the traditional use of audio in games. Although, wouldn't it be interesting if it was the other way around and the audio drove the games graphics and/or game play? Of course, there already is an entire genre and sub-genres of games devoted to music-driven gameplay, classified as music games. However, audio-driven game play and visualizations can be extended beyond that. What we will look at in this chapter, is how audio can be used to drive graphics visualizations and extended to derive game mechanics and game play.

In this chapter, we are going to look at how audio can drive various graphic visualizations. We will look at the background techniques and tools Unity provides us to do this. From there, we will look at how a basic visualizer script can be built, after which we will use it in a couple examples. The following is the list of topics we will cover in this chapter:

- Analyzing audio with FFT windows
- Examining an audio visualizer
- Visualization performance and windowing
- Audio-driven lighting
- Microphone-driven visuals

This chapter will be primarily focused toward the developer and cover more advanced scripting techniques. Sound designers or audio engineers may find it helpful to review the contents in order to understand what is possible. While all readers should give this chapter a try, if you find yourself over your head, then be confident that you tried.

Unlike previous chapters, this chapter will start fresh with a blank new project. The examples in this chapter will assume that the reader has a solid understanding of Unity by this point. This means you should have either covered the introductory chapters or be well versed with Unity. In the next section, we will start with the foundations of how audio can be visualized within Unity.

Analyzing audio with Fast Fourier Transform (FFT) windows

Unity is inherently built with the capability to analyze a playing audio source and determining the various output frequency signal levels. While the mathematics behind this are quite advanced, understanding the theory and background of how this all works will only benefit us later when we build an audio visualizer. Therefore, we are going to cover the theory on how audio can be analyzed for visualization. Starting in the next section, we will look at what comprises an audio signal.

Audio spectrum

Fourier's theorem states that all signals are the sum of sines. This is another way of saying that all audio signals are comprised of component sound waves, called sine waves. Let's look at an example of this in the following diagram:

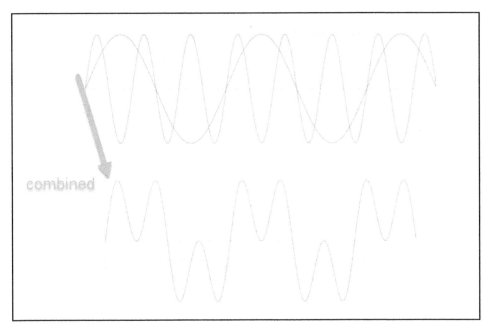

Two different frequency sine waves combined into a signal

The preceding diagram shows an example of two different frequency sound waves (sine waves) being combined into a single signal. Unfortunately, you still may not understand what makes one sine wave different from another aside from frequency. So, let's hear some examples of the audio frequency range we are capable of hearing in the form of single sine waves, given in the following table:

Frequency range	Frequency values	Sample sine wave
Sub-bass	20 to 60 Hz	https://packt-type-cloud.s3.amazonaws.com/uploads/sites/1086/2017/03/sine-wave-50hz.wav
Bass	60 to 250 Hz	https://packt-type-cloud.s3.amazonaws.com/uploads/sites/1086/2017/03/100hz.wav
Low midrange	250 to 500 Hz	https://packt-type-cloud.s3.amazonaws.com/uploads/sites/1086/2017/03/300hz.wav
Midrange	500 Hz to 2 kHz	https://packt-type-cloud.s3.amazonaws.com/uploads/sites/1086/2017/03/1000hz.wav
Upper midrange	2 to 4 kHz	https://packt-type-cloud.s3.amazonaws.com/uploads/sites/1086/2017/03/3000hz.wav

Presence	4 to 6 kHz	https://packt-type-cloud.s3.amazonaws.com/upload s/sites/1086/2017/03/5000hz.wav
Brilliance	6 to 20 kHz	https://packt-type-cloud.s3.amazonaws.com/upload s/sites/1086/2017/03/10000hz.wav

 If you are unable to hear the audio files in your reader or book, go to this page: http://www.teachmeaudio.com/mixing/techniques/audio-spect rum. Be sure to take the time and visit that page and listen to the audio spectrum of the sine waves.

Each of the sound files in the preceding table represents a single sine wave within the audio spectrum or frequency range of human hearing. Recall from Chapter 2, *Scripting Audio*, when we discussed effects and equalization, that the audio spectrum starts with the sub-bass range. This is represented by those low tones often associated with a kick drum or tribal drum sounds that you can feel. Up to the range of brilliance or those very high piercing tones that can hurt your ears and everything in between. The following screenshot shows an excerpt from FMOD showing each of those sine waves in the order of increasing frequency:

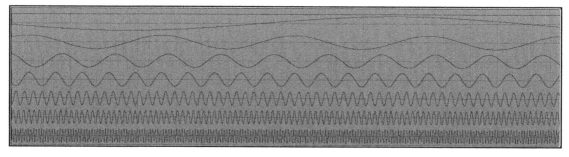

Each sine wave clip represented as a wave form in FMOD

Every sound we hear is composed of those various tones or sine waves all added up together to produce audio such as music or sound effects. Working through this book, you have seen multiple examples of sound wave forms within Unity or FMOD. Yet, to demonstrate a couple of points, we will refer to the picture of an audio clip from FMOD:

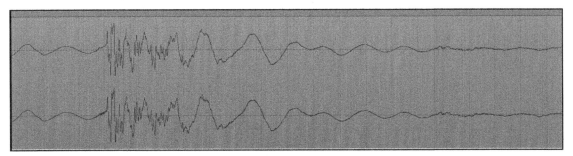

Zoomed in view of audio clip in FMOD showing combined wave form

The preceding image was again taken from FMOD but this time shows a zoomed-in view of a music file. Notice how at the start of the clip you can clearly see what looks like a single sine wave. That quickly changes though to what is obviously a combined mix of multiple waves of varying frequency.

Okay, so now we have a basic understanding of what the audio spectrum is and how audio signals are composed. What does this have to do with visualizing sound? Well, what if there was a way to decompose an audio signal back to its individual sine waves that could be measured. We will look at how that problem can be solved in the next section.

Deconstructing signals using FFT and windowing

As you can well imagine, breaking down an audio signal back to its component waves is not mathematically simple. The process is based on the study of representing complex functions using simpler trigonometric functions, which is called Fourier analysis. It is named after Joseph Fourier who first demonstrated these concepts. The algorithm we use to break down a signal is called a Fast Fourier Transform (FFT) and many different forms have been developed. Of course, we won't go into the maths here, but it will be helpful to understand how the algorithm works.

An FFT algorithm essentially works by breaking down a signal based on time into its frequency component amplitudes as shown in the following diagram:

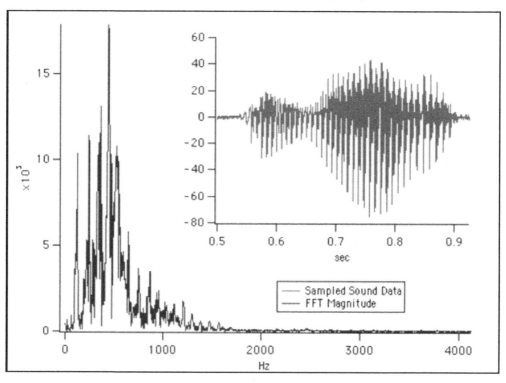

FFT of audio signal into frequency and amplitude

The preceding diagram shows the FFT algorithm transforms our audio signal into frequency amplitudes or essentially into the amplitude of the individual component waves. However, as you can see in the diagram, it may still be difficult to measure specific data points. This can be caused by leakage or aberrations in the data and/or transformation. Fortunately, this is solved by a technique called **windowing,** which is essentially applying another function to transform our data into more measurable containers or windows. The following is an example of the `Hanning window` function being applied to an FFT:

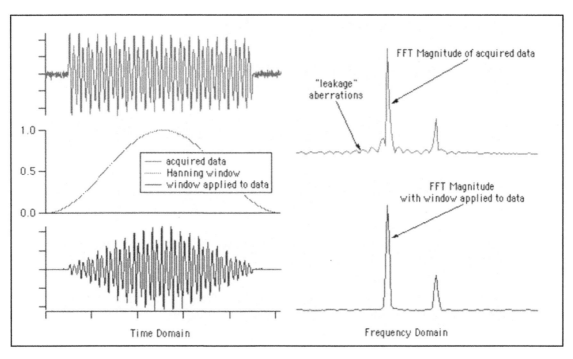

Hanning window being applied to FFT magnitudes

By applying this window function, we now have the data divided into distinct channels we can measure. This allows us to read the frequency signature of an audio signal at any point in time. In the next section, we will look at how all this theory is put into practice when we examine an example of audio signal visualization.

 If you are interested in understanding the mathematics, there is plenty of information available online about the subject of FFT and windowing. Here is a great link that explains the basic mathematics of FFT: `https://betterexplained.com/articles/an-interactive-guide-to-the-fourier-transform/`.

Examining an audio visualizer

Even if you are still a little fuzzy on what an FFT does and how it does it really will become more clear after we look at a completed example. Since this is more of an advanced topic, we will actually look at a completed example first and then break it down to see how it works. Follow the instructions given to add the chapter assets to a new Unity project:

1. Open up Unity and create a new project called `GameAudioVisualizations`.
2. From the menu, select **Assets** | **Import Package** | **Custom Package** and then use the **Import Package** dialog to locate and import the **Chapter_8_Start.unitypackage** found in the `Chapter_8_Assets` folder of the downloaded source code.
3. After the assets are imported, locate the **Chapter_8_Start** scene in the **Project** window and double-click to open it.
4. When the scene has finished loading, press play to run it. As the scene plays, listen carefully and watch the colored cubes as they grow and shrink with the music. The following is a screenshot of the scene playing:

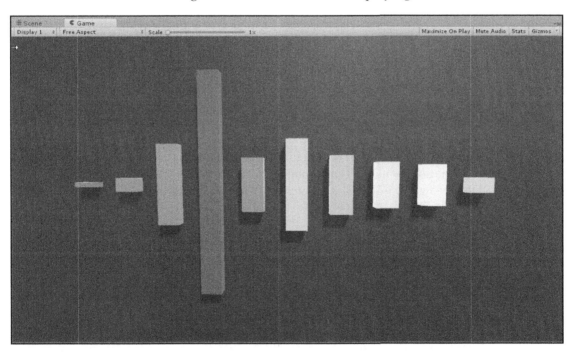

Example of audio visualization scene running with music playing

5. Listen for a while and when you are ready to continue with the demonstration, stop the scene.

6. Locate and select the **Visualizer** object in the **Hierarchy** window and then in the **Inspector** window change the **AudioClip** of the **Audio Source** component to 1000hz as shown in the following screenshot:

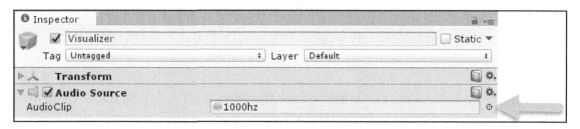

Setting the AudioClip to the 1000hz sine wave audio file

7. Press play again to run the scene. You will hear the single tone at 1000hz and the cyan cube (sixth from the left) should grow to about the same size as the dark blue region did (fourth cube from the left) in the preceding diagram. Stop the scene again when you are done testing the example.

What you are seeing here is how our FFT windowing functionality in Unity is being used to isolate the frequencies of the music or the sample sine wave and show the results graphically. What we have done here is very similar to any of the classic audio-driven screen savers. In the next section, we will dig into the inner details of how this is working.

Uncovering the details

Now that we have seen the completed demo, let's see how this all works under the covers by following the instructions:

1. Open up Unity and locate the VisualizeSoundManager script in the **Project** window and double-click on the script to open it in your preferred editor. Unlike previous chapters, we are not going to look at the entire script but just look at the highlights.

2. Start by scrolling down to the Start method, as shown here:

```
void Start () {
    audioSource = GetComponent<AudioSource>();
    samples = new float[sampleNo];
    CreateFrequencyBins();
}
```

3. The `Start` method should be very familiar to you by now. First, we get the `audioSource` component, initialize an array called `samples`, and finally call the method `CreateFrequencyBins`. We will look at the `CreateFrequencyBins` method later. Next, scroll down to our old friend the `Update` method:

```
void Update () {
    audioSource.GetSpectrumData(samples, 0, FFTWindow);
    BinSamples();
    audioSource.GetSpectrumData(samples, 1, FFTWindow);
    BinSamples();
}
```

4. As we know, the `Update` method is our worker that runs every frame. In this `Update` method, we are calling a special method on `audioSource` called `GetSpectrumData`. `GetSpectrumData`, as you may have already guessed, is an FFT windowing function, which breaks down the audio signal from the currently playing file into an array of floats called `samples`. The array being passed into the method needs to be of a specific size from 64, 128, 256, 512... and up. Since this is such a special method, we will break down each of the parameters in more detail in the following diagram:

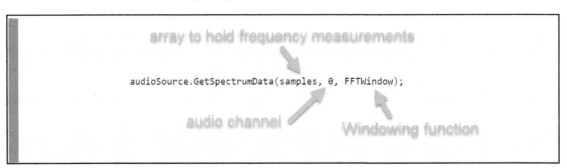

5. We have already seen how the samples array was initialized. The channel represents which audio channel we want to measure. Next comes a parameter called `FFTWindow`; this just represents the type of windowing function we want to use in order to measure our signal. We will look into this parameter later.

6. Before we get into the details of the rest of the script, let's go back to Unity and look at how the component is configured in the **Inspector** window. Go back to Unity and look at the **Visualize Sound Manager** component in the **Inspector** window while the scene is stopped and then run the scene and pay attention to how the component changes. The following is a screenshot of the component not running and while running:

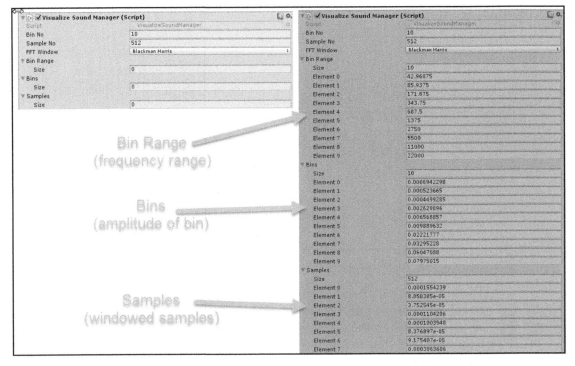

VisualizeSoundManager component not running and running

7. Notice that in the component, the samples array is 512 elements in size when running and the values in that array represent the amplitudes at each frequency step of about 47 Hz over a sampling rate range from about 47 - 24000 Hz. If we were to visualize these amplitudes in a graph by rate, we would see something like the following:

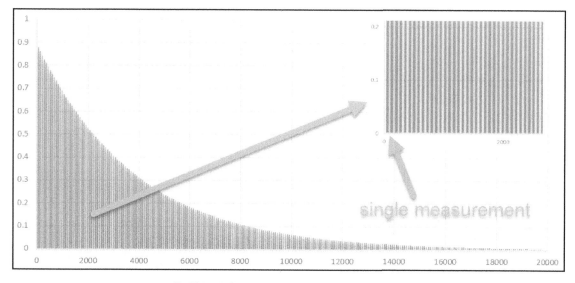

Simplified graph of an audio signal measured by Unity's GetSpectrumData

The graph shows how `GetSpectrumData` measures audio signal data, based on a sample rate or play rate. While the rates and frequencies are similar, it is not on the same scale. However, for our purposes we will treat them as if they are on the same frequency scale in order to simplify things.

8. What may not be immediately apparent, however, is that the first bar measurement covers the whole range of the sub-bass (20-60 Hz). In fact, if you consult the preceding audio spectrum table, you will see that our first four spectrum ranges (sub-bass, bass, low midrange, and midrange) are all within the first label at 2000. So what is happening here and how do we fix it?

    The answer is that the `GetSpectrumData` method returns a linear representation of the audio signal measurements. It isn't broken; that is the way it works. The problem is that we don't perceive sound on a linear scale, but rather on a logarithmic scale. Consult the preceding audio spectrum table again and this time pay attention to the ranges. The following is a graph showing the sub-bass range on a logarithmic scale:

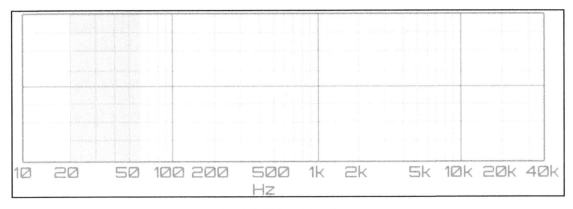

Logarithmic graph of highlighted sub-bass audio spectrum range

    In order to properly visualize the audio signal, we need to convert back the linear sample data we get from `GetSpectrumData` to a logarithmic scale. While this may sound complicated, it really isn't and that is the next piece of code we will look at.

9. Remember the `CreateFrequencyBins` method we saw in the `Start` method? Scroll down to the `CreateFrequencyBins` method and we will show it in the following code snippet as well:

```
private void CreateFrequencyBins()
{
    var maxFreq = AudioSettings.outputSampleRate / 2.0f;
    minFreq = maxFreq / sampleNo;
    binRange = new float[binNo];
    bins = new float[binNo];
    for(int i = 0; i < binNo; i++)
    {
```

```
            binRange[i] = LogSpace(minFreq, maxFreq, i, binNo);
        }
    }
```

10. The `CreateFrequencyBins` method creates the frequency ranges that converts our data from 512 linear sample points to a set number of bins/buckets on a logarithmic or log space. If you look back to Unity, you will see that the `VisualizeSoundManager` has the **Bin No** set to `10`, which matches the number of colored cubes we are using for our visualization. There are a couple of lines in this method that are important to understand, so we will look at them in more detail:

    - `var maxFreq = AudioSettings.outputSampleRate / 2.0f;`: This line determines the maximum sampling rate or frequency of the data. `AudioSettings` is a global Unity variable that determines the current sampling rate of the mixer. This setting can be adjusted at runtime and if it is, it will break the visualizer.
    - `minFreq = maxFreq / sampleNo;`: This calculates the minimum frequency or sample rate.
    - `binRange[i] = LogSpace(minFreq, maxFreq, i, binNo);`: Inside the loop, this line of code calculates the `binRange` using a method called `LogSpace`, which just converts a linear scale to a logarithmic or log scale.

11. The important take away here is that the **Bin No** parameter determines the number of cubes, lights, lines, or whatever we want to use to display an audio visualization. However, you have to be careful on what you set this value to as it will also determine how the audio spectrum is visualized.

Readers, who are interested, may review the rest of the script at their leisure but the parts we covered is sufficient for our understanding. It should be noted, the **VisualizeSoundManager** is really just a starting point for developers to build upon based on the learning we have covered in this chapter.

The final piece of the puzzle is to look at the script that powers the cubes visualization. From the **Project** window, locate and open the `VisualScaler` script in the editor of your choice. The following is the code for review:

```
using UnityEngine;

public class VisualScaler : MonoBehaviour
{
    public float scale;
```

```
    public int bin;

    void Update()
    {
        var val = VisualizeSoundManager.Instance.bins[bin] * scale;
        transform.localScale = new Vector3(1.0f, val, 1.0f);
    }
}
```

As you can see, the script is fairly simple. There is a couple of `public` variables that set a `scale` factor and the `bin`. The `bin` represents the index value to the `bins` variable on the `VisualScaler`.

All the action of course takes place in the `Update` method, where the script grabs the value from the `VisualizeSoundManager` for the `bin` based on the position set. A scale factor is used to modify the value since the original may be quite small in range. After that the `transform.localScale` is set based on the `val` variable previously calculated. In the previous version of the script, only the Y is scaled but you could do any combination of scaling or other combinations of transform you want. Change the last line of the script that does the transform to this:

```
    transform.localScale = new Vector3(1,val, val);
```

Save the script and go back to Unity. Run the scene and watch how much a quick change altered the visualization. Feel free to add or modify other elements of this script. The possibilities are endless here so have fun changing this script.

Now that we have covered the basics of audio visualization, we still need to address some considerations with respect to performance. Audio visualization is a hungry process, and in the next section, we will look at some performance tips on using the visualizer.

Visualization performance and windowing

As we have seen, we are calling `GetSpectrumData` in the `Update` method, not once but twice. Now that you understand some of what is happening under the covers, you can likely appreciate that those calls are quite expensive, which they are. Of course, there are some things we can do to make those calls run quicker, but as always there are trade-offs and your visualizations could suffer. Although, if your game scene is running at a poor frame-rate that really is not much better.

If you wanted to run an audio visualization through a game you built for a mobile platform, such as phone, you would likely want to turn the number of samples down to 64.

Let's look at some settings we can tweak to improve the performance of the visualizer and the effect they have on the audio visualizations by following the instructions given here:

1. Go to Unity and set the **AudioClip** of the **Audio Source** component to the music track we started with. Then, press play to run the scene. This will be our base or control we will refer back to. Look and listen for a while, and when you are happy or you have seen enough, stop the scene.

2. This time change the **Sample No** to 64 on the **Visualize Sound Manager** component. Run the scene again and look at the differences in the way the visualization has changed. You will likely see a more responsive visualization but the cubes to the left (red, magenta, and purple) will almost always be active. This is because the lower frequency bins had to grow in size to encompass more of the spectrum. You can see this by expanding the **Bin Range** parameter as shown in the following screenshot:

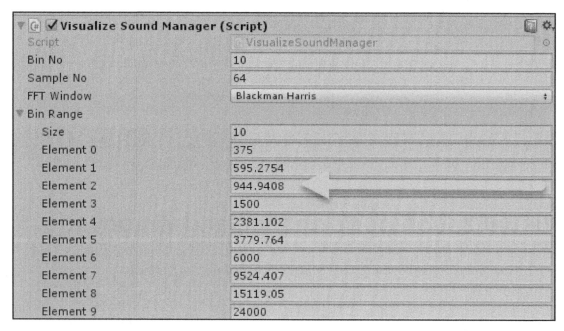

Bin Range when Sample No is set to 64

3. Stop the scene now and change the value back to 512. Run the scene again and notice the difference in **Bin Range** sizes and how this affects the visualization. Stop the scene after you are done reviewing.

4. Now, set the **Sample No** to 4096 and run the scene. Depending on your system, you may notice two things. First, the visualizer is barely crawling along now and the frame-rate is low. Second, you are now seeing the opposite visualization to what we saw with a setting of 64. You can confirm this by looking at the **Bin Range** again, and this time, you will see very small ranges. So small, that the left cubes in the visualization don't even move.

5. At this point, you can try different settings in between 64-4096 for the **Sample No** and run the scene again. Just remember that the **Sample No** needs to be a power of two (that is, 64, 128, 256, 512...).

As you have seen, the **Sample No** can have a significant affect on how the visualization looks and runs, so it is important you understand how to set or adjust that parameter. Of course, there is one last parameter that we need to cover that also can influence the visualization and, to a lesser extent, performance, and that is the FFT window setting.

If you remember back to our discussion about how FFT transforms the signal, there was one last step we did to make the data more readable called windowing. You can think of windowing as just applying a smart filter function that cleans up the data. However, a windowing function typically is specialized to a frequency range and different window functions will clean the data differently. As well, the various window functions will perform differently depending on the type of signal being processed. While this all sounds quite complicated, and it is, fortunately we can quickly see the differences of this by just changing the FFT window parameter on the visualizer. Follow the directions, to test the changes to the FFT window parameter:

1. Go back and change the **AudioClip** on the **Audio Source** to the sine-wave-50hz file. For this example, it will be easier to see the differences by starting out with just a simple audio signal.

2. Change the **FFT Window** parameter on the **Visualize Audio Manager** component to **Rectangular**. Then, run the scene and notice how the visualization looks. Stop the scene.

3. Repeat step 2 for each of the different windowing functions (from **Triangle** to **Blackman Harris)** and notice how they alter the visualization.

As you can see, the differences can be quite substantial and you may want to alter the **FFT Window** to produce different behaviors based on song or something else entirely.

4. Now, repeat step 3 again, but this time also adjust the **Sample No** to a value of **64**, **512,** or **1024** and run them all again.

Depending on your system, you may notice differences in performance between the various windowing functions by turning on the **Stats** window. Just click on the **Stats** button at the top of the **Game** view to turn the window on as the scene is running. Then, look for the Graphics / FPS (frames per second) performance stat. Ideally, you never want your FPS to drop below 30.

5. Go back and try the same exercise with different sine waves or music clips. At this point, there is no right and wrong answers to what setting choices you make as it will come down to your visual preference or style choice.

We have spent a significant amount of time explaining an advanced concept in this chapter. However, spending the time now to understand the internals of how the audio visualization works will help us when we go to build new visualizations later. In the next section, we will extend our growing cubes sample with a bit of dramatic lighting.

Audio-driven lighting

After having seen a working example of how the technical parts of audio visualization come together, you should be well on your way to becoming an AV master. One of things that is predominant in the area of audio graphic visualizations is the use of lighting. Being able to add dramatic and dynamic lighting to a scene can take your visualizations to the next level. In this section, we will look at adding some audio-driven lighting. Follow the instructions, to add some audio-driven lights to our scene:

1. Open up Unity and the **Chapter_8_Start** scene. From the menu, select **File | Save Scene As** and then use the **Save** dialog to save the scene as `Chapter_8_Lights` to the `Assets/GameAudio/Scenes` folder.

2. Locate the **Directional Light** in the **Hierarchy** window (at the top) and disable it in the **Inspector** window by unchecking the game object checkbox.

3. From the menu, select **GameObject | Create Empty**. Rename the new object `Lights` in the **Inspector** window and then use the **Add Component** button to add the **Light Controller** component. Set the properties on the object to match those in the following screenshot:

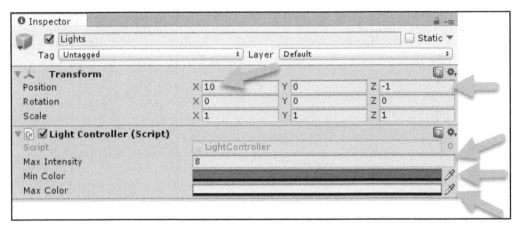

Setting the properties on the Lights game object

4. If you are unable to see the shown colors or dislike the current color choice, you can use the Color dialog to choose different values. The important thing to note is that you are selecting a range of colors and not just two colors. Thus, your **Min Color** should be at the top of the color spectrum and the **Max Color** at the bottom as shown in the following screenshot:

5. Right-click (*Ctrl* + click on Mac) on the **Lights** object and from the context menu select **Create Empty**. Rename the new object Light_1 and then use the **Add Component** button to add a **Light** component. Set the properties of the object to what is shown in the following screenshot:

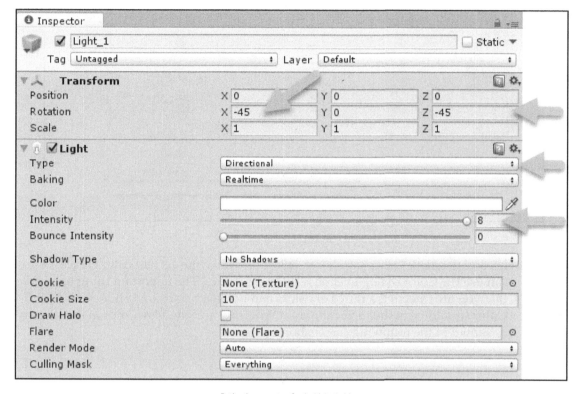

Setting the parameters for the Light_1 object

 There is huge amount of options you can modify in order to explore different lighting techniques. If you are unfamiliar with Unity lighting, then take some time to modify and play with those options on your own. It will also be very helpful to view the changes to the lights within the **Scene** and **Game** views. Here is a link to a great Unity tutorial series on lighting: https://unity3d.com/learn/tutorials/topics/graphics/int roduction-lighting-and-rendering

6. Select the the `Light_1` object in the **Hierarchy** window and type *Ctrl + D* to copy the object. Do this eight more times so that you have 10 children objects attached to the **Lights** object. Use the following table to name the objects and adjust some of the required parameters:

Name	Parameter	Value
Light_2	Transform.Rotation.X Transform.Rotation.Y Transform.Rotation.Z	45 0 45
Light_3	Transform.Rotation.X Transform.Rotation.Y Transform.Rotation.Z	45 45 0
Light_4	Transform.Rotation.X Transform.Rotation.Y Transform.Rotation.Z	-45 45 0
Light_5	Transform.Rotation.X Transform.Rotation.Y Transform.Rotation.Z	0 -45 0
Light_6	Transform.Rotation.X Transform.Rotation.Y Transform.Rotation.Z	0 45 0
Light_7	Transform.Rotation.X Transform.Rotation.Y Transform.Rotation.Z	45 -45 0
Light_8	Transform.Rotation.X Transform.Rotation.Y Transform.Rotation.Z	0 -45 45
Light_9	Transform.Rotation.X Transform.Rotation.Y Transform.Rotation.Z	-45 -45 0
Light_10	Transform.Rotation.X Transform.Rotation.Y Transform.Rotation.Z	0 45 0

7. Open up the **Audio Visualization Manager** component in the **Inspector** window and adjust the **Decay** parameter to a value of `.005`. The parameter is at the bottom of the component.

The `Decay` parameter sets or influences the amount of time a visualization will display the measured values for. A low value will show very quick bouncy changes, while higher values will show very slow changes that will degrade over longer periods of time. Determining the best value to set this parameter will again come down to personal preference or style.

8. Before you run the scene, consult with you doctor. Just a word of caution to readers that suffer from photosensitive epilepsy or are just photosensitive. This scene uses flashing lights, and if you are sensitive to this, you should NOT run this exercise.

Notice that we have omitted the use of shadows for the lights. This is because adding shadows can have a significant impact on performance. If you have a system you think is powerful enough, then enable shadows for all the lights and run the scene again.

9. Run the scene, and now you will see a series of bright lights flashing and keeping rhythm with the music. You can of course alter this scene as much as you like. When you are done testing, stop the scene and save your changes.

As you can see, we were quickly able to enhance the visualization using just some very basic lighting tricks. We will leave it up to the reader to review the `LightController` script on their own. This script is similar to other scripts we have already looked at so adding to it or deriving from it should be easy for those developers out there.

QUIZ TIME
Answer the following questions:

What frequency range do we typical humans hear in?
a) 10 000 - 20,000 Hz
b) 20 - 20,000 Hz
c) 20 - 2,000 Hz
d) 300 - 9,000 Hz

What range would a frequency of 254 Hz fall in?
a) Sub-bass
b) Opulence
c) Brilliance
d) Low mid-range

What does FFT stand for?
a) Fast Frequency Transformation

b) Fast Fast Transform
c) Fast Fourier Transform
d) Fourier Frequency Transform

As always, the answers will be provided at the end of the chapter.

Feel free to modify the scene to create your own lighting visualizations. Another completed example of an audio visualization has been provided in the scene Chapter_8_AV_End. Be sure to open it up and take a look at it. It provides for two audio channel visualizations with the cubes being on channel 0 and the lights on channel 1. Hopefully, this will give you further ideas on how to extend with your own ideas. In the next section, we are going to extend our base scene again but this time using a different audio source.

Microphone-driven visualizations

In just over the last decade, our interaction with computers and games has progressed substantially. Starting in 2006 with the release of the revolutionary Wii, mainstream gaming changed overnight from being entirely controller/keyboard driven to physical human interaction. This evolution further continued with the Kinect and later multi-sensor mobile devices. Now, there appears to a new trend in gaming and that is mobile games controlled by voice or microphone. For this section, we will look at how to convert our previous light visualization sample to use a microphone as an audio source.

If you don't have a microphone, you could also try using a speaker or headphone jacks as a microphone. Just plug your speaker into the microphone jack. You will need to shout to see any form of signal, but it will work if you don't want to go out and buy a microphone for just this book.

Follow the instructions, to add the microphone as an audio source to our visualization scene:

1. Locate and open up the **Chapter_8_Start.scene** in the Unity editor.
2. From the menu, select **Window** | **Audio Mixer** to open the mixer window. Click on the **+** button beside the **Mixers** list to create a new mixer. Name the new mixer `Master`. Select the new **Master** group and then click on the **+** beside the **Groups** to create a new group and rename it `microphone`. When you are done, the **Audio Mixer** window should look like the following screenshot:

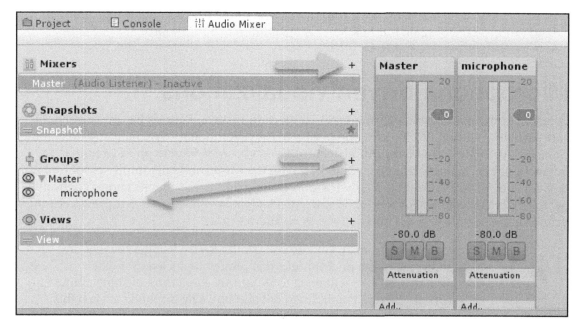

Creating a Master mixer and child group called microphone

3. Select the **microphone** group, and then in the **Inspector** window right-click (*Ctrl* + click on Mac) on the **Volume** parameter and from the menu select **Expose 'Volume (of microphone)' to script** as shown in the following screenshot:

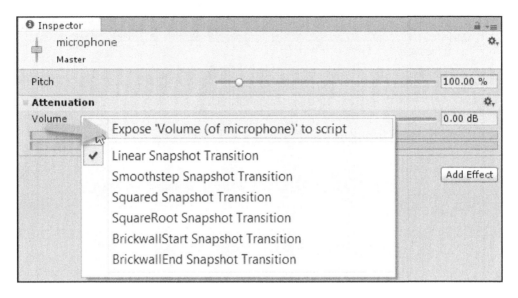

Exposing the Volume parameter to scripting

4. Click to open the **Exposed Parameters** drop-down on the **Audio Mixer** window and then double-click on the **MyExposedParam** text to rename it. Rename the parameter MasterVolume as shown in the following screenshot:

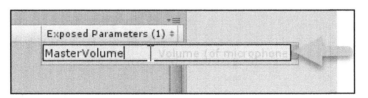

Renaming the MyExposedParam to MasterVolume

5. Find and select the **Visualizer** object in the **Hierarchy** window. Then, use the **Add Component** button to find and add the **MicrophoneListener** script to the object. Set the component parameters on the **Audio Source** and new **Microphone Listener** to what is shown in the following screenshot:

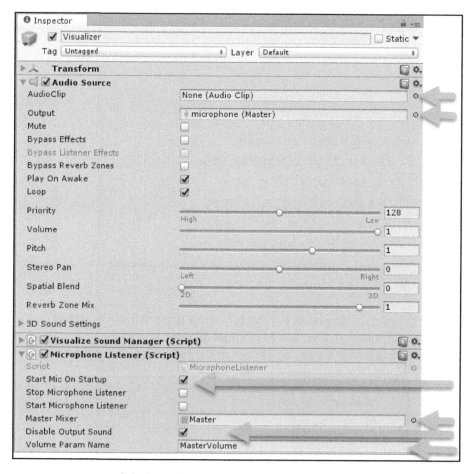

Setting the Audio Source and Microphone Listener component parameters

6. When you are done making changes, save the scene using a new name. Start the scene by pressing play. You can talk or yell into the microphone and watch the visualization your voice makes. Are you able to get all the colored cubes to move using your voice or are you speaking in the range you expect?

7. When you are done testing, go ahead and stop the scene.

So all we did here was to convert the audio source using a new component script called `MicrophoneListener`. Essentially, the `MicrophoneListener` script just uses the Unity `Microphone` object and routes it through the Audio Mixer in real time. We won't go into the details of that script here, but if you are interested feel free to review it in your own time. The end result is for us to be able to analyze the microphone input in real time to perform visualizations but surely you can see how this could easily be extended to control a game in some fashion?

We won't go into any further details to build a complete game but having the ability to read the range of a voice could be quite powerful. In the next chapter of this book we will go into more details about vocal processing and visualizations.

QUIZ TIME ANSWERS
Answers have been shown in bold.

What frequency range do we typical humans hear in?
a) 10,000 - 20,000 Hz
b) 20 - 20,000 Hz
c) 20 - 2,000 Hz
d) 300 - 9,000 Hz

What range would a frequency of 254 Hz fall in?
a) Sub-bass
b) Opulence
c) Brilliance
d) Low mid-range

What does FFT stand for?
a) Fast Frequency Transformation
b) Fast Fast Transform
c) Fast Fourier Transform
d) Fourier Frequency Transform

Summary

In this chapter, we spent a significant amount of time talking about sound, the audio spectrum, and signal processing. From the base of knowledge, we covered at a basic level how the technique of FFT and windowing could be used to process an audio signal into a visual representation of that audio. We then looked at the native support in Unity that allows us to break down an audio signal into bits we can generate visuals with. After that, we extended that example by adding more dramatic visualizations with lights. Breaking away from imported audio, we then looked at other sources of audio we could visualize, by adding support for using the microphone as a real-time audio source, where we discussed using a microphone or voice as a way to control a game.

In the next chapter, we are going to continue looking at vocals and dialog. This time we are going to create visualizations for vocals, where we will look at various sources for vocals and vocal dialog and how they can be used in gaming.

9
Character Lip Syncing and Vocals

Real-time character lip syncing is a powerful tool for any game that needs to showcase character dialog. Traditionally, most character lip-syncing is rendered by animators to pre-recorded vocal tracks. While this works well and is still the method preferred by some, being able to dynamically lip sync a character reduces the need for animation entirely. Character lip syncing, on its own, is an advanced concept we could spent several chapters on. However, for our purposes, we are going to show just what is possible by extending the audio visualization techniques we developed in the last chapter and applying them to character lip syncing. Along the way we are going to get familiar with lip-syncing best practices and ultimately how these techniques can be applied to other environments, characters, or languages.

For this chapter, we going to extend the knowledge we have gained about audio visualization, with our goal being to provide real-time character lip syncing. Along the journey, we will need to understand some basics about speech and animation. Then, we will follow up with some techniques for character dialog and recording vocals. Here is a summary of the main topics we will cover in this chapter:

- Basic lip syncing
- Speech and phonemes
- Blend shape animation
- Real-time character lip sync
- Recording vocals

This chapter is going to continue from where we left off in the last chapter. If you have not read or reviewed that chapter, then it is highly recommended you do so. The previous chapter and this chapter include advanced topics that not all readers may be initially comfortable undertaking. Yet, we will try and address the content at a level all readers who have made it this far should be comfortable with.

Real-time lip syncing

Before we get into the details of speech, phonemes, and animation, we will construct a simple example of how our previous work with developing audio visualizations can be easily applied to character lip syncing. Follow the instructions here to create a new project and set up the scene:

1. Open Unity and create a new project called `GameAudio_Vocals`. After the empty project initializes, select `Assets - Import Package - Custom Package` from the menu and use the file dialog to find the `Chapter_9_Assets` folder in the book's downloaded source code. Select the **Chapter_9_Start.unitypackage** in the folder and click on **Open** to import the assets.

2. Locate the **Chapter_9_Start.scene** in the **Project** folder and double-click to open it. Connect a microphone if you need to and press play to run the scene. After the scene starts running, talk or make some noise and just confirm the colored cubes are moving as you expect. Your **Game** view should look similar to the following screenshot:

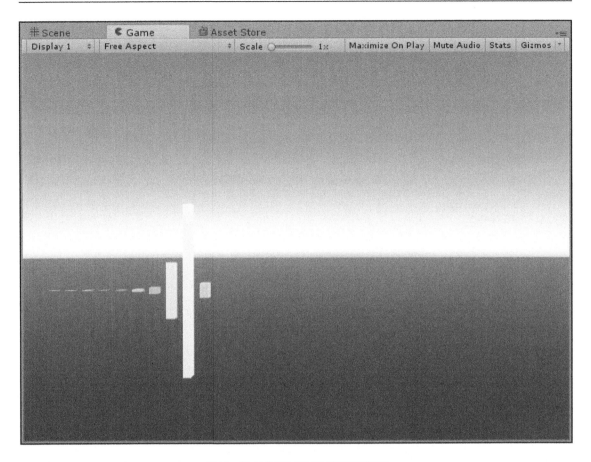

Update audio visualization scene with microphone listener

What you are looking at is the microphone listener example we looked at in the end of the last chapter. The difference is that the spectrum visualization cubes have been scaled down and moved to the side. This will allow us to see the audio spectrum as we expect, while we wire up our lip synced character. Again, if you have not read or reviewed, Chapter 8, *Visualizing Audio in Games*, be sure to do so before continuing this chapter.

3. When you are done testing the scene, stop the scene.

4. From the menu, select **Window** | **Asset Store**. After the **Asset Store** window page loads, type `reallusion iclone` into the search bar and hit *Enter*. This will yield you a search with a choice of three iClone characters plus some other assets as shown in the following screenshot:

Asset Store search for iClone characters

5. Select one of the iClone characters (*Izzy, Max,* or *Winston*), and then download and import the asset into the project. Any of the characters will work, but the examples we will use in the book will be based on the *Izzy* character. Note that unlike other 3D character assets, the iClone characters are not shown fully nude. However, some readers may still find the *Izzy* or *Max* character offensive. For those readers, it is strongly suggested they use the Winston character instead. The iClone characters from Reallusion are for demonstration purposes but also are an excellent asset source for prototyping. Unlike many other free character assets on the store, they are lightweight and work well on any platform. If you want to create your own iClone characters, you will need to use the Reallusion character creator platform. There is a free trial available at `https://www.reallus ion.com/iclone/game/` if you want to test the product.

6. After the iClone character is imported, open the assets {name]/prefab folder in the **Project** window, where the name is saved as the name of the character you downloaded. Inside the folder, you will see a prefab with the same name. Drag this prefab into the scene as shown in the screenshot here:

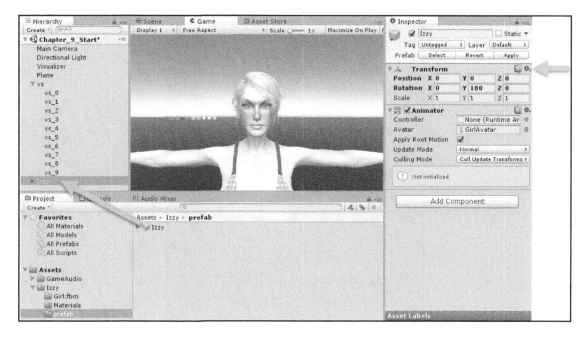

Dragging and placing iClone character prefab into scene

7. After you drag the prefab in, you will also need to reset the **Transform Position** to 0, 0, 0 as shown in the preceding screenshot.

8. Expand the character's object hierarchy in the **Hierarchy** window until you can select the **RL-G6_JawRoot** object as shown in the screenshot here:

Expanding the characters transform bone hierarchy

You could also search for the object in the **Hierarchy** window but be sure to clear the search after the object is done, so you can see the expansion as shown in the screenshot.

9. Then in the **Inspector** window, use the **Add Component** to add a **Visual Transformer** component and set the parameters to the values shown in the following screenshot:

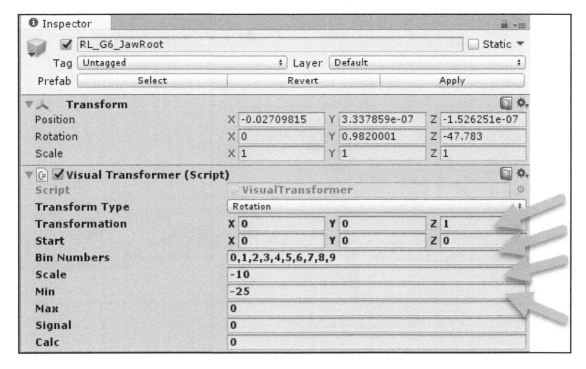

Setting the RL_G6_JawRoot parameters of the Visual Transformer

The `VisualTransformer` is a more generic and extended version of the `VisualScaler` script that was developed in the last chapter.

10. Save the scene as `Chapter_9_LipSync` and then press play. Make a noise and talk; notice now that along with the cubes, the character's mouth now moves with the sound. Here is a screenshot showing an example of this:

Real-time very simplified character lip syncing in action

11. When you are done testing, stop the scene and save the project.

What we just quickly developed here is an example of a very simple character lip sync in real time. While this may seem simple, considering what you have learned, this is just a demonstration of some powerful possibilities. Of course, our character's current lip syncing is nothing more than a ventriloquist dummy. However, as we will start to see in the next section, we really aren't that far away from producing some realistic results.

Speech and phonemes

As you have seen in the last section, we created a character lip sync demo driven by real-time microphone input. While the demo is fun to play, it starts to show what is possible, but it could hardly be mistaken for real speech. After all, we don't just flap our jaws when we speak. Speech and vocalization are a very complex process requiring a synchronization of your larynx, tongue, lips, and even teeth. So as much as we understand how to visualize sound, we will need to go a little further into understanding the key elements in our speech patterns in order to build a more authentic lip syncing simulation.

Animators have been performing realistic lip syncing for many years now, and there are plenty of well established practices for creating speech animation, which means we will be able to use some of those learning and best practices. However, real-time character lip syncing is unique in a few areas and certain practices are less well established. Fortunately, we can still use the basis for character lip sync animation and apply it for our purposes.

Years ago, animators realized that basic sounds of speech called phonemes (pronounced fo-neme) also equate to specific facial expressions. Here is a simple animators chart that shows the common phonemes and how they look when the speaker is speaking those sounds:

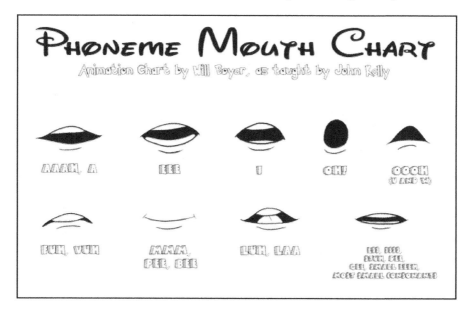

Animators, phoneme mouth chart

Do a quick exercise and work through the chart making each of the sounds. Does your mouth look or feel the same as when you make each of those phonemes? Chances are they follow pretty close. Of course, there are several other phonemes (up to 44 and more) for all sorts of different sounds an English speaker could make. We won't be worrying about all those other phonemes, at least not for this demonstration, and the nine shown in the preceding chart will work just fine.

So at this point, you may be asking yourself how do we go from our signal processing and binning visualization code to controlling phonemes on the character? Well, that is the part that is going to require a little finesse on our part and what we will be doing won't be far from how an animator may do it. There are other real-time lip syncing tools out there, but they use speech recognition APIs to do the work of extracting phonemes. Our audio animation approach won't be perfect, but it will provide you with a character lip syncing tool that you can apply to other languages and speech patterns.

The first thing we need to do is to map the preceding basic speech phonemes to our audio visualization bins. Follow the instructions here to establish your vocal baseline:

1. Go to Unity and open and run the `Chapter_9_VoiceTest` scene.
2. Work through the table and vocalize each of the phonemes by speaking into the microphone loudly:

Phoneme	Sound	Bins
	AAAAAH, A	[0][1][2][3][4][5][6][7][8][9][10][11][12][13][14][15]
	EEE	[0][1][2][3][4][5][6][7][8][9][10][11][12][13][14][15]

	I	[0][1][2][3][4][5][6][7][8][9][10][11][12][13][14][15]
	OH!	[0][1][2][3][4][5][6][7][8][9][10][11][12][13][14][15]
	U AND W	[0][1][2][3][4][5][6][7][8][9][10][11][12][13][14][15]
	FUH, VUH	[0][1][2][3][4][5][6][7][8][9][10][11][12][13][14][15]
	MMM, PEE, BEE	[0][1][2][3][4][5][6][7][8][9][10][11][12][13][14][15]

	LUH, LAH	[0][1][2][3][4][5][6][7][8][9][10][11][12][13][14][15]
	ESS, SSSS, DEE, GEE, EEEEH	[0][1][2][3][4][5][6][7][8][9][10][11][12][13][14][15]

3. As you work through the table and make the sounds, extend the sounds and consult the **Console** window. If you are speaking loud enough into your microphone, you should be able to see at least one, two, three, or more bars. Here is a screenshot of how this will look in the **Console**:

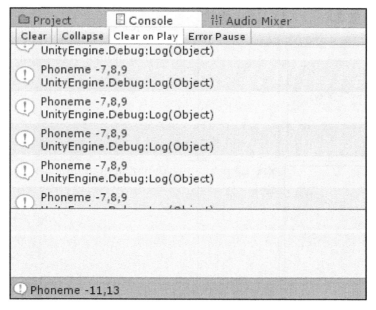

Log output showing the currently activated bins when sounding out a phoneme

4. Work through the table again but this time black out or mark the numbers that show up in the **Console** window. These will essentially be the corresponding bins that match the sound you make when speaking that phoneme. As long as you consistently get from 1-4 bin numbers for each phoneme you are doing well. If you get more than four bin numbers for each phoneme, you will need to turn up the **Min Signal** parameter on the **Phoneme Controller** component. This component is located on the `PhonemeController` game object. The object, component and parameters are shown in the screenshot of the **Inspector** window here:

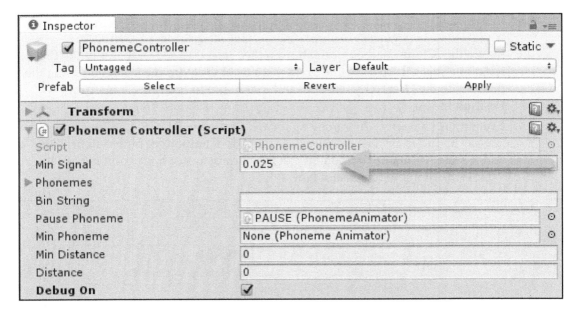

Adjusting the Min Signal threshold parameter on the Phoneme Controller

You may have already realized that the Visualizer in this scene is set up with 16 bins or visualization channels. This was required because using 10 bins would not provide enough distinction in audio binning. There would be just too much overlap in the phoneme sounds.

5. When you have filled in values for the table, stop the scene. If you notice that more than a couple of the phoneme entries in the table have the same bin range, then try adjusting the **Min Signal** parameter on the **Phoneme Controller** to a larger value, as shown in the preceding screenshot. Be sure that you are also over vocalizing the phoneme so that you can extract distinct patterns. This may require a little trial and error on your part.

 If you are having trouble identifying consistent bin ranges, then practice your vocalization and do your best to hold the note while simulating the phoneme. It may also be helpful too ask a friend to try and read the phonemes into the microphone while you watch the bin range response.

6. Locate the **iClone** character prefab from the {name}/prefab folder in the **Project** window. This will be the same prefab you used to set up the last scene. Drag the prefab into the **Hierarchy** window and make sure to reset the **Transform Position** to 0, 0, 0.

7. Expand the character's hierarchy again and locate the **RL-G6_JawRoot** transform just as you did in the last exercise. Use the **Add Component** button to find and add a **Bone Animator** component. Set the parameters of this component to the values shown in the screenshot here:

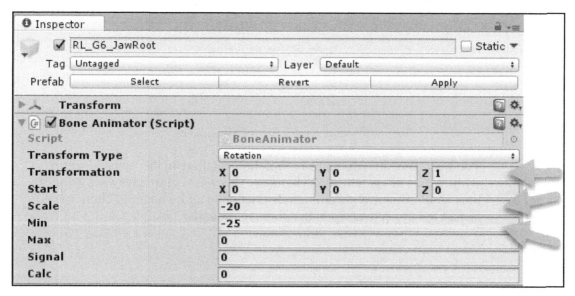

Setting the parameters for the Bone Animator component

The `BoneAnimator` script is another generic variation of the `VisualTransformer` we used in the last exercise. The difference is that the `VisualTransformer` will fetch updates from the `VisualizeSoundManger`, whereas, the **Bone Animator** only updates itself based on the **Signal** set by another component.

8. When you are done editing, save the scene.

Now that we have identified the sounds that match your basic phonemes and some other additional setup, we can start to use that information to update the real-time lip sync character animation. In the next section, we are going to use the bin ranges in controlling what phonemes we animate for our character.

Blend shape animation

During the first exercise in this chapter, we animated the character's jaw transform or what is often called a bone in animation speak. While animating this bone worked for our first pass at a simple lip sync animation, it lacked the authenticity of real speech facial expressions we now understand as phonemes. What we really need is a way to control and animate the character's facial muscles to produce the appropriate speech phoneme animations. Fortunately, animators have solved this problem with the use of what is called blend shapes. In order for us to produce a realistic looking lip sync animation, we are going to have a learn a little bit about blend shapes.

Blend shapes or per-vertex morphs are an animation tool that allows for the warping or altering of the vertexes of a mesh at runtime. They are almost always constructed by the modeler building the model but there are third-party tools that allow for them to be added after the fact. Here is a combined screenshot showing the bones of the character beside a wire-frame model showing the vertexes and connections:

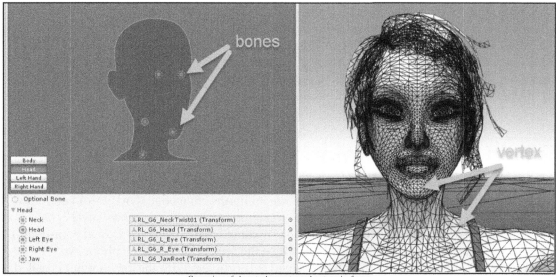

Comparison of character bone setup and vertex wire frame

Explained simply, the difference between bone and per-vertex (blend shapes) animation is the location of the control point. In bone animation, not unlike our own bones, the bone controls an entire wrapped area of vertices, where per-vertex (blend shapes) animation allows for finer control of the vertices in an area controlled by a bone. Another way to think of this is that bones are similar to real bones and per-vertex (blend shapes) are akin to muscles.

So, let's take a look at how this is controlled on our character by following the directions here:

1. Jump back to Unity and locate the RL_G6_Body object in the **Hierarchy** window and select it.

2. Go to the **Inspector** window and expand the **BlendShapes** list and then scroll through the items. As you can see, several blend shapes have been added to our character. A cut-off view of the **Inspector** window screenshot is shown here:

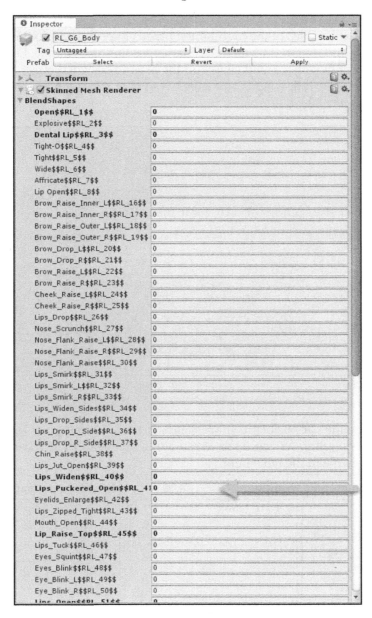

Inspector window showing an abbreviated list of blend shapes

That is quite a list, and for our iClone character there are 46 blend shapes. The list shows more than that, but there are only 46 blend shapes that we modify at runtime.

3. Increase the values of the highlighted blend shape from [0,100] in the **Inspector** window and as you do watch the character's lips also change. Do the same thing to some of the other blend shapes in the list and see what effect it has on the character. The following is an image of our character with numerous blend shapes set to 100:

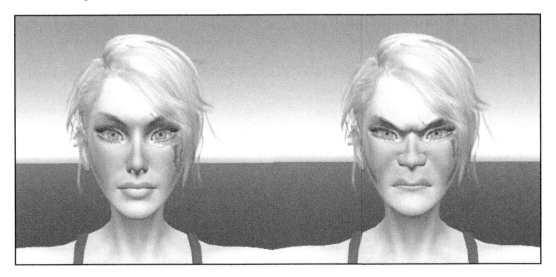

Side-by-side comparison without blend shapes applied and with multiple blend shapes applied

4. Now use the various blend shapes and start modeling each of the phonemes we reviewed earlier. As you do so, write down the blend shapes you used to mimic the phoneme in the table here:

Phoneme	Sound	Blend shape (name/setting)
![phoneme mouth]	AAAAAH, A	

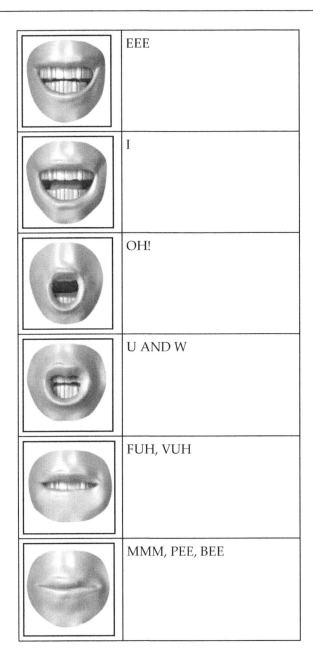

	EEE
	I
	OH!
	U AND W
	FUH, VUH
	MMM, PEE, BEE

| 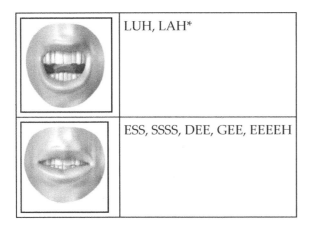 | LUH, LAH* |
| | ESS, SSSS, DEE, GEE, EEEEH |

* Do not worry about getting the tongue to stick out in this exercise. The tongue actually uses it's own separate mesh with a different set of blend shapes.

5. In some cases, you may need to use more than a single blend shape to mimic the phoneme. After you work through each item in the table, be sure to reset the values back to 0. When you are done mimicking all the phonemes, reset everything back to 0.

After completing that exercise, you will certainly understand how phonemes can be added and a better appreciation for how we speak and vocalize sounds. In the next section, we are going to use all the previous work you did in the previous couple exercises and build a better real-time lip sync.

Real-time character lip sync

Now, we are ready to pull all our previous work together and setup our real-time lip syncing character. However, before we do that, we probably should set some expectations on the negatives of using this method as well as the benefits. Take a look at the list of **Negatives** versus **Benefits** in the following table:

Negatives	Benefits
• Vocals need to be tuned to the speaker or speakers vocal range. It may be possible for males to share vocal sound charts but not with a female. • Depending on the vocal range, there may still be some overlap in phoneme vocalizations. For instance, a speakers MMM and U vocalization may register the same, but the phonemes look completely different.	• Real-time and dynamic character lip syncing that once tuned can be reused over and over again. Pre-recorded vocals can also played to generate character lip syncing as well. • A lip sync system that can easily be applied to other languages, dialects, or voice distortions, can be real or constructed. This is especially useful if you need to provide character lip syncing for alien or fantasy languages. • The knowledge of how we tune vocals to phonemes, use blend shapes to animate phonemes, and do this in real-time. This knowledge can then further be applied to other lip sync strategies or even just to better understand how speech vocalization works.

When it comes right down to it, would you use this system if you have to provide character lip syncing for a **AAA** game or movie CGI effect? Probably not, as they likely have the budget to hire full-time animators that can spend their time to do the character lip syncing. However, if you are a small low-budget indie shop or just a game developer prototyping, then this system will work well for you. As well, the knowledge you have thus far gained can easily be transferred to any commercial lip sync software.

As we mentioned earlier, other real-time character lip sync software uses speech recognition to identify the phonemes in the vocals. This removes the step of manually generating the phoneme vocal chart and thus the system will work for any speaker. However, speech recognition software is often tightly coupled to the hardware platform so being able to demonstrate that capability for multiple platforms would not be possible in a single chapter. It will be up to the individual reader at this point, if they choose to integrate speech recognition into the provided real-time lip sync tool.

Now that we have all the preliminary work performed, setting up the character for real-time lip syncing should be relatively straightforward. Follow the exercise here to finish setting up the scene:

1. Open up Unity and the last scene we were working in. Locate and expand the `PhonemeController` object in the **Hierarchy** window. Notice that the object contains all the phonemes and a couple new ones as shown in the screenshot here:

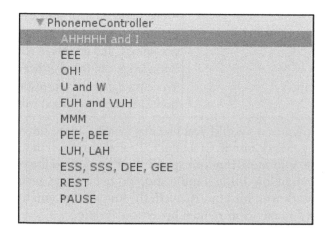

Expanded view of the PhonemeController showing contained objects

2. Select the `AHHHH and I` object from the children as shown in the preceding screenshot. Then, look to the **Inspector** window and set the parameters of the **Phoneme Animator** component as shown in the screenshot here:

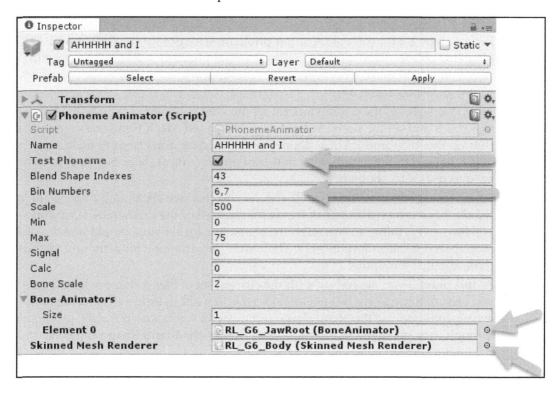

Setting the parameters on the AHHHH and I, Phoneme Animator component

3. Don't worry about setting the blend shape indexes you wrote down in the last exercise just yet. Do make sure to set the bin numbers you jotted down in the phoneme vocal chart. Each number should be separated by a comma with no spaces, as shown in the example. At the bottom of the component, be sure that the component slots are set correctly.

4. Run the scene with a microphone attached and practice vocalizing the **AHHHH** sound. Assuming you set the bin numbers correctly, then you should see the character make the phoneme as you vocalize it. When you are done testing, stop the scene and set the **Test Phoneme** parameter to false (unchecked). It is important you do this last step as you can only test a single phoneme at a time.

If you run the scene and nothing happens, be sure to check that the Debug On parameter is set to true (checked) on the Phoneme Controller.

5. Repeat steps 2-4 for each of the other phonemes, except for the REST and PAUSE phoneme objects. REST and PAUSE are special phonemes. REST is the mouth state you would make when generally speaking, while PAUSE is the mouth state when not vocalizing at all.

6. After you have set the parameters for all the vocal phonemes, you will now need to go back and set the **Bone Animator** and **Skinned Mesh Renderer** component slots on the REST and PAUSE phoneme objects. You don't need to make any other changes to the parameters on those components at this time. You do not need to test these phonemes.

7. When you are done editing, run the scene and practice vocalizing a speech or just words. Try a range of words that encompasses all of the phonemes. Assuming you have everything set correctly, the characters lip syncing should match your own speech vocalizations closely. There may be variations for some sounds but those should be minimal.

8. At this point if you are happy with the current set of blend shape settings, then you can continue using those. However, if you want to improve on some of the expressions and use the blend shape settings you wrote down earlier, just go back through each phoneme in test mode and change the **Blend Shape Indexes** parameter setting.
   NOTE: The index numbers shown on the mesh don't line up to the actual index value. You will likely need to set a value and open the RL_G6_Body object in the Inspector to verify the correct index is being set. Here is a screenshot showing an example of this:

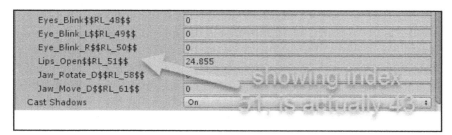

showing differences in labelled versus actual indexing

9. When you are done setting the new blend shape indexes in each of the phonemes, you will also need to open the PAUSE object and set all the index numbers you used into that list as shown in the screenshot here:

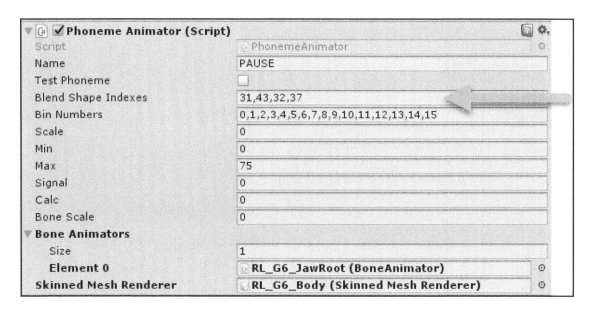

Setting all the Blend Shape Indexes for reset during PAUSE phoneme

The **PAUSE** phoneme is used as a reset to no vocalization. Therefore, it needs to be able to reset any of the blend shapes that may have been modified by the other phonemes.

10. After you are done making your various edits, make sure everything is off test and run the scene again. Hopefully at this point, you are happy with the lip syncing, but if not, you can try and go back to tweak the settings as needed. Just be aware of the limitations that this lip sync system has.

Now that we have everything set, you should have a reasonably good lip sync mimic of your vocals or anyone else you want to use. Remember, there are limitations with this lip sync system, which could be overcome with better phoneme detection algorithms, like those you would find in a speech recognition API. We will leave it up to the reader on their own to open the various new scripts and understand how they work if they so desire. In the next section, we are going to cover recording vocals with Unity for later playback through the character lip sync system.

QUIZ TIME
Answers to the quiz will be provided before the end of the chapter.

Which of the following is not a phoneme?
a) AHHHH
b) OH
c) DOH
d) FUH

What would be the best way to animate eye blinking?
a) Animate the eye bone
b) Animate the eye blend shape
c) Animate the eye lid blend shape
d) Animate the eye blink blend shape

Which of the following is NOT a key element in character lip syncing?
a) Phoneme detection in vocals
b) Animations of character bones and/or blend shapes
c) The size of the speakers mouth
d) The speakers language

Recording vocals

As much as we now have a real-time lip sync system running, you will of course still want to have in game characters lip sync vocal instructions to your players. In order to do that, we need the ability to record vocals or other sounds. How about instead of using different audio recording software we use Unity to record the audio directly. That way, we can also use this recording system to record sounds in a game just like those Foley artists do.

Open up Unity and follow the directions here to create a recording scene:

1. From the menu, select **File** | **New Scene**.
2. After the new scene is created, select from the menu **GameObject** | **Create Empty** to create a new object in the **Hierarchy** window. Rename this new object `Recorder` and make sure the **Transform Position** is set to 0.
3. Locate the **MicrophoneRecorder** script in the **Project** window and drag it onto the new `Recorder` object in **Hierarchy** window. This will automatically add a new **Audio Source** and **Microphone Recorder** components to the object.

4. Set the parameters on the **Microphone Recorder** component to those shown in the screenshot here:

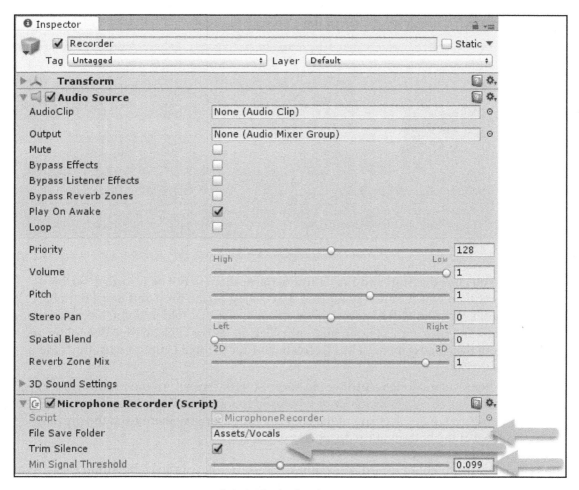

Setting the Microphone Recorder parameters

Setting those parameters allows for the recorded files to be saved and also trimmed of any leading or ending areas of silence. Trimming silence can be quite useful in recording and eliminates the need for you to do this later. As well, the Min Signal Threshold will allow you to block out background noise or any other noise distractions that can be common if you don't have a proper recording room. Of course, there are much better ways to record audio and we will look at one of those in Chapter 10, *Composing Music*.

5. When you are ready, run the scene. After the scene starts, you will see a **Record** button on the **Game** view. Click on the button to start recording and then press either the stop button to stop and save or stop and play the recording. The interface buttons are shown in the screenshot here:

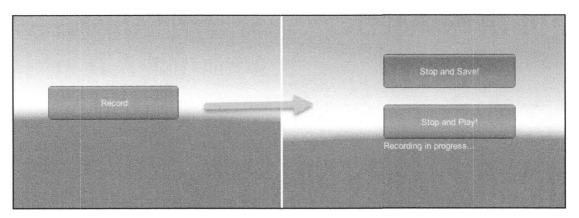

The button interface for the MicrophoneRecorder script

6. If you click the **Stop and Play!** button, the audio will not be recorded. So, be careful on which button you press. By clicking on the **Stop and Save!** button, audio wav files will be saved to the `Assets/Vocals` folder. If you are unable to view any files in this folder, just right click on (*Ctrl* + click on Mac) the folder and from the context menu select **Refresh** in order to force Unity to relist the folders contents.

7. When you are done recording the audio stop the scene. All the recordings will be in the `Assets/Vocals` folder or whatever you set it to. They will all be auto numbered. Just select any of the clips and you can play them from the preview panel at the bottom of the **Inspector** window.

You now have the ability to record some quick vocals or other audio right within Unity. We won't spend anytime looking at the scripts that are used to do this since they are complicated and likely only of interest to the more developer focused reader anyway. Feel free to extend those recorder scripts for any other application and purpose you require.

QUIZ TIME ANSWERS
The answers are marked in bold.

Which of the following is not a phoneme?
a) AHHHH
b) OH
c) DOH - for Homer Simpson maybe, covered by OH
d) FUH

What would be the best way to animate eye blinking?
a) Animate the eye bone
b) Animate the eye blend shape
c) Animate the eye lid blend shape
d) Animate the eye blink blend shape

Which of the following is NOT a key element in character lip syncing?
a) Phoneme detection in vocals
b) Animations of character bones and/or blend shapes
c) The size of the speakers mouth - mouth size could affect vocal tone but this is covered with answer a
d) The speakers language

Summary

During this chapter, we extended our audio visual capabilities we developed in the last chapter into real-time character lip syncing. We first put together a novel lip sync example using just our basic audio visualizer. From there, we looked at how we could make our lip syncing more realistic and natural by understanding speech phonemes. After that, we ran through an exercise on understanding how to classify speech phonemes by using our audio visualizer. This lead to our need to animate the characters jaw and facial muscles using a combination of bone and blend shape animation. We also took time exploring by attempting to model each of the base speech phonemes. With all that knowledge gained, we then put everything together and tested the real-time lip syncing. Finally, we looked at a component that would allow us to use the microphone to record directly to Unity. Something we certainly could find useful.

In the next chapter, we enter a new more fundamental area of audio development, composition. Here, we will explore a number of techniques and methods to compose sound and music for games.

10
Composing Music

There are numerous websites available that provide free access to great sound effects and music. However, most of these sites are essentially artist demo and portfolio sites, where they feature their wares or talents. While in some cases this will work for games that only require a few effects or music, it certainly doesn't scale well; especially, if you plan to incorporate adaptive music throughout your game. In such a case, having the ability to compose or mix and match your own music becomes essential. Composing your own music does require additional knowledge and time, but with the advent of excellent software, it may not be as difficult as you think. Furthermore, even if you don't have the time to compose your own music at a minimum understanding, the basics of music theory and composition will make you a better adaptive music designer or developer.

In this chapter, we are going to explore music and sound composition. We will start with downloading a music composition tool called **Reaper**. After that, we will cover the basics of music theory and composition. We will then use that knowledge to develop a unique score and record it. Here is a summary of the topics we will be covering in this chapter:

- Getting started with Reaper
- MIDI and virtual instruments
- Basic music theory
- Enhancing the composition
- Recording music and vocals

In this chapter, we will have no contact with Unity or FMOD, yet we may still put things in the context of those software products. If you have jumped ahead to this chapter and have a basic understanding of audio mixing, then you should be alright to continue. However, if you have no background in audio mixing then you should go back to the start of the book and review the first three chapters.

Getting started with Reaper

There are numerous music composition tools that range from free basic tools that will allow you to quickly and easily compose music to full-fledged pricey professional tools that will let you do everything else and more. Reaper falls on the more high end of professional tools, but it is priced very reasonably and provides for a substantial trial period of 60 days. It only makes sense then that you learn to work with a more capable tool. If we started with a free basic tool, it is likely you would quickly outgrow it. Let's get started by downloading and installing Reaper by following the instructions as follows:

1. Open you web browser to `http://www.reaper.fm/`.
2. At the top of the page, click on the **Download Reaper** link to go to the downloads page.
3. Scroll to the bottom of the page and select the version **Windows** or **Mac** and 32 or 64 bit, that best matches your operating system and click on the link to start downloading the software.

 Linux installation of Reaper is supported through the use of WINE. WINE is the compatibility layer that will allow you to run supported Windows applications on top of Linux. You can learn more about WINE at `https://www.winehq.org/`.

4. Wait for the software to download and then launch as you normally would any other application.
5. Follow the software installation utility to install the software into it's default location.
6. When the software has finished installing, launch Reaper as you normally would any application. Depending on your installation, the software may automatically run after being installed.

7. After the software launches, you will see an interface similar to the following screenshot:

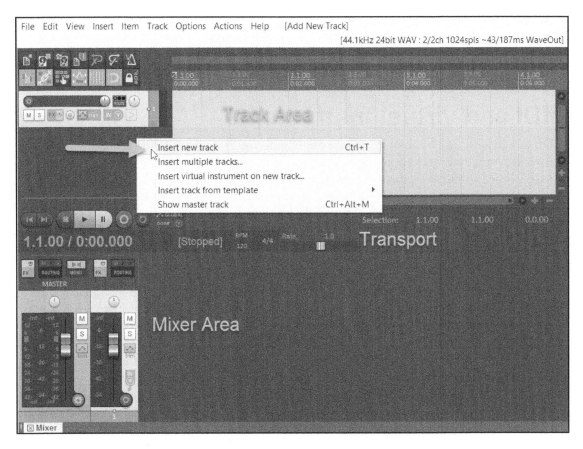

Basic Reaper interface with track loaded

8. Right-click (*Ctrl* + click on Mac) on the dark gray area beside the track area, and then from the menu, select Insert new track. This is also shown in the preceding screenshot.

9. If you want, you can press the play button, but there is no audio tracks so there will be nothing to hear.

Reaper is a professional commercial tool for music composition, so don't be surprised if the interface is a little overwhelming at first. However if you have followed along through the book or done sound design previously, then several elements of the interface will seem quite familiar by now. While the first part of the installation was straightforward, we still need to configure some other elements in order to get completely up and running, which we will do so in the next section.

MIDI and virtual instruments

MIDI, which is short for Musical Instrument Digital Interface, is a standard that describes an interface or way for computer devices to recognize musical input. While the standard was developed in the early days of computer-synthesized music, it really has become the interface for everything we do in modern music production. However, many people still confuse the use of MIDI to represent the digital representation of music, which it is not. Perhaps the simplest way to think of MIDI is as a complex form of music notation. In order to help demonstrate that concept, we will open up Reaper and import an MIDI song by following the instructions given here:

1. Open Reaper, and from the menu, select **File | New Project**. This will clear out the workspace and reset any changes you may have made. If you are asked to save the current project, just click on **No**.

2. From the menu, select **Insert | Media item**. An **Import file into project** dialog will display. Use the dialog to navigate to the location you downloaded the book's source code and to the `Chapter_10_MIDI` folder. Select the **Movie_Themes_-_The_Sting_-_The_Entertainer_by_Scott_Joplin.mid** file and click on **Open** to load the song.

3. An **MIDI File Import** dialog will prompt you to choose some options. Just confirm that both of the options are selected and click on **OK** as shown in the following screenshot:

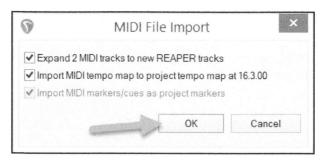

MIDI File Import dialog and options

4. After the MIDI file is imported, you will notice two new tracks have been added to the track area. These tracks look somewhat different than the audio wave files we are used to working with. The following is a screenshot showing how this will look in Reaper:

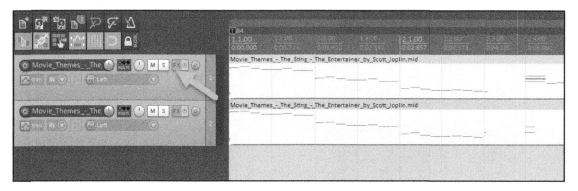

MIDI tracks imported into Reaper

 The MIDI tracks are actually showing the musical notation or notes that will be played at any point in time. Looking at MIDI in this way, you can see that it is not unlike the old punch cards or rolls that were used in the old western player pianos. If you have ever watched the opening credits to the HBO drama Westworld, that analogy should be quite clear now.

5. Press play and listen. There is no sound. The reason for that is because we need to add a MIDI instrument to our tracks.

 While we do have the musical notation defined, what we don't have is an instrument to play those notes, which, in our case, it might be a synthesizer or any virtual instrument. Now, that doesn't mean we need to have a MIDI keyboard or other MIDI instrument, as we can get using a virtual instrument instead.

6. Click on the small **FX** button on the first track in the list; the button is highlighted in the previous screenshot. This will open a couple of dialogs. Select the Add FX to bring the dialog to the front. Then, select the Instruments group on the right panel and after that select the **VSTi:ReaSamplOmatic5000(Cockos)** instrument as shown in the following screenshot:

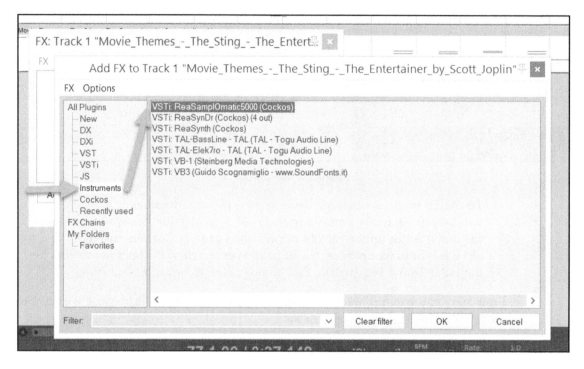

Selecting the ReaSamplOmatic5000 instrument

7. After you select the instrument, click on the **OK** button. The background **FX:** dialog will now take center stage with a confusing set of options. Click on the **Browse** button and use the **Open media file:** dialog to locate the books downloaded source code `Chapter_10_Audio` folder. Select the `sting_piano_c6.wav` file and click on **Open** to load the file. Then, select the **Freely configurable shifted** option from the **Mode** drop-down as shown in the following screenshot:

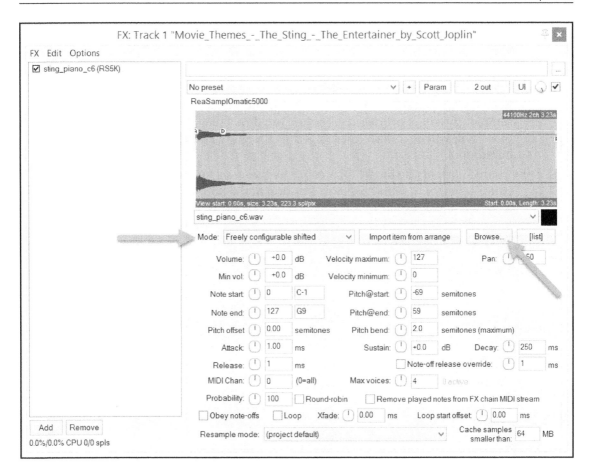

Setting up the ReaSamplOmatic5000 instrument sampler

The virtual instrument we are using here is called a Sampler. By setting the media file into the sampler, we are essentially telling it how one note sounds. The sample then creates the other notes as needed, very much like we did with our simple keyboard we built back in `Chapter 2`, *Scripting Audio*. You will learn more about virtual instruments later in this chapter.

8. Click on the start of the project home button at the far left of the control panel. This will move the play head to the beginning of the tracks. Then, press the play button to start the playing and listen/watch. As the play head scrolls across the tracks, you will see and hear the notes play.

9. Repeat steps 6 and 7 for the second track and just use the same settings for the sampler virtual instrument. After you are done, play the composition again. Now, you will hear both tracks playing a melody and chords, using the same instrument.

10. Double-click inside the MIDI area of the first track and this will open the MIDI editor window. Use the zoom in + button at the bottom right of the new window to zoom in to a few similar to the following screenshot:

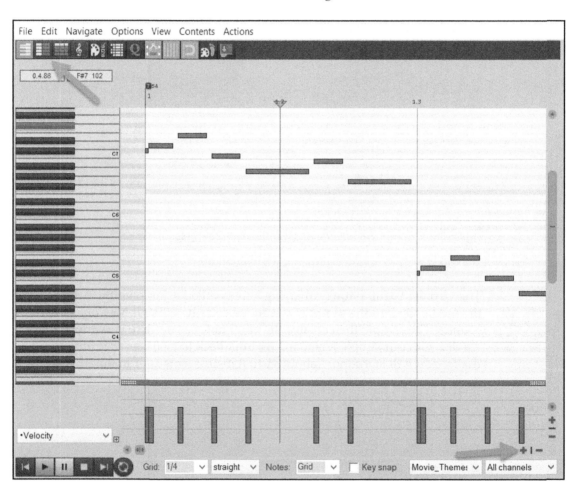

MIDI editor showing a piano roll view

The default view for the MIDI editor is called the piano roll. The name piano roll is well suited because the notes look like cutouts in an old piano player roll. You can change the view by clicking on the various toolbar buttons. There is even a musical notation view on the end (musical staff) that can show you how the MIDI track would look on sheet music.

11. Use your mouse to click on the piano keys on the keyboard at the left, and you will hear each of the notes. From here, you can also add or edit the notes on the track. We will leave doing that until later. For now, just look through the menus and play some piano.

To be clear, we have only just scratched the surface for what MIDI fully encompasses. However, the preceding exercise should provide you with a basis now for how we can use MIDI to compose sound or music. As you move through the software, you can also likely appreciate now how powerful and fully functional Reaper is. It may not be as slick as other packages, but for the price, it is remarkable. In the next section, we will cover another aspect of MIDI, the use of virtual instruments.

Virtual instruments

MIDI is a broad standard that covers many aspects for the interface of musical instruments with computers. The piano roll view of notes we looked at, in the end of the last section, could be thought of as a message from an instrument to a computer or vice versa. Yet, since the standard also covers the instrument interface for MIDI devices such as keyboards and synthesizers, it only follows that it could be extended to create effects and virtual instruments or VSTs. A VST or virtual studio technology is another way of describing an audio interface. The instrument we used in the last exercise is known as a sampler, because it creates notes from sampled media. The following is a list of the types of VSTs available:

- **VST-FX**: This group covers audio effects like reverb, echo, equalization, and so on. If you have been a consistent reader throughout the book, you should feel right at home using many of those effects by now.
- **VST-MIDI**: This is a type of effect that allows for the transpose and/or routing of MIDI to other instruments. It's not something we will worry about in this chapter.
- **VSTi**: This stands for virtual studio technology instrument or just virtual instrument. There are different types of virtual instruments described here:
    - **Synthesizer**: These create tones/notes from any sound generation technique. Synthesizers were very characteristic of MIDI music for the longest time. Now, they are as common as any other instrument.

- **Samplers**: These sample a media file and then use that to generate tones/notes. An extension of this is called a ROMpler, which has predefined media already tuned to sound like a physical instrument. The ROM in ROMpler stands for read only memory, which just means these instruments are read only. We will explore some of these in the next exercise.
- **Drum machine**: Similar to synthesizers, these instrument creates tones/notes that are specific to drum sounds.

In most cases a VST will be a software plugin that is specific to the operating system. A windows VST will not work on a Mac for instance. There are a huge number of freely available VST plugins available for Windows but unfortunately Mac users will have less luck finding good plugins. This is because Apple's competing protocol Audio Units is often more preferred.

 An excellent music composition tool called **GarageBand** is freely available for the Mac. It uses the Audio Unit protocol to describe effects and virtual instruments. While the software won't have all the options of Reaper, it still may be a platform worth investigating for some Mac users, if you haven't already done so.

Open up Reaper again and we will take a look at how to set up and install a third-party VSTi ROMpler plugin by following the instructions:

 The following exercise is specific to Windows installations so certain details may be different if you are a Mac user. However, the concepts should be the same on both platforms.

1. From the menu, select **Options | Preferences**. This will open up the **REAPER Preferences** dialog. Look on the left side of the dialog and select the **VST** group and you will see the following dialog:

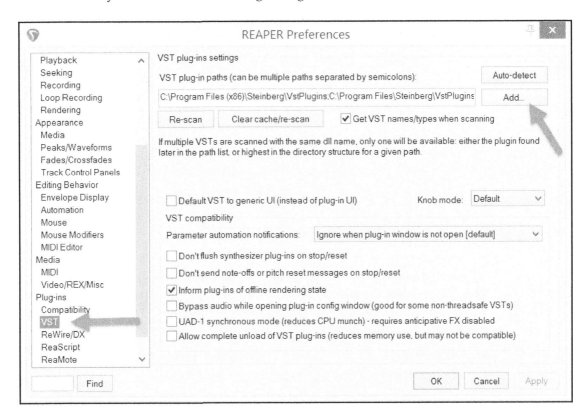

Adding a VST plugins folder

2. Click on the **Add** button, as shown highlighted in the screenshot, and use the **Browse for Folder** dialog to find the `Chapter_10_VST` folder in the book's downloaded source code. An example of how this will look on Windows is shown in the following screenshot:

Selecting the VST folder that matches your OS platform

 If you plan to use Reaper extensively and will be downloading numerous plugins, then you should create a new VST folder on a drive with lots of space. VST folders have been known to grow into the 10's or 100's gigabyte range.

3. Click on **OK** after you set the folder. Then close the preferences dialog.
4. Click on the **FX** button on the top track to open the **FX:** dialog.
5. Then, click the **Remove** button at the bottom left of the dialog to remove the sampler VST we previously configured.
6. Click on the **Add** button and this will open the **Add VST to Track** dialog. From the dialog menu, select **FX | Scan for new plugins**. This will load the new plugins, or in this case, VST instrument. Select the **VSTi:VSCO2 Piano (Bigcat)** instrument from the instruments group and click on **OK**. This will open the ROMpler settings panel. Stick with the defaults and then close both dialogs.

 It is customary for most VST plugins to showcase a cool looking interface that may represent a hardware version of the device or something more abstract. In most cases, plugin interfaces will rarely share anything in common and you will often need to just fidget with the controls to see how things work.

7. Press the play button to play the audio and try to listen for how this virtual instrument sounds compared to the sampler we used earlier. If you pay attention to the high and low tones on the first track, you will notice that the new instrument plays much better. This is because ROMplers sample from a wider variety of preset media files and they have already been preset for the best experience.

8. When you are done listening, stop the audio. If you are still unsure of the difference in the way the instruments sound, repeat the previous exercise to load the sampler and play again.

Windows users may have noticed that included in the book's source code is a whole collection of other ROMplers from DSK Music. Victor with DSK Music was gracious enough to provide us rights to distribute several of his excellent instruments. Each of the plugins from DSK actually contains, in most cases, numerous instruments. Here is an example screenshot from the **DSK Overture** ROMpler:

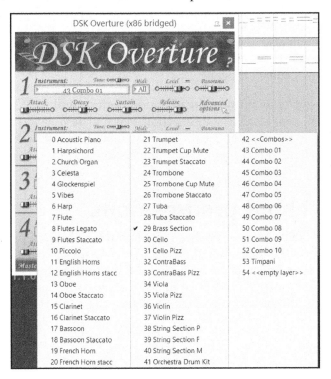

DSK Overture showing it's orchestra of instruments

There are literally thousands of VST instruments and effects out there freely available for download. However, not all VSTs are alike, and many can be unstable or just do not work right. So, finding the VSTs that work for you may take some time. Commercial VSTs are another option, but keep in mind these plugins are made for industry professionals. This means they will be at a premium cost but also better in quality.

Now that we have Reaper set up with virtual instruments and MIDI tracks, it is time for us to move onto some basic music theory in the next section.

Basic music theory

First off, we will start with a disclaimer and state that this section is not intended to teach you music theory. In fact, a whole book could be written on just teaching basic music theory. The goal of this section is to teach you a few basics on music theory and some simple tricks to prototype music for your game or just fun. It is hoped that the knowledge of music composition will also assist you with working with sound designers or developing adaptive music for games. If you like composing your own music, you can certainly explore more learning resources online or locally.

 For those of you with an already good understanding of music theory, you may still want to review this section as it will be relevant to the later sections in the chapter. However, remember that this section is intended for people with no knowledge of music theory.

Chords and chord progressions

A chord is a harmonic set of notes or pitches that sound as if they are played simultaneously. They are the root of tonal classic western music. This is the style of music now common in games and the one we will compose in. To keep things simple, we will just look at the major and minor triad chords, so named because they comprise of three notes. The following is a diagram showing an example of the major and minor triad chords:

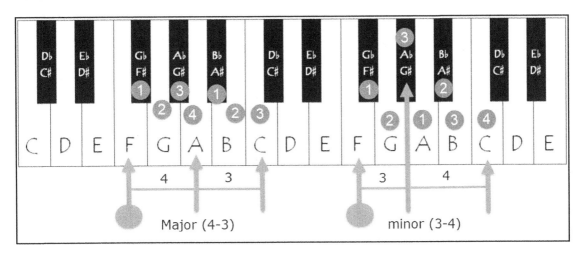

Example of Major and Minor chords in F

The diagram shows an example of a major and minor chords in F. We call it an F chord because our first note is F, as you can see in the diagram. From there, it is just a matter of counting. For a major chord, we count four notes (white and black keys) to the next note, an A. After that we count another three notes to the last note, a C. With minor chords, it is the opposite. Starting again with F, we count three notes to G# and then another four notes to C. In order to understand this better, how about we drop these two chords into a MIDI track by following the instructions:

1. Open up Reaper, and from the menu, select **File** | **New Project** and when prompted to save the project select **No**.
2. From the menu, select **Insert** | **Virtual instrument on new track**. This will open the **FX:** dialog. Select and configure the sampler piano we used earlier or another VSTi piano or keyboard you may have downloaded. Close the dialog when you are done setting up the virtual instrument.
3. From the menu, select **Insert** | **New MIDI item**. This will add an empty four bar MIDI item. Double-click within the MIDI item to open the MIDI editor.

4. Find the F key; somewhere around **C4** or **C5** is good. The F key is always the white key left of the grouped three black keys. Click on the key to list to the note. Then, use your mouse to draw the notes across the track to fill one bar (four notes at 1/16). Count four notes up from F and draw another set of four notes. Do this again, but this time count three notes up from the last note and again draw the notes. When you are done, your screen should resemble the following screenshot:

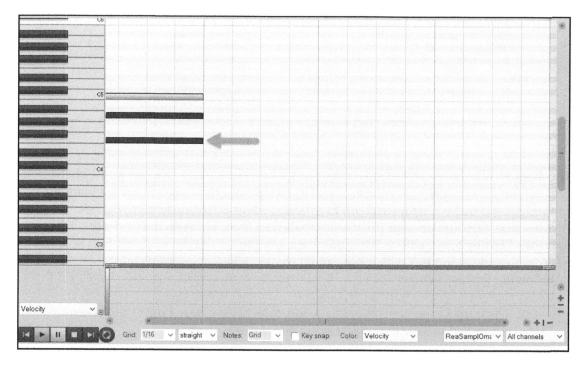

Writing the F Major chord on the MIDI track

5. Press the play button at the bottom of the window to play the track. When the track plays, it should sound harmonious; if it doesn't, then you may have done something wrong.

6. Now, we will repeat the process for the minor chord. Again, start at the F note just above the last chord, but this time start drawing notes after the first chord on the second bar. Then, just as before, start counting. Remember though a minor chord is three notes first and then four notes. After you have drawn the minor chord, your MIDI track should resemble the following screenshot:

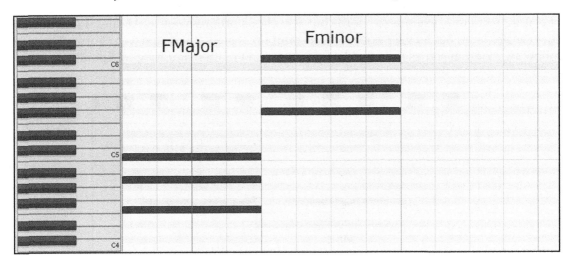

Major and minor chords added to the MIDI track

As a matter of convention, we will always refer to Major with a capital M and minor with a lowercase m. Thus, the shorthand form of F Major would be FM or often just shortened to F. For F minor, the shorthand form is Fm.

7. Again, play the track and listen to the two tracks together. If you only want to hear the minor chord, move the play head at the top of the timeline to the second bar just before the minor chord. When you are done listening, save your project so we can return to it later.

One thing you may notice is that those two chords when played together sound harsh. Now assuming we don't want this harshness, how do we know which chords will work together and provide the basis for our theme? We will cover some basic chord progression tips and how they can be applied to themes in the next section.

Chord progression

Probably the first time you played with any musical instrument, you quickly realized that just mashing keys or notes just sounds awful. However, what you may not have realized is that there are actually some basic rules or theories we can use to make music. So far, we have covered the basic counting rules for constructing a major or minor chord. This method of counting not only extends to chords but also chord progressions and scales. We will cover scales later, but let's see how we can count the distance between two chords. The following diagram shows two chords, the key doesn't matter, and how we count the distance between chords:

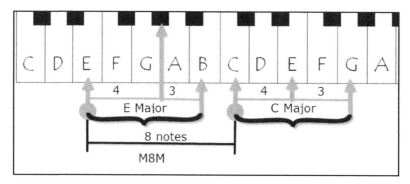

Counting the distance between two Major chords

We count the distance between two chords from the root or the starting note of the chord. In the diagram, we start with E and then count the keys up from there to the next root of the second chord. Try counting the distance between the two chords on your own. Remember that counting starts on the next key, and we count all keys (black and white). Go back and count the keys between the last chords in the last exercise. Since we went from an F major to F minor, there will be 12 keys or one octave. In the preceding diagram, we use a form of shorthand to denote the chord type and distance (M8M).

Interestingly enough, some smart people have identified how the distance between chords relates to the theme of music in movies, television, and games. The following table shows chord progression distances that are common among the various themes:

Theme	Chord Progression	Shorthand	Examples
Protagonism	Major 2 Major	M2M	Back to the future
Outer space	Major 6 Major	M6M	Star trek
Fantastical	Major 8 Major	M8M	Lord of the rings
Sadness, loss	Major 4 minor	M4m	Lost
Romantic	Major 5 minor	M5m	Stargate
Wonder	minor 5 Major, Major 7 minor	m5M, M7m	Night at the museum
Dark mysterious	minor 2 Major	m2M	Batman
Dramatic	minor 11 Major	m11M	Dark knight
Antagonism	minor 6 minor, minor 8 minor	m6m, m8m	The Empire strikes back

In order to demonstrate this concept, we will extend the example we showed in the preceding diagram. As we can see from the diagram or counting the notes, the progression is M8M using our shorthand. Then, if we consult our preceding table, we will see that relates to a fantastical or fantasy theme. So, let's see how this sounds by drawing this on our MIDI track by following the directions:

1. Open up Reaper and go to the MIDI editor window. Right-click (*Ctrl* + click on Mac) and drag the mouse around all the notes we previously drew. When you release the mouse, the notes will be selected and a context menu will appear. Select **Delete** from the menu to delete all the notes.

2. Locate the **E** key around **C4**. You can easily find **E** as it is the white key just to the right of the grouped two black keys. Draw the notes on **E** to fill a measure (four notes). Then, continue the process and count 4-3 to finish drawing the chord.

3. Right-click (*Ctrl* + click on Mac) and drag select all the notes you just drew. From the menu, select **Edit** | **Copy** to copy the notes. Then, select the area just past the root note on the E chord, and from the menu select **Edit** | **Paste**. You will now have a duplicate of the E chord as shown in the following screenshot:

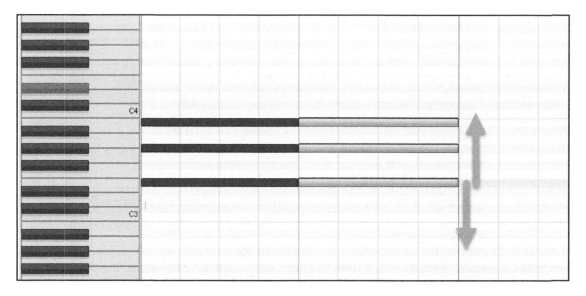

Duplicating the Major chord

4. Now, click to drag the selected notes, the second chord, up or down eight notes. Notice that you don't have to count keys, you can instead just count the grid lines. Since this chord is already a Major chord, no matter where we move it, up or down, it will always be Major.

Duplicating a chord and then just dragging it up or down is a great way to test various themes. At this point, you could quickly make any of the other chord progressions: M2M, M6M, or M8M.

5. After you are done editing, play the track and listen. This sounds much more natural, but with only two measures, it is difficult to tell.

6. Select all the notes and copy them. Then, click in the area on the third measure and paste the notes. Adjust the chords so that they are inverted and look like the following screenshot:

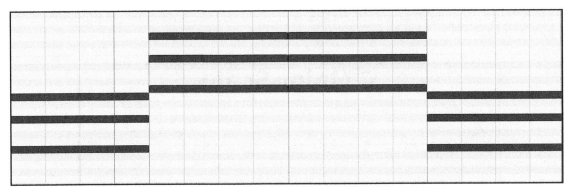

Inverting the chords to fill the four bars of the measure

7. When you are done editing, play the tracks and listen to the composition. We can of course alter those chords any way we like, but follow along with the notes and chords we have chosen in this example for now.

Now that we have some chords down, the next thing we generally will do is add a melody and this is what we will cover in the next section.

Melody and scale

A melody could best be described as the interesting or distinct part of a tune. While the chords establish the base notes and tone, a melody is what we often recognize a song for. Now, you probably are not going to compose a classic melody in your first session, but you will be surprised at what simple melodies you can create.

Before we jump into composing the melody, we need to understand a little about what a scale is. A scale is a set of notes or pitches that we know will sound good together. Now, there are many different forms of scales and how they are defined. For our purposes, we are going to use a classic form to derive the scale or notes we can use when constructing our melody. The following diagram shows how a diatonic scale is derived by counting whole and half tones:

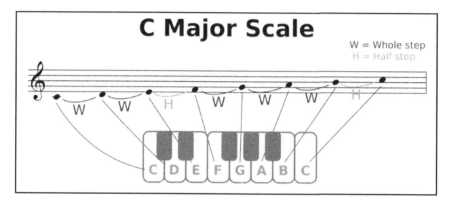

The C Major scale

The preceding diagram shows how you count out the notes for a C Major Scale. A W represents a whole tone or two notes and an H represents a semi-tone or single note. Looking at the diagram, you can see how we could just count out the notes of any major or minor chord. However, we are going to use an even simpler method to generate the notes for our scale. Of course, if you have some music theory under your belt and are comfortable finding all the notes on a scale, by all means use that.

The C Major Scale, as you may have noticed in the diagram, is all the white keys. This can make composing simpler in C Major, but realize that at some point, you will likely want to introduce other scales to your music.

In order to demonstrate our simpler scale method and start writing our melody, follow the instructions:

1. Open up Reaper from where we left off in the exercise. Move the MIDI editor window down and out of the way but don't close it.
2. Hover your mouse over the left end of the MIDI chord track and it will change to the drag symbol. Hold the mouse down and drag the end of the MIDI item so that it is covers 12 measures as shown in the following screenshot:

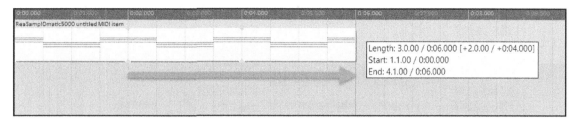

Length: 3.0.00 / 0:06.000 [+2.0.00 / +0:04.000]
Start: 1.1.00 / 0:00.000
End: 4.1.00 / 0:06.000

Extending the MIDI item

 You will notice that as you drag the MIDI clip over, it repeats the chords. This is because an automatic repeater has been added. If you open the MIDI editor for the chords, you will see a dark grey bar, denoting the repeat point has been added.

3. From the menu, select **Insert | Virtual instrument on new track**. Use the **FX** dialog to select and configure the same instrument you used for the chords track above it.
4. From the menu, navigate to **Insert | New MIDI item** and then drag the item to fill the same area as the track above it. Double-click on the MIDI clip to open another instance of the editor window.

5. Do your best to overlay the melody MIDI window over top the chord window but to the right so you can see the first set of notes. Scroll the melody up to around **C6** or **C7** and try to match the keys (C to C), but the melody side should be at least an octave higher. Then, draw single notes that match the chord keys as shown in the following screenshot:

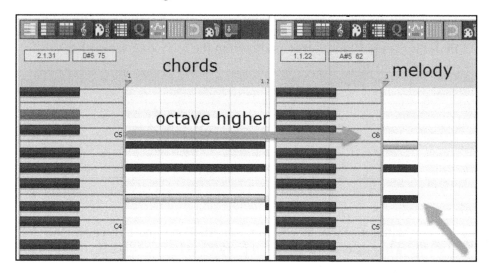

Placing the keys for the melody

You will almost always want to create a melody that is higher in pitch. A higher pitch puts more focus on the melody.

6. The three notes you drew will be our scale for the first chord. At this point, you can move those notes horizontally within the range of the first chord. Remember, you can't move the notes vertically as that would change the pitch and therefore the key. When you are done moving the notes, play the track and listen.

Using just three notes, we are obviously simplifying our songs. Yet, by only using three notes in each chord area we also force the use of space. Often, many beginning composers will want to fill every beat with a note, when it is better to compose some rest or space in your compositions. You certainly don't have to use all three notes and if you want you can optionally eliminate some.

7. Repeat steps 5 and 6 for each of the three remaining chords. Remember, you can only move the notes horizontally or 12 notes vertically (1 octave). As you add notes to your melody, keep playing the tracks and listen to the changes you are making. When you are happy with your melody, be sure to save the project.

Instead of trying to place notes randomly, when composing a melody, it is often helpful to have lyrics or an idea of the song's voice. If you are not a poet, just use a poem or other verse that fits the intent of what you are after. Then as you compose, sing the poem and place the notes where you want to highlight key phrases or emotions. Even though your song may not have vocals, you will likely be pleasantly surprised how well things come together.

If this is your first composition, don't worry about it sounding perfect. There will be plenty of time for improvement later. Just be satisfied that you have composed your first tune. In the next section, we are going to show you how to add some simple enhancements to the composition.

Enhancing the composition

Music, much like anything else, can be improved upon by adding some additional elements, such as a bass line and drums. This is no different than us enhancing the look of a scene through better lighting, shaders, or post effects. The overuse of enhancements can drown out the original intent. We, therefore, need to be careful and self-edit, in order to not go too far.

We are going to add a couple of additional tracks in order to enhance our very simple song and hopefully give it more depth and interest. Follow the instructions to add the new tracks to our composition:

1. Open up Reaper and from the menu and select **Insert | Virtual instrument on new track**. Then, when the **FX** dialog opens, this time select the **VSTi:ReaSynth(Cockos)** instrument. This is a synthesizer we are going to use as our bass line track. Select **OK** and then configure the instrument as shown in the following screenshot:

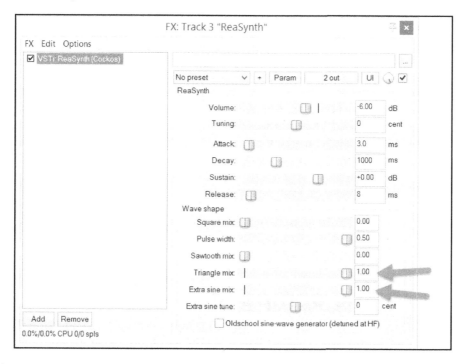

Configuring the ReaSynth synthesizer as a bass instrument

If you have other instruments that you have downloaded and would prefer to use for the bass, then go ahead. This is after all your song and you are in complete control.

2. From the menu, select **Insert | New MIDI track**. Drag the track to fit the same region as the tracks above it. Then, double-click on the MIDI region to open the editor.

3. For our base line, we are just going to alternate back and forth between the main key chords (E and C). Focus the editor on or around **C4** and draw the notes as shown in the following screenshot:

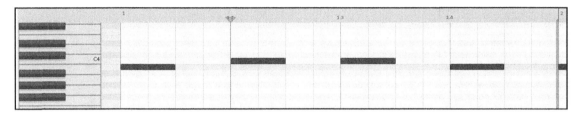

Drawing the notes for the bass line

4. Play the tracks and listen to how the bass line enhances the song. Of course, if you feel those bass line notes collide with the melody, then feel free to move them around or choose different notes. Just remember to use the same three-note scale. When you are done testing, close the bass line editor window.

5. From the menu, select **Insert | Virtual instrument on new track,** and when the FX dialog opens, select the **VSTi:ReaSynthDrum(Cockos)** instrument. You will be prompted with a **Build Routing Confirmation** dialog; just select **NO** to add any additional tracks.

6. From the menu, navigate to the **Insert** | **New MIDI** item and drag the MIDI clip to cover the same area as the preceding tracks. Double-click to open the editor and notice that this time some of the keys are labeled with drum sounds as shown in the following screenshot:

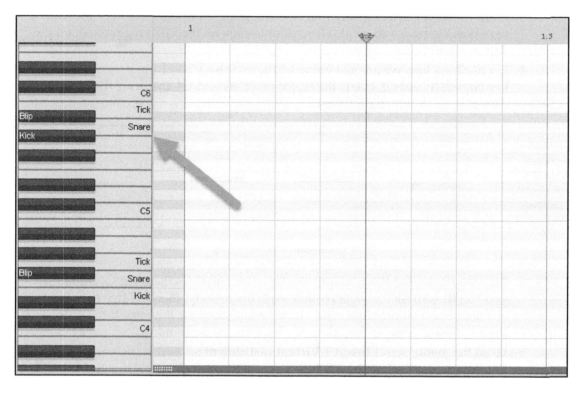

The labeled keys of the ReaSynthDrum instrument

7. Use your mouse to click on the various keys, and you will see only the labeled keys make sound. You can add a simple rhythm to your tune by drawing one note every three columns on the Snare. Try that beat and see how it sounds with the rest of the tracks. Chances are it may not blend with your melody, in which case you will need to adjust the notes to a more pleasant beat.

8. Try adding just a couple notes/tones in a beat or rhythm that works with your melody. At this point, you are on your own, but if you keep things simple, you should be fine. When you are done editing and are happy with your song, save the project.

If you are still having trouble composing anything you like, and it will happen, there is always another option. You can download other MIDI tracks of almost any music you want online. You can then use those MIDI tracks as a basis for editing and rebuilding your own music. This will even allow you to change instruments, tempo, and more from the original song. Unless you are going to purchase the rights to the song, just be careful on how much inspiration you use from well known music in your game score.

Now that we have a simple song completed, in the next section we are going to record it to file, for later playback in our game.

QUIZ TIME
Answer the following questions:

What does VSTi represent?
a) Visual Studio Technology Instrument
b) Virtual Studio Technology Instrument
c) Virtual Sound Technology Instrument
d) Visual Sound Technology Instrument

What counting sequence would you use to derive a Major triad chord in C#?
a) 3-3
b) 2-2-1-2-2-2-1
c) 3-4
d) 4-3

How many notes would you count going from C4 to C5?
a) 11
b) 7
c) 12
d) 10

Answers will be provided to the quiz before the end of the chapter.

Recording music and vocals

Now that we have our music composed, we can proceed to record or render our tracks as a combined song or perhaps just the individual tracks. Having the individual instruments on each track can, of course, be beneficial, especially when developing adaptive music using vertical remixing techniques. Likewise, understanding how the music changes can also help you horizontally re-sequence multiple songs more easily.

Follow the instructions to render the song we constructed to a media file:

1. Open Reaper to the project you have been developing your song in. From the menu, select **File | Render**. This will open the **Render to File** dialog. Enter a name for your song and then select the options as shown in the following screenshot:

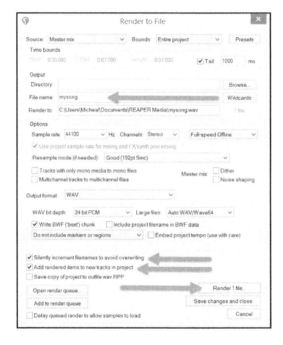

Setting the file name and options for rendering to a file

2. After you name the file and set the options, click on the **Render 1 file** button on the dialog. This will open another dialog where you will see in real time how the song is rendered to the file and what the resulting waveform looks like.

3. Click on the button labeled **Close** to close the dialogs. You will now see a new track has been added with your rendered audio clip. At this point you can solo the track by pressing the **S** button and listen to how the render went.

From this point, if you are not happy with how the song rendered, you can alter the mix using the controls to adjust the volume/output. At this point, in the book, you should be fairly comfortable mixing or adjusting the tracks as you need to. In the next section, we are going to showcase one other excellent use for Reaper, recording and optimizing vocals.

Recording and optimizing vocals

Recording vocals or any other sound you may need for your game can be frustrating. What you think should be easy often doesn't turn out that way. To make matters worse, if you need to record multiple vocal tracks with a proper recording space, the end result will be inconsistent and noisy. Fortunately, since Reaper is a commercial audio generation tool, it has a number of good effects that can optimize your vocals or other sounds.

Follow the instructions to record and optimize your vocals:

1. Open up Reaper and from the menu select **File | New Project**. If you haven't already saved your last project, you probably want to do so.

2. Double-click on the gray area beside the track area. This will add a new track. Click on the **Record Armed** button on the track and make sure that the **Record Input** option is selected on the input options as shown in the following screenshot:

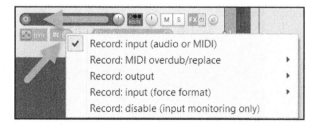

Setting the track recording options

3. When you are ready to start recording, type *Ctrl + R* (*command + R* on Mac). As the sound is recording, you will see a wave form being generated on the track. Wait for a count of three and then start recording the vocals. After you are done type *Ctrl + R* (*command + R)* to stop recording.

The reason we waited for a three count before we start, is to establish a base for the audio recording. This base will contain just the ambient noise of your recording room or equipment. This could be noise like hissing, heating vents, and other sounds you may not even notice.

4. Click on the red button on the track to disarm recording. Press play to listen to the vocals and you will likely notice some obvious noise now at the start of the recording. We will use an effect to remove that background noise from the recording.

5. Use your mouse to drag and select just below the audio clip track the region just before the vocals start. Don't worry about getting all of it; if you waited 3 seconds, there should be plenty to select. Then, click on the green **FX** button to open the **FX** dialog. Click the loop or repeat button on the play head controls located next to the record button.

6. On the **FX** dialog, select the **Cockos** group and then select the **VST:ReaFir(FFT EQ+Dynamics Processor)(Cockos)** effect. Click on **OK** to open the effect parameter settings. Set the **Mode** and option as shown in the following screenshot:

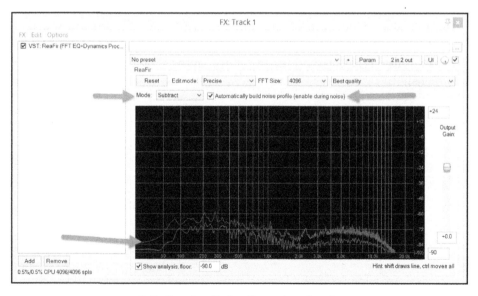

ReaFir effect settings with subtract filter set and recording audio

7. Press play to play just the leading section of the vocals. As the audio plays, you will see the noise sound being captured in the **ReaFir** effect as shown in the preceding screenshot. When you have let the audio section loop a couple of times, press the stop button. Uncheck the option **Automatically build noise profile** to turn off the noise capture.

8. Close the **FX** dialog and right-click (*Ctrl* + click on Mac), and from the context menu, select Remove Selection. Then, click on play again to play and listen to the audio. As you will hear, the noise in the audio has been completely removed.

Generally at this point, you would trim out the leading noise area and then add an EQ, compression and normalization effect. All of these effects are available in Reaper, and it is up to the reader to explore those in order to better optimize the vocals.

That covers our quick demo on recording vocals in Reaper. As you can see, there are plenty of capabilities and other effects you can apply to clean up and improve the audio recording.

QUIZ TIME ANSWERS

What does VSTi represent?
a) Visual Studio Technology Instrument
b) Virtual Studio Technology Instrument
c) Virtual Sound Technology Instrument
d) Visual Sound Technology Instrument

What counting sequence would you use to derive a Major triad chord in C#?
a) 3-3
b) 2-2-1-2-2-2-1
c) 3-4
d) 4-3

How many notes would you count going from C4 to C5?
a) 11
b) 7
c) 12
d) 10

Summary

In this chapter, we took a complete diversion from working with Unity and dove into music theory and composition using a professional composition and recording tool called Reaper. We started by downloading, installing, and configuring Reaper for basic use. After that, you learned about MIDI and how that could be used to allow us to compose our music. From there, we covered the use of virtual instruments within Reaper and how they would allow us add virtual sound to our MIDI tracks. With the background out of the way, we moved on to a very quick look at some music theory and simple composition rules we could use to build songs for our games. From there, we looked at adding a melody, bass line, and drum tracks. Then, we looked at how to render our songs to audio files. Finally, we covered the recording tools in Reaper and how you could clear up noisy sound.

In our next and final chapter, we will jump back into Unity and FMOD, where we will explore troubleshooting and performance tips.

11
Audio Performance and Troubleshooting

While Unity has done an excellent job redesigning it's audio system, it still manages to have difficulty optimizing audio resources. This default mismanagement of resources may cause performance issues for your target platform. Likewise, while FMOD is an excellent and powerful tool, it also has some performance pitfalls you need to be aware of, if it is your chosen audio system. In fact, understanding the performance limitations of either audio implementation may be a deciding factor for which system you use for your game and target platforms. After all, game development is always about squeezing every little bit out of your platform, in order to provide the best experience for the player. Finally, we will finish with various troubleshooting tips that can help you in your current and future audio development efforts.

In this chapter, we will cover audio performance and troubleshooting with Unity and FMOD. Performance tuning is an essential process for any aspect of game development and audio is no exception to this. After covering performance for both audio systems, we will review some helpful troubleshooting tips. The following is a summary of the main areas we will cover in this chapter:

- Audio performance considerations
- Profiling performance with Unity
- Audio optimization tips and tricks for Unity
- FMOD performance and optimization
- Audio troubleshooting

This chapter will work off from previous developed exercises. It is suggested that the reader should have at least reviewed the relevant chapters with Unity and/or FMOD, in order to cover the corresponding sections on performance. A reader with experience in Unity/FMOD could get by, assuming they have mastered the relevant software. This means, you should at least do a quick review up to `Chapter 5`, *Using the Audio Mixer for Adaptive Audio*, for Unity performance optimization and/or `Chapter 7`, *FMOD for Dyanmic and Adaptive Audio*, for the section on FMOD performance. For readers here looking for troubleshooting tips, jump ahead to the last section in the chapter.

Audio performance considerations

Before we dig into the details of profiling and tuning audio performance, we probably should go over the primary factors that determine an efficient audio system. When we talk about an audio system, we refer to all the components (Audio Source versus FMOD), resources (audio clips), mixes (Mixer versus FMOD), and effects. The major contributors to performance will be driven by the quality, size of resources, and/or the use of mixing and effects. Ultimately though, it all comes down to your chosen platform and the expected limitations of that platform. Since the type of platform is so important, we will consider those options first:

Platform	Performance benchmarks	Considerations	Pitfalls
Desktop (Windows/Mac/Linux)	**CPU:** excellent **Memory:** GB range **Disk space:** GB range	Less restrictive than other platforms, but may also be limited by other game systems such as physics or graphics	Using high quality or too many resources and audio components
Tablet (iOS, Android, and Windows)	**CPU:** good **Memory:** MB to GB range **Disk space:** MB to GB range	More restrictive than desktop due to lower memory and CPU.	A tablet deployment may share the same footprint as a phone, unless targeted explicitly for the tablet

Phone (iOS, Android, and Windows)	**CPU:** poor to good **Memory:** MB range **Disk space:** MB range	Memory and disk space will often be a prime concern	May require significant downgrading of the audio system if the game is targeted for multiple platforms.
Web	**CPU:** poor **Memory:** MB range **Disk space:** none	At present this will be the most restrictive platform. You need to be especially careful of resource memory and streaming	Unique restrictions on audio system make it best suited for single web target deployment

Now, we don't have time to go into the specific details for profiling and tuning performance for each platform, but we will talk about the main factors. It will then be up to the reader to apply those tips to their target platforms. The following table breaks down the elements of an audio system and how they can affect performance:

Element	Performance Considerations	Optimization	Notes
Audio sources or FMOD events	• Number of different audio sources in a scene • Instantiation of game objects with audio components	Carefully manage the number of sources in a scene	Object pooling is a good solution
Resources (audio clips)	• In game memory for each loaded audio clip • Loading time from the disk • Decompression impact on CPU	*Optimize audio resources by type	Unity defaults are poor and almost always need customization
Mixes	• Impact on CPU performance	Not a significant impact on performance but need to be careful with hidden effects	Be careful not to unintentionally replicate effects through groups or other levels of deep nested mixes

Effects	• Impact on the CPU • Impact on memory	*Optimization through careful use or reuse of effects	Easy to unintentionally replicate effects through mixing

As identified in the preceding table by the asterisk(*), the two critical elements of a Unity audio system will generally come down to resources and use of effects. That isn't to say that you couldn't get yourself into trouble with the other elements as well. Yet, for our purposes, we will focus on optimization tips and tricks for resources and effects. In the next section, we will go over audio performance profiling with Unity.

Profiling performance with Unity

There is no better way to understand performance profiling and optimization than by doing it. Therefore, in this section, we are going to get hands on and profile the example Viking village project as we last left it in Chapter 5, *Using Audio Mixer for Adaptive Audio*. Follow the instructions to open up Unity to the previously saved project:

1. Open up Unity and load the GameAudioBasics project you created earlier.

   If you have not previously created the GameAudioBasics project, create a new project in Unity called GameAudioBasics and download and/or import the Viking Village example project from the Asset Store. You can use the walk-through in Chapter 1, *Introducing Game Audio with Unity*, if you need help setting up the base project.

2. From the menu, navigate to **Assets | Import Package | Custom Package** and use the **Import** dialog to locate and open the Chapter_11_Assets folder within the book's downloaded source code. Select the **Chapter_11_Start.unitypackage** and click **Open**. Follow the dialog directions to import all the assets.

   If you have modified the original project and want to keep your changes then either make a copy of the project folder or create a new project and download the Viking Village starting project again.

3. After the package has finished importing, locate the Chapter_11_Start scene in the **Project** window and double-click on it to open it.

4. From the menu, navigate to **Window | Profiler**. This will open the **Profiler** window. Use your mouse to drag and dock the window beside the **Inspector** window so that it is docked like the following screenshot:

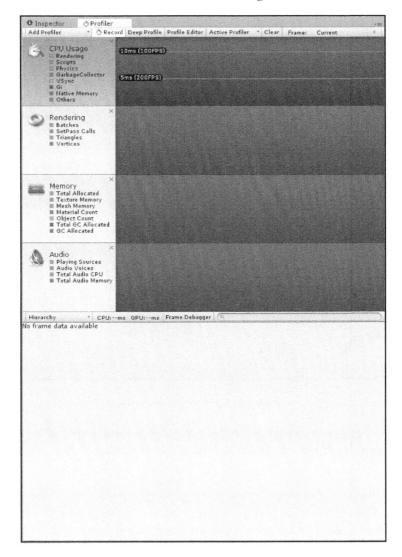

Profiler docked beside the Inspector window

5. Press play to run the scene now. Move around the scene with the *W*, *A*, *S*, *D* keys. Press *Esc* to unlock the mouse and then select the **Audio** panel on the **Profiler** window. This will display details about the audio performance as shown in the following example screenshot:

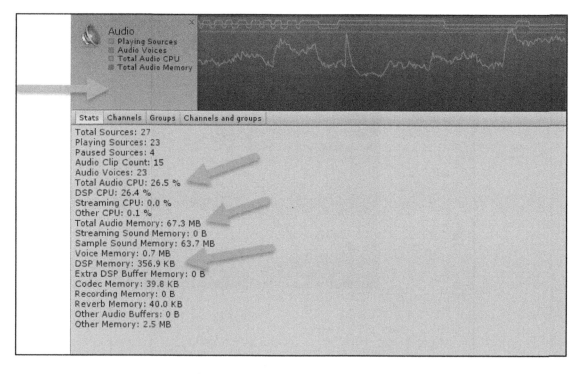

Examining the audio performance Profiler window and Stats

The stat percentages you see on your computer may be quite different. The important thing is to just watch how much and when they change.

6. There is obviously a lot going on here. For now though, focus on the highlighted **Stats** as indicated in the preceding screenshot. Continue to move around the scene and watch how the graph and **Stats** change.

7. When you are done, unlock the mouse and stop the scene.

This initial test has shown us that some good and bad things are happening with our scene. First, our memory usage is quite consistent and minimal at only around 67.3 MB. Of course, if this was to be a mobile game that number would likely be an issue, but for now we will consider it good. Second, our audio CPU usage is hovering around 20-25% on average and may peak as high as 30%. That is a significant problem, and if we look below the **Total Audio CPU** stat, you will see the culprit is the **DSP CPU**. **DSP** stands for **Digital Signal Processing**, or in other words, the audio processing the audio system is performing. In order to better understand how DSP affects performance, open up Unity and follow the given exercise:

1. Press play to run the scene and make sure the **Audio** panel is highlighted on the **Profiler** window. Move around the scene until you find an area where the **DSP** and **Audio CPU** usage is high.

2. From the menu, navigate to **Window | Audio Mixer**. If the **Audio Mixer** window doesn't dock beside the **Console** window, drag it into place. Select the **Master** group and make sure all the child groups are visible.

3. Hover your mouse around the pause button at the top of the editor and wait for what looks like a peak **Audio CPU** usage. When you think the stat is peaking, press the pause button to freeze the scene.

4. With the scene paused, click on the **B** button on all the mixer groups in the **Audio Mixer** window. When you are done, you mixer window should look like the following screenshot:

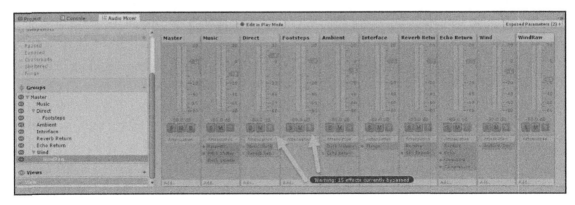

Bypassing all the effects on the Audio Mixer

If you recall, pressing the B button causes all the effects to be bypassed for that group.

5. After you are done bypassing all the groups, then press the pause button again to unfreeze the game. Watch closely the Audio graph and **Stats** panels on the **Profiler** window. You will see a very clear drop in CPU usage after the scene starts running again. An example of how this will look is shown in the following screenshot:

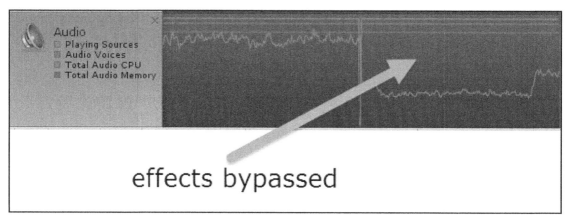

```
Audio
□ Playing Sources
■ Audio Voices
□ Total Audio CPU
■ Total Audio Memory
```

effects bypassed

Observing the impact on Audio CPU performance after bypassing effects

 You may notice that even as you turn off all the effects, after a while, the graph goes back to being high again. This is because the plots are normalized to show a maximum value. What this means is that you want to watch the chart for any significant changes, as we saw in the preceding screenshot.

6. Go back to the **Audio Mixer** window and click all the **B** button's again to enable all the effects. Then, click on the **Channels** tab on the **Profiler** window as shown in the following screenshot:

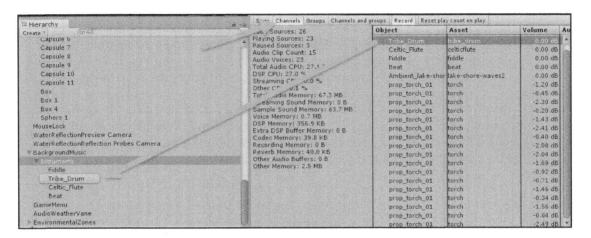

Viewing the currently active Channels (audio sources)

7. This tab will show you the currently active **Channels** or audio sources. Go through the list and double-click on the object to highlight it in the **Hierarchy** window. Select the object in the **Hierarchy** window and then disable it in the **Inspector** window. As you go through the list, make a note of the channels which appear to make the largest impact on performance. When you have disabled all the channels, your **Profiler** window will look like the following screenshot:

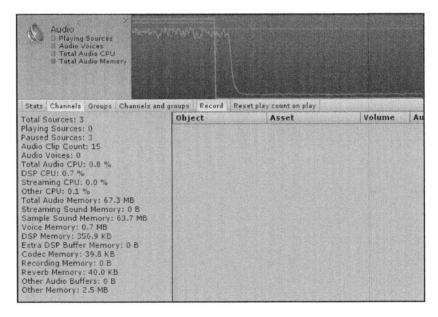

Audio Profiler view after all the Channels (audio sources) have been disabled

8. If you want, you can go back through the list of items again just by stopping and restarting the scene. Remember, that any changes you make to a game object during runtime will be reset when you stop the scene. After you have identified the list of sources and group effects that may be problematic, stop the scene.

What you may find surprising is that the four musical instruments are actually consuming more than half the DSP CPU. This is because of the adaptive music with vertical remixing we put together in Chapter 6, *Introduction to FMOD*, the adaptive and dynamic audio, is consuming the CPU. We will look at some options for this later, including considering FMOD for implementing adaptive audio.

That simple technique of just walking through the audio sources and bypassing effects will generally help identify CPU problems. However, it will not usually identify areas where audio memory may be a problem. We will look at techniques to resolve those memory and CPU performance issues in the next section.

Audio optimization tips and tricks for Unity

Now that we understand how to profile the audio performance system, we can more easily identify our potential problem areas. Keep in mind though, that not everything may be an issue and quite often fixing an issue in one area may cause problems in others. This is why you should constantly go back and profile the audio system with every optimization you perform. What you may see is that not every tip or trick works the way you think it should or the fix may be more costly in other areas.

As we mentioned in the first section, our primary interest will be in optimizing audio system memory and effects of DSP CPU usage. Therefore, we will break up both of these topics into sub-sections and start with audio memory optimization in the next section.

Memory optimization tips and tricks

In the previous profiling section, we observed a static usage of audio memory, which is very good. Yet, what if we wanted to deploy this same game to a mobile platform and needed to cut down on memory? Fortunately, there are a few tricks we can use in order to reduce the memory footprint of our audio clips in memory usage and on disk. We will review a few of those options and the trade-offs in the following exercise:

1. Open up Unity and open the `Assets/Audio/Ambient` folder in the **Project** window. Select the `lake-shore-waves2` audio clip. Then select the **Inspector** window and change the **Load Type** to **Streaming** as shown in the following screenshot:

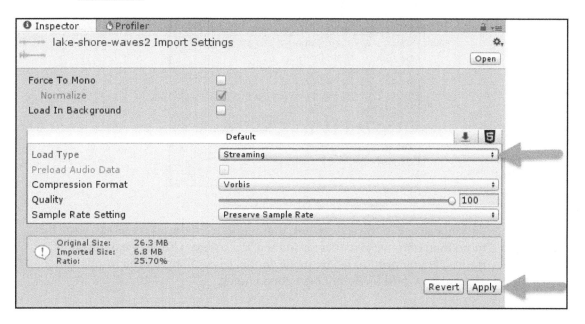

Changing the Load Type on an audio clip resource

2. Then, click on the **Apply** button to apply the changes to the resource. Locate the `viking_music` clip in the `Assets/Audio/Music` folder in the **Project** window. Select the clip and change the **Load Type** to **Streaming**, just as you did with the previous clip.

3. Press play to run the scene and open the **Profiler** window. Notice now how the memory usage has been cut by more than half. However, you will also notice that the `Streaming CPU` stat is now showing a value that is affecting our total CPU usage as shown in the following screenshot:

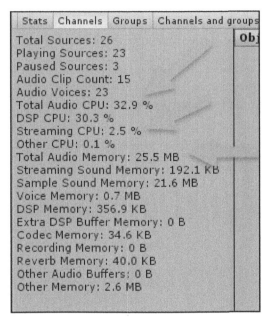

Stats	Channels	Groups	Channels and groups

Total Sources: 26
Playing Sources: 23
Paused Sources: 3
Audio Clip Count: 15
Audio Voices: 23
Total Audio CPU: 32.9 %
DSP CPU: 30.3 %
Streaming CPU: 2.5 %
Other CPU: 0.1 %
Total Audio Memory: 25.5 MB
Streaming Sound Memory: 192.1 KB
Sample Sound Memory: 21.6 MB
Voice Memory: 0.7 MB
DSP Memory: 356.9 KB
Extra DSP Buffer Memory: 0 B
Codec Memory: 34.6 KB
Recording Memory: 0 B
Reverb Memory: 40.0 KB
Other Audio Buffers: 0 B
Other Memory: 2.6 MB

Obj

Profiling the audio system after making changes to the resources

 As you can see in the screenshot, that while we reduced memory usage by more than half, we also increased the CPU usage. This is one of those trade-offs you need to be aware of. In this case, changing the resources to streaming would likely not be a good choice.

4. Go back to each of the audio clip resources you changed to Streaming and reset them back to **Decompress On Load** and make the changes as shown in the following screenshot:

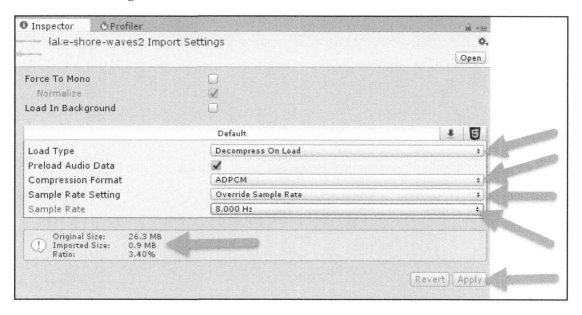

Resetting the audio clip to Decompress On Load and reducing the Quality

5. Click on the **Apply** button and notice how this changes the **Imported Size**. Be sure to do this for both of the clips.

> This is an extreme example where we are trying to reduce the file size as much as possible. In most cases, you may not want to reduce the Sample Rate as much.

6. Run the scene again and again bring up the **Profiler** window. You will now see the audio memory usage is half of what it was and there is no Streaming CPU usage. The trade-off here is the drastic reduction in the quality of the audio. Although, if you closely listen to the lake waves sound before and after the quality reduction, it will be difficult to tell there is a difference with all the other audio playing.

7. Locate the `grunt` audio clip in the `Assets/Audio/Direct` folder in the **Project** window and select it. Then, in the Inspector window, change the **Compression Format** to **PCM** and click on **Apply**. Notice, as shown in the following sample screenshot, how the **Imported Size** changes:

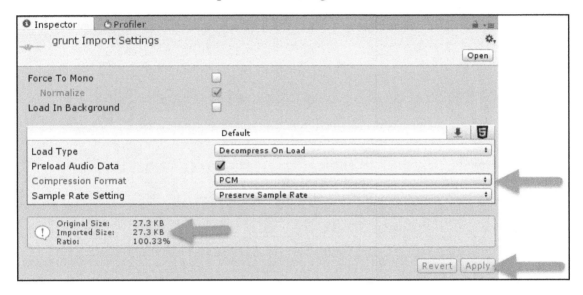

Changing the compression settings for the grunt audio clip

 Converting an audio clip, such as the grunt sound effect, to use a different compression format, is an excellent way to reduce memory usage. When this clip was imported, it used the default of vorbis. Vorbis is a good format for medium and long playing clips, but is not well suited to short clips.

8. Run the scene again and see if you can notice a difference in audio memory.

9. After you are done testing, stop the scene.

What we just demonstrated is a few ways in which we can reduce the memory footprint of audio resources. While there are more strategies to reduce the memory and CPU usage of audio resources, it becomes a balancing act on when to use them and for what type of audio. For instance, certain types of audio will work better with different strategies and the following table breaks this down for us:

Resource Type	Usage	Strategy	Notes
Ambient sounds or music	Continuously playing and medium to long in length	**Load Type :** Streaming **Compression Format :** Vorbis	Constantly loads the resource from disk. Low memory footprint but at the cost of Streaming CPU. Works well if the audio clip is especially large and playing constantly.
Ambient sounds, sound effects, instruments, music, or vocals	Rarely played but requires quick playback, medium to long in length	**Load Type :** Compressed in memory **Compression Format :** Vorbis **Quality :** Less than 100	Compresses the audio clip in memory. Reduction in memory footprint but at a cost of CPU. A good strategy for medium to large audio clips that need to play rarely but quickly.
Ambient sounds or music	Audio quality is not critical and medium to long in length	**Load Type :** Decompress On Load **Compression Format :** PCM or ADPCM **Sample Rate Setting :** Override sample rate	Reducing the quality of audio in order to save disk space and memory. A fallback strategy to use when you need to reduce platform deployment size. Depending on the audio and where it is used, this may be a good option.
Sound effects or instrument loops	Frequently played and short in length	**Load Type :** Decompress On Load **Compression Format :** PCM	PCM will load without any compression and play very quickly. In most cases, you will want to change all your imported short clips to use this setting.

Sound effects or instruments	Frequently played but medium in length	**Load Type:** Compressed in Memory **Compression Format :** ADPCM	ADPCM will create files 3-4x smaller than PCM. The file is compressed in memory, so it will consume CPU to play, but much less than Vorbis. Try using this setting on the four instrument looping sounds we used for the adaptive music vertical remix.
Sound effects	Rarely played and short in length	**Load Type :** Compressed in Memory **Compression Format :** ADPCM	Since the files are rarely played, it is better to use compression and suffer a small CPU penalty when playing.

Use the preceding table as a guide to adjusting the resource audio clip settings in order to improve your game's memory usage. If you are struggling with which strategy to use, try a couple of different ones and constantly profile the results. It may also be helpful in some instances to profile audio clip settings in isolated scenes. That way you can more easily determine the impact your changes make. In the next section, we will look at how we can optimize effects for better performance.

Effects optimization tips and tricks

During the previous profiling exercise, we noticed a significant use in DSP CPU, which as shown is a result of mixing effects and other signal processing. Unfortunately, unlike the memory optimization strategies we looked at in the last section, strategies for optimizing effects are more cut and dry. This means that, in most cases, if effect performance is a concern, you may need to remove those offending effects entirely. Another option is choosing to use another DAW tool saw as Reaper to premix the audio or another audio system such as FMOD.

Since we have already covered how to identify and disable problem effects, we will focus on the standard list of Audio Mixer effects in the following table and possible tips and/or tricks for optimizing performance:

Effect Type	Examples	Tips/Tricks	Notes
3D Spatial	Audio source 3D spatializer Occulus spatializer	Limits the number of audio sources using this effect. Changes the **MaxDistance** on the Audio Source 3D Sound Settings to a lower value.	Most developers may forget that this an effect that requires DSP. You will almost never want to go with the default **MaxDistance** of 500 for the standard Audio Source. The larger the effect distance, the longer this effect will consume DSP.
Frequency Filter	Lowpass (simple) Highpass (simple) ParamEQ	Limits the use of these effects to dynamic or script controlled. Balances or filters the audio before importing as a resource.	These effects can be quickly abused as a way to fix poor audio resources. Still very useful effects for dynamic scripting or vertical remixing.
Delay	SFXReverb Echo Chorus Flange	Routes multiple groups through a return with a single delay effect. Limits the use to one delay effect per mix if possible.	These are generally the most expensive effects and SFXReverb is at the top of the list. Use them sparingly and try to send multiple groups through the same effect.
Compression	Normalize Compressor Duck volume	Routes these effects through a return when possible.	If you are using Compressor and Normalize to fix vocals or other sounds, consider doing that offline in another DAW before importing. Duck volume is expensive so when possible route multiple groups through the same effect.

Bypass	Send Receive	Useful for processing multiple groups through the same effect.	Remember that a Send effect duplicates the signal, which creates additional DSP usage. Yet, this may be a good trade-off if routing multiple sources to a delay effect.
Snapshot	Snapshot	Limits the number of parameters being set within a snapshot to only what is needed.	Transitioning snapshots can be expensive if you have multiple parameters and have chosen non-linear transition methods.

Take your time reviewing the preceding table and use it as a reference when you find yourself profiling effect performance. It is also helpful to understand the impact an effect has on performance, when you are creating your mix within the mixer. While we mentioned snapshots, it is important to realize that a lot could be going on with transitions, none of which is shown in the profiler well. Often the only way you can profile snapshot transitions is by disabling the controlling component (script) and monitoring the effect on performance.

Before you take the time to make radical changes and eliminate effects it is usually best to determine if the DSP performance is in fact a problem. One way to monitor this is by seeing how the rendering frame rate performs as the DSP usage peaks. Chances are if the frame rate drops, you have a problem. At some point, it all becomes a bit of a balancing act on priorities between the rendering, physics, AI, and audio.

In the next section, we are going to take a look at how to profile and optimize performance when using FMOD as our audio system.

FMOD performance and optimization

The FMOD Studio audio system we worked with in Chapter 6, *Introduction to FMOD* and Chapter 7, *FMOD for Dyanmic and Adaptive Audio*, is external to Unity. It is helpful to remember that Unity actually uses FMOD for its core audio system. Therefore, many of the optimization strategies we have already discussed will apply equally well when working with FMOD Studio. What we will cover in this section is how to profile with FMOD and where to tweak settings in order to optimize performance.

This section on working with FMOD Studio will require you to have reviewed Chapter 6, *Introduction to FMOD* and Chapter 7, *FMOD for Dyanmic and Adaptive Audio*, at the least. Ideally, you should have worked through the FMOD Studio set up to install the software and be able to find your way around the interface.

We will start with getting the Unity and FMOD projects set up by following the instructions:

> If you have worked through to the end of Chapter 7, *FMOD for Dyanmic and Adaptive Audio*, and not modified those projects, you can jump ahead to the next exercise.

1. Open Unity and create a new project called GameAudio_FMOD.
2. From the menu, select **Window** | **Asset Store**. To open the store page, find the Viking Village Unity asset and download and/or import it.
3. From the menu, select **Assets** | **Import Package** | **Custom Package** and use the dialog to locate the FMOD Unity integration package you previously downloaded from FMOD. If you are unable to locate the package, you will need to go to FMOD.com, login, and then download the package again.

> Be sure you have installed the FMOD Unity integration package into your Unity project before continuing.

4. From the menu, select **Assets** | **Import Package** | **Custom Package** and use the Import dialog to open the Chapter_11_FMOD folder from the book's downloaded source code. Then, select and import the **Chapter_11_FMOD.unitypackage**.

5. Located within the `Chapter_11_FMOD` from the book's source code is another folder called `GameAudio_FMOD`. You will need to copy that entire folder to your Unity `GameAudio_FMOD` project folder. After you copy the folder, the contents of your project folder should look similar to the following screenshot:

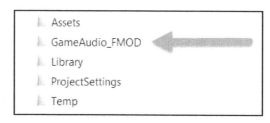

Copying the GameAudio_FMOD folder into the Unity project folder

6. Launch FMOD Studio and from the menu and select **File | Open**. Use the dialog to locate and open the `GameAudio_FMOD` folder you just copied. Select the `GameAudio_FMOD.fspro` to open it in FMOD Studio.

7. From the menu, select **File | Build** to build the project.

8. Return to Unity and from the menu select **FMOD | Edit Settings** and set the **Studio Project Path** using the **Browse** button to locate the FMOD project file and set it as shown in the following screenshot:

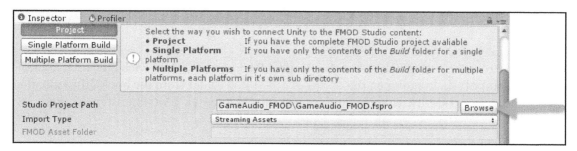

Setting the Studio Project Path in the FMOD Settings

9. Locate the `Chapter_11_FMOD` scene in the **Project** window and double-click on it to load it. At this point, you can run and test the scene to make sure everything works as expected.

With the project set up, we can now look at how to profile and implement some performance optimization strategies by following the directions:

1. By default, a **FMOD Studio Debug** overlay will be shown within the **Game** view when you run the scene. This overlay will look like the following screenshot:

FMOD Studio Debug overlay showing performance profiling stats

 Try not to directly compare the values in this window with the project running the Unity audio system. If you recall, we did not implement all the effects or ambient sounds in the FMOD project.

2. From the menu, select **Window** | **Profiler** to open the **Profiler**. Select the **Audio** panel again to look at the stats, and you will see everything is running at minimal levels. What is happening is that, for the most part, FMOD is running external to the Unity audio system; we already knew that.

3. Keep the scene running in Unity and then open FMOD. From the FMOD menu, select **Window | Profiler**. This will open the **Profiler** window. Switch to the **Profiler** window, and from the menu, navigate to **File | Connect to Game**. You will be prompted with a **Connect to Game** dialog. Just use the defaults and click on the **Connect** button. Nothing will happen until you click on record.

4. Click on the **Record** button as identified in the following screenshot and watch as the **Profiler** comes to life and starts capturing data:

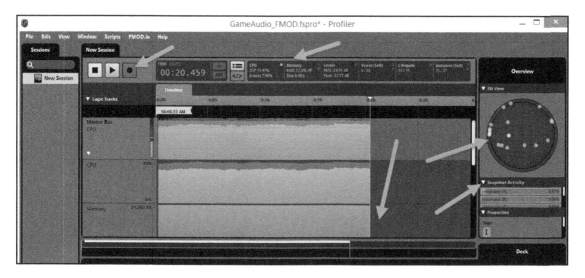

FMOD Profiler window capturing performance stats from a running game

 There is a lot of information being captured here, and it is important not to be overwhelmed. Just remember the stats are going to be similar to the Unity stats we already looked at.

5. Look through the interface as the game keeps running. You can always go back to Unity and move around the scene returning to the **Profiler** window, when you want to see how the performance has changed. This is best done with multiple monitors or moving the Unity and FMOD windows beside each other.

6. When you are done profiling, stop the scene in Unity and then stop the profiling session in the FMOD **Profiler**.

While we won't have time to review every detail about the FMOD Profiler, there is some very helpful profiling that can identify potential problem areas immediately. If you go back to the profiling session and look through each of the tracks, you should immediately notice that one of the tracks is showing especially high usage, as shown in the following screenshot:

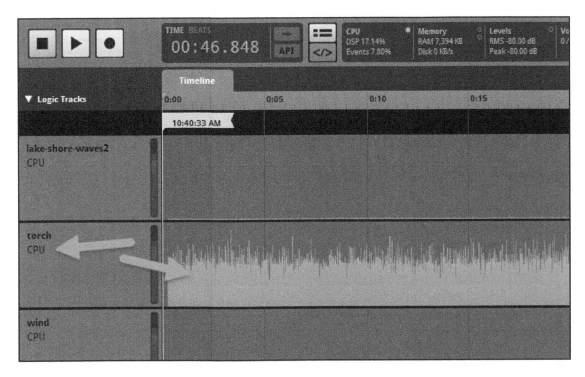

Profiler performance for a torch showing possible performance issues

While we know the torch uses a spatial effect, should the CPU usage be this high? We definitely were not seeing this an issue in Unity, so let's look at the following torch event:

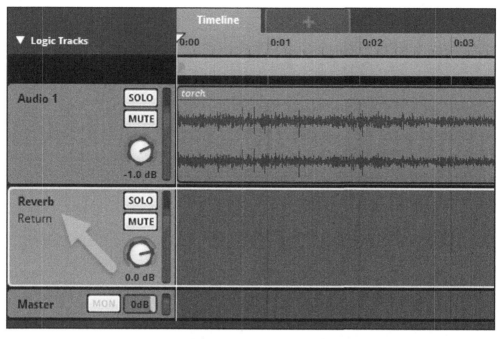

Torch event showing a Reverb return effect added

We only have to look at this event for a few seconds to quickly realize that this **Reverb** effect is the likely culprit. If you look back at our optimization strategies, one of our rules was to be careful not to overuse delay effects like reverb. What we did here is apply a reverb effect to every single torch event. The simple way to fix this is to remove the **Reverb** effect here and instead apply it through a group mixer. We will leave the reader to figure out how to do that on their own.

Before we leave this section on FMOD, we want to cover managing audio resources by following the instructions:

1. Open up the FMOD **Event Viewer** and select the **Assets** tab. This will show the list of project assets and a summary of how the resource is managed. Click on the **torch** asset and look to the settings at the bottom of the panel as shown in the following screenshot:

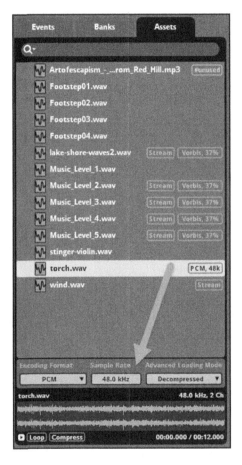

Examining the project audio resources in the Assets panel

2. What you will see here are the same options for optimizing the audio resources in your project. You will also notice that as you add new resources, FMOD is a little smarted on the options it chooses for the default settings. From here, you can override the settings using the previously discussed optimization strategies.

There is of course much more we could cover about FMOD performance but for most readers this will be a great starting point. In the next section, we complete the chapter by talking about troubleshooting tips.

QUIZ TIME

Answer the following questions:

What type of compression should you use for short frequently played audio resources?
a) ADPCM
b) Vorbis
c) PCM
d) MP3

What type of loading would be best suited for long running audio clips?
a) Compressed in Memory
b) Vorbis
c) Decompress on Load
d) Streaming

What does DSP stand for?
a) Digital Sound Processing
b) Dynamic Sound Processing
c) Dynamic Signal Processing
d) Digital Signal Processing

Answers will be provided before the end of the chapter.

Audio troubleshooting

This section is intended to be a resource for any issues readers have while working through the book's exercises. It can also be used as a reference for your future game development efforts. The following table lists a number of common problems you may encounter and questions that hopefully will lead to a solution:

Problem	Question to Solution
Unable to hear sound from Audio Source.	Is there an **Audio Listener** added to the scene? Is the **Audio Source** or GameObject enabled? Is the **Audio Clip** parameter set? Is **Play on Awake** enabled or is the source playing in script? Is Volume set to maximum? Is Output set to an active mixing group? Is **Audio Listener** within range of the the source's 3D Sound Settings? Is the source being output to a muted mixing group? Are you able to play the audio from the resource import settings view?
Unable to hear audio output from mixing group.	Is the mixing group muted? Is another audio group soloed? Is the volume or attenuation turned up to max? Is the mixing group being routed to another group (master or parent)? Is the audio being muted by another effect such as Duck Volume?
Unable to hear an effect applied to a mixing group.	Is the effect set in the right order? Does the effect require a feedback or return signal like a delay, such as SFX Reverb or Duck Volume? Are the effect parameters adjusted correctly? Is the effect set before or after a receive effect?

Unable to hear FMOD Studio Event Emitter.	Is there an FMOD Studio Event Listener in the scene? Has the FMOD project been built? Is the event name correctly set; try resetting the name? Is there a parameter controlling volume that needs to be set? Is the effect being routed to a mix that is muted or bypassed by another solo group? Is the `Project Path` and `Streaming Assets` folders set in the FMOD settings panel?

If you are still having issues with audio then the Unity community is an excellent resource. Also FMOD has an excellent forums site where you can look for answers or ask new questions.

QUIZ TIME ANSWERS

What type of compression should you use for short frequently played audio resources?
a) ADPCM
b) Vorbis
c) PCM
d) MP3

What type of loading would be best suited for long running audio clips?
a) Compressed in Memory
b) Vorbis
c) Decompress on Load
d) Streaming

What does DSP stand for?
a) Digital Sound Processing
b) Dynamic Sound Processing
c) Dynamic Signal Processing
d) Digital Signal Processing

Summary

In this chapter, we covered an always important concern in game development, performance. We first looked at the considerations you should take into account when developing for your platform. After that, we looked at how to use the Unity Profiler and specifically looked at profiling audio performance. From there, we broke down some strategies for optimally handling resources and effects. This diverted us to cover profiling the FMOD audio system with FMOD Studio and how to identify and resolve issues. Finally, we looked at a troubleshooting section which is intended to help readers having issues with book's exercises or with the issues in the future.

That completes our journey through game audio development with Unity. Hopefully, you are able to take away a number of audio development skills that you can apply to your own games. While we tried to cover all aspects of game audio, in truth, not a single book could ever encompass all of it. Instead it is hoped that you use this base of new knowledge as a platform to build on and expand. There is plenty of excellent information online in many areas of game audio and other audio development that you can use now to extend your knowledge. We wish you the best of luck in your future game development, sound design, or music production efforts.

Index

1

12-tone equal temperament (TET) method 56

3

3D sound 42, 43, 45

A

adaptive audio cues
  building 162, 163, 164, 165, 167, 168
adaptive audio
  about 160
  event triggers 161
  examples 161
  game state 161
  proximity triggers 161
adaptive music, FMOD 245, 247, 248, 250
adaptive music
  mood, creating with 170
ambient audio 10
audible frequency range 101
audio changes, recording with snapshots
  about 126
  scene, pausing 128, 129, 130, 131
audio clips 41
audio effects
  breakdown 110
audio equalization
  visualizing 98, 99, 101
audio file formats, Unity
  .aif 26
  .mp3 26
  .ogg 26
  .wav 26
audio layers
  ambient audio 10
  background music 11

direct feedback audio 10
environmental audio 10
interface audio 11
theme music 11
weapons 65
audio listeners 35
Audio Mixer
  about 88
  basics 88, 90, 91, 92
  groups, creating 93, 94
  scripting, with parameters 132
audio optimization tips and tricks, Unity
  about 362
  effects optimization 368, 370
  memory optimization 363, 364, 365, 367
audio performance
  considerations 354, 355
audio scenes
  ax, throwing 70, 72, 73, 74
  axController script 75, 77
  sounds, playing on collision 78, 80
audio signals
  routing, in mixer to effects 104, 105, 106, 108
audio source
  about 35
  adding, to scene 38, 39, 41
audio spectrum 262, 263, 265
audio visualizer
  examining 268, 269, 272, 274
audio
  analyzing, with Fast Fourier Transform (FFT)
    windows 262
  importing, into Unity 26, 27, 29
  issues, troubleshooting 379
  randomizing 81, 82, 83
  shaping, with effects 95, 96, 97
auto-driven lighting 278, 280, 281

B

background music 11, 84, 85
basic music theory
  about 332
  chords 332, 334
  melody 339
  scale 340
basic speech phonemes
  mapping, to audio visualization bins 298, 301, 302
Blend shape animation 303, 304, 306, 308

C

chord progression 336, 337
chords 332, 333
components, game audio
  music 8
  sound 8
  vocals 9
compression 115
Compressor effect 116, 117
cross fading 255

D

delay effects, breakdown
  about 111
  Chorus 114
  Echo effect 111
  Flange 113
  SFX reverb 112
diegetic sound
  versus non-diegetic sound 9
Digital Audio Workstation (DAW) 10, 88
Digital Signal Processing (DSP) 359
direct feedback audio 10
duck volume effect 118, 119, 120, 121
dynamic audio wind effect 133, 134, 136, 137, 138, 140, 141
dynamic music mixing 153, 154, 156, 157
dynamic range compression 115
dynamic wind, FMOD 226, 228, 230, 231, 232

E

Echo effect
  default settings 111
effects
  audio, shaping with 95, 96, 97
environmental audio zones
  creating 142, 143, 144, 146, 147, 148, 149, 151
environmental zones, FMOD 226, 228, 230, 231, 232
equalization effects, breakdown
  about 110
  Highpass and Highpass simple 111
  Lowpass and Lowpass simple 111
  ParamEQ 111

F

Fast Fourier Transform (FFT) windows
  audio, analyzing with 262
Fast Fourier Transform (FFT)
  used, for deconstructing signals 266
Flange effect 113
FMOD Studio
  about 194
  installing 194, 195, 197
  reference 194
FMOD
  about 193
  adaptive music 245, 247, 248, 250
  audio, controlling with snapshots 217, 218, 219, 221
  audio, controlling with triggers 217
  audio. controlling with parameters 217
  dynamic wind 226, 227, 231
  effects, applying 207, 208, 210
  environmental zones 226, 227, 230, 231
  mixing, in reverb effect 210, 211, 212, 213, 214, 216
  performance, optimizing 370, 372, 374, 376, 377
Foley artists 8
footsteps example
  updating 241, 242, 244
footsteps
  with adaptive sound 182, 184, 185, 188

G

game audio
  about 8
  components 8
GameObject 36
GarageBand 328

H

Highpass filter 97
horizontal re-sequencing
  about 170, 252
  advantages 170
  disadvantages 170

I

intellisense 55
interface audio 11

L

Lowpass effect 96

M

master mixer 101
melody
  about 339
  writing 341
microphone-driven visualizations 283, 285, 286
MIDI track 64
mood
  creating, with adaptive music 170
music composition
  enhancing 343, 345
music demarcation branching 255
music
  about 8
  recording 348
musical demarcation branching 254
Musical Instrument Digital Interface (MIDI) 322
musical keyboard
  building 54, 55, 56, 58
  enhancing 62, 63, 64
  notes, importing 58, 60, 61
  notes, playing 59, 60, 61

N

non-diegetic sound
  versus diegetic sound 9
normalization 115
Normalize effect 115

O

Ogg Vorbis 26

P

ParamEQ graph 101
performance profiling 356, 358, 359, 360, 362
phonemes 297
phrase branching 252, 254
Pitch Shifter effect 114
Prefab 70

R

real-time character lip sync 309, 311, 313
real-time lip syncing 290, 292, 293, 295
Reallusion character creator platform
  reference 292
Reaper
  about 319, 320
  reference 320
ROMpler 328

S

scale
  about 340
  demonstrating 341
scripting, Unity 50, 51, 52, 54
scripting, with FMOD 233, 234, 236, 238, 240
SFX Reverb
  default settings 112
signal flow
  controlling 101
signals
  deconstructing, FFT used 265
  deconstructing, windowing used 265
snapshots
  audio changes, recording with 126, 127
sound
  about 8

diegetic sound 9
non-diegetic sound 9
spatial blending 42, 43, 44
speeches 297
stinger-based sequencing
  about 171
  advantages 171
  disadvantages 171
stingers 251, 254, 255

T

theme music 11
transition timelines 251, 253, 256, 257

U

Unity Asset Store 20
Unity project
  creating 17, 18
Unity
  about 11
  audio file formats 26
  audio, importing into 26, 27, 29
  downloading 11, 12, 14, 15
  imported audio files, inspecting 31, 33, 35
  project assets, downloading 20, 22
  project assets, importing 20, 22
  project scene, loading 24, 25
  scripting 50, 51, 52, 54

V

vertical remixing (layering)
  about 171
  advantages 171

disadvantages 171
  with Audio Mixer 172, 174, 176, 179, 180, 181
Viking Village asset
  importing, into project 199, 201, 202, 203, 204,
    207
virtual instruments 322, 327
virtual studio technology (VST)
  VST-FX 327
  VST-MIDI 327
  VSTi 327
visualization performance
  and windowing 276, 277
vocals
  about 9
  optimizing 349, 351
  recording 314, 316, 349, 351
VST-FX 327
VST-MIDI 327
VSTi ROMpler plugin
  installing 328, 330
VSTi
  about 327
  drum machine 328
  samplers 328
  synthesizer 327

W

windowing
  about 266
  used, for deconstructing signals 266
WINE
  about 320
  reference 320